Camelot-on-Hudson. To Fowler, the Manhattan of his day was Camelot, and his fellow newsmen—Grantland Rice, Westbrook Pegler, Heywood Broun, Arthur Brisbane—were knights of the round table, which was usually a bar. Fowler's personal idol and friend was Alfred Damon Runyon. Despite his Broadway camaraderie, Runyon was a brooding, lonely man, and there were distinct traces of rube in his makeup. He believed that to count as a New York know-it-all, he had to unearth a champion heavyweight. Over the years he maintained a series of fighters who ate like lions and fought like lambs. One of these disgraces to Cro-Magnon man was stabled at the Gotham Hotel. "This canvas inspector finished several breakfasts one Sunday morning," Fowler tells in one of the book's funnier anecdotes, "and was trying to read the comic pages of the *American*. He had just about mastered the spelling of the hard word 'Wow!' in a Barney Google episode when the bells of nearby St. Patrick's began to ring. Down went this fighter to the rug. He roared out 'Foul!' The house dick burst in upon him to see the splendid athlete holding his groin, moaning like a busted pipe organ, and refusing to come out for another round."

To Fowler's generation of writers, New York was always the Big Town, a drink was *spiritus frumenti*, and Broadway was the Rue Regret. Reading *Skyline* with or without *spiritus frumenti*, one question is bound to arise: Where are the monkey glands of yesteryear?

SKYLINE

ALSO BY GENE FOWLER

TRUMPET IN THE DUST

SHOE THE WILD MARE

THE GREAT MOUTHPIECE

TIMBERLINE

FATHER GOOSE

SALUTE TO YESTERDAY

THE GREAT MAGOO (*a play
in collaboration with Ben Hecht*)

ILLUSION IN JAVA

THE JERVIS BAY GOES DOWN (*poem*)

GOOD NIGHT, SWEET PRINCE

A SOLO IN TOM-TOMS

BEAU JAMES

SCHNOZZOLA

NEW YORK

SKYLINE

A REPORTER'S REMINISCENCE OF THE 1920S

BY **Gene Fowler**

THE VIKING PRESS ～ 1961

LIBRARY OF CONGRESS CATALOG CARD NUMBER: 61-5860
PRINTED IN THE U.S.A. BY VAIL-BALLOU

To

HARRY BRAND

SKYLINE

———————————

For the noblest deeds do not always show men's virtues and vices; but oftentimes a light occasion, a word, or some sport makes men's natural disposition and manners appear more plain than the famous battles won. . . .

—PLUTARCH

Prospectus

So long as we may,

Let us enjoy this breath,

For nought doth kill a man

So soone as Death.

—DRUMMOND OF HAWTHORNDEN

THE building of castles in the air made architects of us all. It would seem harder now to shape the towers of reverie than in the gone time when a man dared send the children of his mind out-doors, and expect them to come home unmarked by the blows of cynics and immune to the contagions of despair.

That was long ago when you piled fancy upon wishfulness, the hall of make-believe uprising—and never a fallen column nor a crumbled arch to mar the daydream. King Ludwig of Bavaria decreed no castles as extravagant, nor Sir Christopher Wren cathedrals as vast as yours. That was long ago. That was once upon a time.

Men still would dream glad dreams, I think, could they but fend off the cudgels of dissent and dodge the stones of mistrust. Nor does the night bring serenity to our young ones in their beds. Someone has kidnaped the Sandman. What ransom must we pay for his return?

As far back as my own memory goes I heard the doomsayers foretell a time of fire and sword. An angry God had tired of America. See what happened to Babylon, they said; not to mention old "Silver Dollar" Tabor and the panic of 1893. As a child I became almost persuaded that the world was about to make a swan dive into hell. I found sanctuary in daydreams.

There now are few daydreams in which to spend a sheltered hour. So I do the next-best thing when weary of the dirge singers: I make long-distance calls to the way stations of the past. Then the sense of wonder that always has been mine—transcending the fears, the cares, or even the recollection of misdeeds—seems unimpaired. And age for a little while quits pounding on my door.

Every man has a favorite decimal, I would imagine—that is to say, the best ten years of his past. Laughter came the more readily then; the handshake had not yet gone out of style; tears did not fall upon yellowed valentines. A knocked-about fellow might speak of the struggle to keep body and soul together, but managed somehow to keep them apart, sensibly quarantined in the pesthouse, with a warning: "Mind your own business, you."

I used to hear my elders speak with much relish of the "Gay Nineties." I do not make long-distance calls to that time, because too often I went hungry then for bread as well as for affection. But if most storytellers avow that the nineties were gay, who am I to play a mere garden hose against this Niagara of legend?

Besides, I have always thought it a slender errand to disparage anyone's sincere turn of fancy. During my New York days, for example, I saw no point in spoiling an illusion which my grandmother-in-law enjoyed. This gentle old lady, Mrs. Maria West, was born in Warwickshire, England, in 1848. She was quite small, and reminded one of a tea cosy with a china doll's head. Her cloistered innocence made me wonder how she had happened to become a mother.

At twilight on Fire Island, where we spent our New York summers, Mrs. West would go to the front window to await the rise of the evening star. She would say never had it shone so fair, except when she, as a girl, made wishes as the star rose above Warwick

Castle. How, then, she would ask her three great-grandchildren, could anyone question the existence of God when this star shone upon the world! Then she would hum a few bars of "Lead, Kindly Light" in a voice as deep as that of Madam Schumann-Heink.

The evening star which Mrs. West admired was in fact but an electric-light bulb atop the flagstaff in a yacht-club skipper's front yard. And to think that Thomas Alva Edison, the inventor of that lamp, had told me during a birthday interview that there was no God!

Evening star or beacon light, Gay Nineties or the legend of a time, what matters it? Legends are the salad dressing of history. The storytellers allow the "Roaring Twenties" a nostalgic role in the narrative of America. Some contemporaries remember that age as a golden time; others speak of it as the heyday of the foul fiend. I had a ringside seat during that era. I was a newspaperman in New York. What did I see? Or fail to see?

When dealing with the Park Row story of the 1920s, most writers establish their memoirs upon the "big" men and the "big" events of that period. I find no fault with these tales nor with the way in which they are told. For my own part, whenever I make excursions into the past, I like best to remember the offbeat happenings of a time when my good companions and I were reporting the news. That time, it seems to me now, found for us, or else shaped in us, a zest for adventure which the latter-day obsession for easy-does-it security has made obsolete.

I looked upon the same scenes which my Park Row friends witnessed. I shared their reportorial forays among the heroes and the villains of the banner lines. Our interpretations of memorable assignments sometimes differ, one from the other, mainly in terms of social or political ingredients. Then, too, each of us recreates his own New York of forty or more years ago. Perhaps our city of the twenties was not that which one now so confidently says it was; less enchanting than the Camelot one thinks it was. Old men tell themselves white lies about their yesterdays. They do so with the hope that, somehow, they can be young again for an hour or two. But no! We are allowed but one serving at the table of Youth; there can be no second helpings.

As I watched the kangaroo leaps of men who jumped into, then out of, journalistic focus, I tried to find, or at least to approximate, the story behind the story; the *cause* as well as the consequence of a deed. The "underside" of the news and of its makers always stirred my inquisitive faculties. One might come upon clues—or so I fancied—to some of the deeper meanings of life, strong hints in respect to the spiritual aims of mankind among a catalogue of fragments sifted from the dust bins of personal histories.

Each news story, I thought, had enlightening footnotes and marginal comments. Sometimes they were scrawled by the Devil's hand, or at other times by Gabriel's. These points of reference were of little use to the newspapers. News is history shot on the wing. The huntsmen from the Fourth Estate seek to bag only the peacock or the eagle of the swifting day.

I do not pretend to remember and assemble every important thing that happened along old Park Row. I best recollect the bits and pieces of my news-gathering time. And with these I would form a mosaic.

I still can see the incredibly fast flutter of bandit Gerald Chapman's small feet as he dies on the hangman's rope. I again can hear Queen Marie of Romania tell her lady-in-waiting to "get rid of that damned thing!" after the Dakota Indians have given Her Majesty a war bonnet. Once again I am present at Carnegie Hall as the addled Mayor Hylan makes his ghost-written address of welcome to President Woodrow Wilson; but unthinkingly keeps his back turned to Mr. Wilson during the ceremony. I remember also the lean Irish statesman Eamon de Valera, clad in his long underwear, and huge boxing gloves on his hands, as he spars with his bull-necked secretary in a sitting room at the old Waldorf.

Even as I write, there unaccountably springs to mind an occasion when I asked Henry Ford about the sleep habits of his good friend Edison. Was it true, as legend had it, that Mr. Edison, like Napoleon, slept but four hours? Yes, said Mr. Ford, but Mr. Edison slept twice and sometimes *three times* a day!

Little things about big men. Or, if you will, big things about little men. These grace notes stay on in the memory. For poets remember such matters as a woman's glance, a tune played upon the mouth organ by someone in the bleak prison yard of the Tombs, the dust on the law books of a disbarred lawyer, the toy train of a dead child. I was a poet without portfolio. I would always remember these things.

The stories of my day are no longer big in the public attention, or else have been chewed upon until the taste is gone. The once-mighty names are no longer green except upon corroded urns. The 1920s had as many colors as Joseph's coat. At best a man who treats of that period can adequately describe but one or two patches of the garment. No one has marked out the whole design in the novels that have to do with bathtub gin and flaming youth, with the sagas of perforated gangsters, with the tales of Mrs. Astor's defunct smart set, or with the rise of the straw aristocrats of the cafés.

To my mind the best estimation of that whirlwind time—when our country was passing through its age of puberty, the voice changing, and the young glands rebelling against the sober functions of the brain, and while adventure and romance and disappointment and tragedy moved to the flutes, as at a masked ball— the most apt description of the age, the very mood and meaning of it, was expressed in a newspaper editorial.

Perhaps a commemorative tablet designed by Mr. Lucius Beebe, the tall and elegant connoisseur of things past, one day will grace the premises where this editorial had its conception. Alas, the editorial never got as far as the linotype console or the composing-room stones. But plaque there should be, and embossed upon it the name of William Morris Houghton of the *Herald Tribune*.

The memorial plate should be spotted somewhere near the place where once stood the bar at Jack Bleeck's saloon, alias the Artists and Writers Club, in the West Forties of Manhattan.

In the late 1920s Mr. Houghton was second in command of the *Herald Tribune's* editorial page; the late Geoffrey Parsons was his senior. Mr. Houghton—educated at Harvard, Yale, and Bowdoin —long had been popular with the newspaper stars of the Inky Way, not many of whom had attained his degree of Master of Arts (Harvard, 1904) or wore Phi Beta Kappa keys.

Tradition has it that Mr. Houghton had been able as a mere lad to interpret the Old Testament Book of Leviticus at first glance, but dismissed the Book of Numbers as the work of name-droppers. It has been said, but on what authority I cannot remember, that Mr. Houghton had shaken hands with Admiral George Dewey.

On the evening of his oracular editorial, Mr. Houghton was standing at Bleeck's bar, discussing with Mr. Beebe the sorrows of Adam. Mr. Beebe had on a pop-up hat, white tie, and tails. As usual, he looked as though he were on his way to or from the House of Lords. His city editor, Mr. Stanley Walker, once described him as a "peasant-baiter."

This Texas-born Mr. Walker was one of the great desk men of the 1920s. He also was the enunciator of "Walker's Law": "Associate with well-mannered persons and your own manners will improve. Run with decent folk and your own decent instincts will be strengthened. Keep the company of bums and you will become a bum. *But* hang around with rich people and you will end by picking up the tab and dying broke."

I first met Mr. Walker in 1919 as we were covering a hoboes' convention, having arrived there in a hansom cab and amid the "boos" of envious delegates. My friend Walker just recently built a Fowler memorial wall at his Lampasas, Texas, ranch. It serves as a windbreak and shelter for ewes with lambs during blizzards. Mr. Walker has dug a grave for himself near it, and has offered to do the same for me. He has topped the wall, appropriately enough, with cactus plants.

But to return to the Messrs. Houghton and Beebe and the night of the momentous editorial.

Lucius Beebe, the best-dressed of all journalists, past, present, or in eternity, had just left the nearby Metropolitan Opera House during the first act of *Aïda* because, as he put it, the Egyptian scenery somehow reminded him of his days in Harvard Yard. After complimenting Mr. Houghton for having on a Brooks Brothers No. 1 sack coat, Mr. Beebe (also educated at Yale and Harvard but not Bowdoin) chanced to remark that most men blame their woes on others. The precedent for this despicable course, he went on to say, was established by Adam. The father of mankind had maintained even to Jehovah Himself that Eve had persuaded him he was not getting enough pectin in his diet.

Mr. Houghton asked Leo the bartender for a glass of Prohibition dew. He then made a somewhat shrewd observation: "The basic cause of poor Adam's cynical behavior lay in the fact that he had had no childhood. He had been deprived of the fun of hating his mother, or, on the other hand, of a longing to return to the womb. The psychoanalysts are baffled by Adam's case history. They simply must come upon a cantankerous mother to bolster their findings, else throw in the sponge."

A messenger from the *Herald Tribune* now burst in upon the philosophers. He said that a time of crisis was demoralizing the editorial room. Mr. Ogden Mills Reid, amiable proprietor of the newspaper—the son of Whitelaw Reid, one-time Civil War correspondent, author, cotton planter, and late Ambassador to the Court of St. James's—was said to be kicking his desk to pieces.

A ghastly oversight had been discovered as deadline neared. Members of the editorial-writer staff had gone to their respective speakeasies. They had done so without the usual interchange of information as to which one of their scholarly corps had submitted the lead editorial for next day's breakfast-table consideration. No one had written it at all!

The paper could not be put to bed without this daily seven inches of exalted thought. There were fillers on hand, to be sure, among them a vignette having to do with the building of a stockade in 1653 along what is now Wall Street, as well as a plea to rid the statue of Horace Greeley of the irreverent pigeons of Herald Square. Stopgap essays such as these would seem feeble alternatives for a political rouser.

Mr. Houghton responded to the Macedonian cry. He excused himself to Mr. Beebe, then went to his newspaper office next door to compose the editorial. Mr. Reid muttered something to the effect of "Thank God in His infinite wisdom!"

Make-up editors, printers, stereotypers, pressmen—all were alerted. Copy boys were warned not to go near the busy man, not to cough, eat peanuts, or even scratch their behinds until the editor completed his emergency labors. A visiting bootlegger was told to deliver his wares next day.

For perhaps twenty minutes the Harvard Master of Arts crouched like a concert pianist at the keyboard of his typewriter. At last he leaned back. He lifted the hand which supposedly had shaken that of the hero of Manila Bay. Copy boys sprinted toward his desk. A pair of them collided like confused outfielders after a high fly ball. The first to come to his feet and his senses took the editorial on the double to Mr. Reid.

With an air of shocked amazement, the publisher examined the two pages. His hands trembled, and his cheeks turned tallow-pale. He called upon his most trustworthy subalterns to verify what he thought he saw. They assured him that he was not the victim of myopia, nor of brain tumor. Written upon these pages they saw a word, a formidable word, repeated again and again, in the manner of Poe's Raven.

That word was "Nevertheless."

Had not Mr. Houghton's mighty ditto suffered martyrdom upon the editorial-room spike, his "Nevertheless" might have become the true signature of the Roaring Twenties. For it was a world of Nevertheless, a rosy time, the complexion of which now has faded like a clown's face in the rain.

CHAPTER

1

---

*He walked much and con-
templated, and he had in the
head of his staffe a pen and
ink-horne.* —JOHN AUBREY

I LIKE the brown pen best. It is nine or ten books older than the other pens at hand. Though long outmoded—it lacks the twisters and twirlers of, say, the sky-blue pen, which you may have for the asking—the brown one has written a phrase now and then, even a paragraph, that I liked. I am mindful, of course, that its lilts would never make folk dance, as when Yeats' musician played on his fiddle in Dooney.

This pen moved the more readily on the page whenever it explored my quicksilver days as a newspaperman west or east, or in between. The newspaper was my first love, and, come to think of it, my last. I smelled the ink of the press room when I was a printer's devil, and have found no other scent as stimulating except in the heart of a blue-spruce grove, or occasionally in that of a lady.

I have written elsewhere and at some length of my childhood among the mountains and plains of Colorado, and of my apprenticeship on three Denver newspapers. Most editors of that day and place were outstanding mentors, strict and wise. The graduates of that Western school were many and celebrated. I was neither the best nor the worst of the lot, but perhaps the luckiest. I knew but little and believed a great deal, but learned before long that little lives are big to the ones who live them.

Early in this century most young reporters of my bent hoped one day to reach the city rooms of the metropolitan dailies. Now the graduates of schools of journalism find satisfaction and prestige on the staffs of their home-town papers. The editorial unions protect them in terms of pay and hours and give them the five-day week; they cannot be fired willy-nilly by some sourball on the city desk.

In my time New York was the rainbow's end. I shall tell about my journey to New York, with here and there a comment having to do with the occasions when I came home again, home again, *not* dancing a jig. Perhaps these recollections of my newspaper life in the twenties, and my random sketches of half-forgotten journalists, and of other personalities whose lives touched mine, will convey a bit of the carefree feeling which enlivened the years before Mr. World became a great cry-baby.

Anyone who lives long enough among men and women of spirited persuasion is bound to have a legend grow about his name. A legend of sorts has been put upon this alumnus of old Park Row, much to his distaste for ragtag echoes of a madcap yesterday. For he was unpretentious by nature, and somewhat given to studious concerns in private hours, notwithstanding the robust tales which outlasted his work on the newspapers. Whatever else may be said of him, this man who wears my name enjoyed the professional sanction as well as the friendship of the greatest reporters of the 1920s.

My legend seems out of proportion to the measure of name and goods which I possess. Still, no over-all harm has come of the embroidered anecdotes. I am not a candidate for the hall of fame, nor do I have the least anxiety about my social acceptance. Much of this legend is of my own making. For one thing, I have been slow to deny the well-meant fictions with which the old boys spice their jolly memories of me and of our time together on Park Row.

Another circumstance encouraged the fable—my appearance of frivolity when solemnity deadened the air. My unseemly mirth may well have come of false pride. Rather, I think, I raised a shield of levity to hide doubts and perplexities. I believe that I was afraid of success, or of that which passes for success. As a reporter I became convinced that "success" is a snowball. It grows as it rolls along, becomes huge, immovable; then, one warm day, it melts. Possibly my opinion of "success" was perverse and extreme. I shall never know; for now I am seventy and a great-grandfather, and do not much care which way the winds of opinion blow.

Damon Runyon—long before he tasted both the sweetness and the bitterness of "success"—deplored my "odd-ball way of throwing a career up for grabs." He once said to me, "You are on your way to becoming America's foremost self-unmade man. Opportunity not only knocks once at your door; she busts it wide open every day; and then you kick her in the breadbasket. Is that the way to treat a lady?"

"The lady is a whore," I said. "I can't afford her asking price."

Audacious or gay as I may have appeared while at work, I was not always happy with that which I had to do. Actually I felt downright mean of spirit whenever I sought out a troubled stranger, to confront him with evidence of his newsworthy sins, or with those of his wife. Again, when assigned to the death house to report an electrocution or a hanging, my senses performed the somersaults of St. Vitus. I could not, for the time being, think of what the criminal had done against society, but of what society was doing to him. In the paradox of justice, the good chaplain whispers the promises of heaven, while the executioner makes ready to invest the victim with the bolts of hell. The death house is not the ideal place in which to strike a bargain of any sort.

Whatever my fears, I felt that one day I would come upon the meaning of my life, or its lack of meaning, in some flash flood of self-revelation. I think that Aristotle (unless it was "Bugs" Baer) called this "the moment of recognition." I called it "The Idea."

I kept on looking for this John Doe of an idea. I felt that I had a warrant for its arrest.

My mask of flippancy also hid a stubborn and a sometimes costly fault of refusing to bow to reason or expediency. Once committed to an action, I seldom back-tracked—an all-or-nothing player, as the saying goes. I ran up many hills when I should have walked around them. I thought that caution meant hardening of the arteries.

I had learned to fight to a finish when but a child, thanks to my grandmother, who insisted that I wear a sunbonnet when playing out of doors. Young realists of West Denver would invade our back yard to trounce the fellow in the calico bonnet. Their drubbings made me as durable as the next one (excepting young Johnny Loftus, who, I have been told, became a Roman Catholic priest). I learned, by means of trial and error, not to stand still, or spar in the orthodox manner, but to use fists, elbows, knees, and a goat-quick head, which was thick in more ways than one. If I do say so myself, I could deliver an uppercut which made a foe look as though he had caught the mumps.

One of my eccentricities in battle (and I don't pretend to understand it) was to laugh while fighting. This kind of hilarity put an opponent off guard. It puzzled the spectators as well, as it did Mr. Westbrook Pegler, America's Voltaire, at a much later time when, in 1924, I got my lumps at Billy LaHiff's Tavern on West 48th Street, New York. I had made the mistake of boxing the rugged Mr. William Gibson, manager of Gene Tunney, instead of sticking to my own system of blow-the-man-down. Before Spooner, the headwaiter, could intervene, Mr. Gibson raked away part of an eyebrow with his diamond ring.

We resumed our friendship the next day. Mr. Gibson, however, wished to clear up one point. "What the hell was you laughing at last night?"

"I was thinking of sunbonnets."

"Who you kidding?" Mr. Gibson seemed anxious about my

mental status. "Should you not lay down or something for a while?"

I never quite shook off my provincial ways, although at times I tried to pass as one on winking terms with the world. During my first months in New York I felt as frustrated as a sword swallower with the hiccups. I lost my fear of the city, however, the day I flew over it together with ten other reporters. We took off in a Caproni bomber piloted by the Italians Juliano Parvis and poet Gabriele D'Annunzio's younger son Ugo. Two miles below us, Manhattan seemed but a lizard lazing in the sunlight of a September noon.

I did impulsive things in those newspaper days, some of them sophomoric, but, I like to think, this side of malice. All in all, I had a very good time, as well as much good fortune. These turns of chance made me seem a more able reporter than otherwise I might have appeared to be. And great friends were mine.

Afraid of lightning as I was, and still am, I could not help looking upon its flashing turmoil, and then listening to the thunder's roll. To see the lightnings of life best, and at first hand, I thought that a man should work for the newspapers. To see the most of life, and in its most colorful display, I believed that New York was the enchanted place to which a young reporter must go. While considering the ifs and buts and hows and whens, I would walk the streets, or sit at my desk at the Denver *Post*, the last newspaper on which I worked in the West, and think of New York. Each week I would read *Editor & Publisher* from beginning to end (as I still do) to learn what was happening in the world of journalism. I also would study the exchange newspapers from the metropolitan East as though for a master's degree.

Among my various duties I was chief assistant to the veteran sports editor Otto C. Floto. His celebrated out-of-town friends dropped in from time to time: actors, sportsmen, athletes, gamblers, wine agents, circus folk. They told great tales, mostly about their own exploits, some of which were valid.

Otto Floto was a big man in every way. He was a merry man much of the time, but when offended had the mien of an archbishop who had just heard the confession of Gyp the Blood. Otto had been a billposter in Cripple Creek before the turn of the century, a time when Lowell Thomas's doctor-father, "the Colonel," practiced medicine in the gold camps. The Colonel never pressed anyone for the payment of a bill for pills or splints.

Otto become a prize-fight referee, managed champion Robert Fitzsimmons's theatrical tour, and accompanied heavyweight Peter Maher to England. Floto had seen many of the old bare-knuckle bouts. He was a timekeeper at the John L. Sullivan–Jake Kilrain battle of seventy-five rounds on the turf at Richburg, Mississippi, in 1889.

Otto tended bar in his early days, but never drank. Come to think of it, few Western saloon owners or their employees did drink. H. H. Tammen, co-owner of the Denver *Post* (himself an ex-bartender), hired Otto Floto as his sports editor "because his name is so beautiful."

Otto wrote with authority of the sports world and of his own colorful experiences, but thought that plumed words plucked from a thesaurus were preferable to the simpler ones. Nevertheless, he was a first-rate spinner of yarns, and made friends everywhere and in all social climates. He had moved in the horsy set of banker August Belmont and of the great architect Stanford White, as well as that of Wilson Mizner, who lived by his wits, and of Mattie Silks, the pistol-packing madam.

Floto had enemies, to be sure, among them William Barclay ("Bat") Masterson, buffalo hunter, scout for General Nelson A. Miles during the Apache uprising of 1886, and sheriff, when but twenty-two years old, of Dodge City, Kansas. Masterson was a bad man to cross; he had killed several hearties "in self-defense." This tight-lipped fellow had never been known to smile.

Masterson was a card dealer at the Arcade, a gambling house in Denver during the nineties. He entered into a partnership with Floto and Patrick ("Reddy") Gallagher in the promotion of box-

ing and wrestling matches. Gallagher, a former Midwestern prize-
fighter, had an explosive right hand, and the fans used to call out
to him, "Let 'er go, Gallagher!" a popular saying of the day.

The three promoters dissolved their partnership. One day Floto
and Masterson came to grips in front of Bert Davis's Cigar Store,
where tickets were on sale for a match promoted by Floto. Masterson had said the bout would be a fake, a waltz in three-quarter
time.

As ring critics Floto and Masterson were perfectionists. They
would reprimand an athlete for the mistiming of a blow, the
faulty delivery of a punch, or improper stance or ring posture.
What then did these experts do when they themselves went into
action? Well, they began by kicking each other in the belly,
then whaled away with roundhouse rights that stirred up more
wind than the town had felt since the blizzard of 1883. Since
that brawl I have questioned the infallibility of critics, pugilistic or
otherwise.

Bat Masterson went to New York to join the staff of the *Morning Telegraph*, and became the East's foremost authority on boxing. He kept up his attacks upon his Denver enemies. He even denounced a racehorse named "Otto Floto," and whenever it lost
would gloat in print. The hayburner eventually was taken off the
flats and entered in the jumping races, with some success. Bat
Masterson, however, never mentioned its victories. Another horse,
a gelding named "Bat Masterson," one day dropped dead in the
backstretch. Floto thereupon wrote a column entitled "Poetic
Justice." He said that not even the strongest elephant could carry
both a jockey and a bad name.

The never-smiling Bat Masterson died at his newspaper desk
October 25, 1921. On his typewriter was found this paragraph:
"There are many in this old world of ours who hold that things
break about even for all of us. I have observed for example that we
all get the same amount of ice. The rich get it in the summertime
and the poor get it in the winter."

Otto Floto liked everyone to think that he owned a part of the

Sells-Floto Circus. The proprietors of the *Post* actually owned it, and merely made use of Floto's name. That name originally had been Flotow. Otto said that he was the grandson of Freiherr Friedrich Ferdinand Adolf von Flotow, German composer of the opera *Martha*. My editor liked fine clothes. His expensive taste in this respect influenced Runyon (who had worked for him) in the ways of dress. Floto's only criticism of me had to do with my indifference to good clothes, and with my wearing a pair of moccasins given me by Buffalo Bill.

Floto had a lovely wife, one-time queen of the bareback riders. As the "Lady in Red" Kitty Kruger had been a tanbark star with the Sells-Floto Circus. Although Kitty and I eventually became the best of friends, in the days of my association with her husband she looked upon me as something that belonged in a menagerie.

Perhaps her opinion was formed the day after I became Floto's assistant. I had been up all night, a practice which I now most earnestly warn against. I went to the Glenarm Baths for half an hour or so of silent prayer. Floto found me there. Before I could say "Stanislaus Zbyszko," two rubbers whom I had looked upon as friends stood me between them while another attendant played a fire hose, full-blast, upon my body. After this hydrotherapy, and a rubdown which had the tempo of Custer's last stand, I dressed to go to the Denver *Post* to make up the first edition of the sports pages.

It was characteristic of Otto to follow a drastic action with a deed of kindness. After I put the sports pages on the press Floto saw me to bed in his suite at the Brown Palace Hotel. He neglected to leave word for Kitty that I was their guest. In some manner not remembered, I left Otto's bed to continue my slumber underneath it. Kitty came home to see my bare feet sticking out, the moccasins nearby. She assumed that an Indian was lying in ambush there. Her scream brought the house detective.

Otto regarded me as one would a son. My own affectionate feeling for him may have sprung from the circumstance that so far I had not seen my own father, Charles Devlan. My mother had

divorced Devlan some months before my birth. He then had gone
into a hermit-like existence among the mountains. Nor could I
take my father's name because my maternal grandmother, Mrs.
Norman Wheeler, detested Devlan, name and all. So I was a
"Wheeler" until adopted at six by my stepfather, Frank D. Fowler.
Perhaps that early mixup is the reason why I find names so hard
to remember.

Otto Floto's assistants sometimes thought him a difficult person
to work for, but to me he seemed a hearty, life-loving friend. He
condoned my mischievous actions and thus encouraged in me a
strong distaste for discipline. Like Plutarch, he believed that the
wildest colts made the best horses. Floto died in 1929 at the age of
sixty-five. A photograph of me riding one of Mr. Tammen's circus
elephants lay beneath his pillow.

Before World War I, much "scouting" of young newspapermen
was practiced. Editors of the Middle West or the East quite often
saw the work of a likely young man of the lesser newspapers, or
else heard about his abilities from staff correspondents. One's talents might become known in far-off city rooms, though a reporter's
stories seldom were signed. A by-line was a more uncommon thing
than in your modern newspaper, the pages of which carry more
credits than the stud book of a Kentucky breeding farm.

My own name, to be sure, occasionally appeared above a newspaper story—for example, my account of the funeral of Colonel
William F. ("Buffalo Bill") Cody on Lookout Mountain. I super-
vised that ceremony at the request of Mr. Tammen, the scout's
last creditor. It was my unsigned work, however, which caught the
attention of several out-of-town editors, among them Edward Beck
of the Chicago *Tribune*. Mr. Beck's interest in me may have been
prompted by his friendly regard for my mother, with whom he had
gone to grade school. Another editor who offered to hire me was
the remarkable Walter C. Howey. His Chicago career afterward
prompted playwrights Ben Hecht and Charles MacArthur to por-
tray him as "Walter Burns" in their newspaper play *The Front
Page*. Hecht has said that Howey had a roller-coaster for a brain.

This editor had but one good eye, and one ear in working order, but the surviving organs were of the best quality.

Mr. Howey was a proponent of slam-bang journalism. A story of mine had caught his good eye. The lead of it read, "She laid her wanton red head on her lover's breast, then plugged him through the heart." This kind of prose, while slightly inferior to that of Addison, stimulated the sales of our newspaper.

Howey was a persuasive gentleman. I might have gone to work for him in Chicago or for one or another New York editor had it not been for my grandparents. I was their support; they were nearing the eighties.

"There still is plenty of time," Otto Floto would say. "Besides, I'd wait till New York wants you."

New York seldom wants you; you want New York. But it is as easy for a man to turn a fierce desire topsy-turvy in his skull as it is for political candidates or lovers who frequently mistake an echo for a call.

One day Alfred Damon Runyon came to town with Harry Lauder, the comedian from Scotland, whose life story he was ghost-writing. Damon was on leave from his newspaper after having reported with much distinction the Pershing expedition against Pancho Villa in 1916. Runyon had formerly worked on the newspapers of Pueblo and Denver. He left the Denver *Post* in 1910 to go to the New York *American* at the recommendation of the short-story writer and journalist Charles E. Van Loan. Runyon soon made good in New York. He prided himself on his ability to "spot talent." Editors of the Hearst newspapers had respect for Runyon's opinions of reporters of the inland towns.

I first saw Damon Runyon (called "Al" by his Western friends) when he visited Eldorado Springs in 1905 or 1906 with cartoonist "Doc Bird" Finch to do a publicity article for my stepfather, Frank D. Fowler. Frank owned a summer resort at the Springs, a beautiful place which my brother Jack now operates among the mountains near Boulder.

I was but fifteen or sixteen at the time the slender, owl-eyed

Runyon arrived at the Springs. Although I had a nasty case of poison oak after going half-naked in the mountain brush, I made it my business to find out how a great reporter went about his noble calling. Mr. Runyon took no notes. While drinking beer with artist Finch, he spoke not at all about the newspaper world, but of his days as a soldier in the Spanish-American War, and of going grouse-hunting as soon as he could see his way clear to buy a fowling-piece. He chanced to observe my red blisters and advised me to *eat* poison-oak leaves early each summer as a means to immunize my system against the shrub. Otherwise Mr. Runyon seemed unimpressed by my company.

The fact that Runyon drank other than water in those days need not mean that he was alone in that respect. Western newspapering reflected the still restless heritage of pioneer times. Some journalists drank too much, others did not. An editor's main concern was whether or not a man brought back the story to which he had been assigned. What you did in your off hours was a matter to be resolved by yourself, your bartender, your sweetheart, your pastor, or the undertaker.

Runyon quit the bottle when he went to New York. He immediately set out to dissuade his pals, especially his disciples, whenever they took aboard too much of that which Lucius Beebe calls "the ardent." Legend has it that one of Runyon's last misadventures with drink occurred in the company of his sidekick Doc Bird, a lovable little man with a big thirst. Doc Bird's name was Frank Finch. He came by the pseudonym because he drew a finch as a signature to his cartoons.

As the tale goes, the Denver *Post* had just hired Runyon and Finch away from the *Rocky Mountain News*. The *Post* had bought a motor-driven delivery truck, the first to be seen west of Chicago. It was the Christmas season, so the proprietors planned a public celebration. The *Post* invited the children of the city to assemble in the street in front of the newspaper office. The red truck would contain wonderful gifts for one and all. Santa Claus himself, assisted by Doc Bird, would bestow each present.

On the day of this carnival, city editor Josiah M. Ward assigned Alfred Damon Runyon to play the role of Santa Claus. It was an unusually warm day for December; besides, someone had neglected to turn off the heat in the business office used as a dressing room for Kris Kringle and his helper.

Joe Ward belatedly thought Runyon too skinny for Santa Claus, the red costume too large. Mr. Ward borrowed some pillows from the Albany Hotel to fatten the saint. While being costumed for the role Runyon recited one of his own poems to his fellow journalists. It had to do with the seduction of a Mexican lass by a heartless New York gambler, and the anguish of her brother, who asked the villain, "What happened to my seester, meester?"

The padding, the steam heat, the great white beard and wig and cap brought to a simmer the sauce which Runyon had downed. Liquids do not easily come to a boil in the mile-high Queen City of the Plains, but today's drinks must have found the proper barometric pressure for action inside the Runyon gizzard. Then Santa fell asleep.

Doc Bird had been fitted out with a feathered costume. Over his head and face was a papier-mâché bird's noggin with a huge beak. The solid headpiece would keep Mr. Finch from drinking while on duty. But Doc Bird had placed an uncorked quart of rye whisky inside the mask. Whenever he desired refreshment—which was often—he would point his beak to the sky, and swallow as the other birds did.

By the time the truck rolled up for the grand debut hundreds of children and their parents had assembled outside the *Post*. Reporters lifted Santa Claus onto the truck seat. A happy cheer arose. The whoops of the youngsters gladdened the proprietors as they looked down from the iron balcony of the newspaper office.

The publishers were congratulating themselves upon this promotional triumph when a disturbance occurred in the street below them. They saw the children nearest the truck climb to receive their gifts from Santa Claus. Next they saw the white-bearded fellow rouse, blink, look all about, then begin to kick at the clambering kiddies.

The voice of Santa Claus could be heard, "Get outta here, you noisy brats!"

The kiddies could not understand why their patron sought to boot them. Their parents closed in with promises to lynch Santa. Police Chief Hamilton Armstrong and his boys in blue quickly established a hollow square. Sturdy circulation-department men rescued Santa Claus, who once again had fallen asleep. Doc Bird waddled out of view, his beak pointed toward the sky. There were threats to cancel subscriptions. The police eventually distributed the presents, but it is said that several of the children became atheists that day.

It was a sober, "deadpan" Runyon who came back to Denver late in 1916 with Harry Lauder and his kilted entertainers. I went with a newspaper pal, Frank E. White, to call upon the great alumnus of the Denver press. I saw in him a man of restrained manner though friendly. I remarked that he became talkative only when speaking of his adventures as a cub or of the didos of old gamblers or gun toters of the frontier towns. He listened a great deal, and looked with unblinking eyes through the windows of rimless spectacles. He wore a natty suit of clothes, and had a cosmopolitan air.

Runyon spoke of New York's Manhattan as familiarly as if he had been born there instead of in that much smaller town of the same name, Manhattan, Kansas. He talked about New York, especially Broadway, as though he were its discoverer. This air of seeming to have been the very first observer to see the oft-written-of locale, the Big Town, gave his subsequent great short stories their appealing freshness.

Forty-second Street and Broadway had been in business a long time before Runyon first gazed at its electric wonders. But he pounced upon the Great White Way like a prospector jumping a claim. He made the street and its people his literary property.

Damon's ability to impart to the reader his own sense of excitement about something old to others but entirely new to him exactly fitted his genius for style. He underscored the excitement by casting his stories in the present tense, a device borrowed from his journalistic idol, Arthur Brisbane, a devotee of the historical present. Editor Brisbane had cribbed it from Coleridge's "Rime of the Ancient Mariner."

Runyon spoke of his now long-dead father, an itinerant printer. In the years to come he would often speak or write of his father with much affection. Today he said that the elder Runyon had warned him as a mere lad against gambling, especially with strangers.

"Son," Damon's parent had said, "you will go out in the cold, cold world. And soon you will find yourself alone on a railway train. A slick stranger will come up to where you are sitting. He'll show you a brand-new deck of cards. He'll offer to lay you six to one that he can make the jack of hearts pop right out of the deck and piddle in your left ear. Don't take that bet, son! Don't take that stranger's bet, I'm telling you, my boy—unless, of course, you want to get a mighty wet left ear!"

"Well, fella," Runyon then said (and he often addressed me that way in the after years), "I've had my eye on you. How'd you like to work in the Big Town?"

"Think I could make the grade?"

He looked me over for a moment or so, then removed his spectacles to polish them with a small handkerchief of fine linen. I remember that he appeared very young for his thirty-eight years, with or without eyeglasses. He always seemed much younger than he was, until his last illness etched the real years on his face.

He carefully refolded the handkerchief. "Modest, eh? Well let me wise you up to something: He who tooteth not his own horn, the same shall not be tooted."

Two winters would pass before I was to see Runyon again—pass by with snows that paled the fifty-four blue peaks of the great watershed. The Chinook wind spilled down the eastern slope of the high range, a miracle of dry warm air which each new year frees the gates of spring. For two successive springtimes I would watch the surrounding prairie go again from gray to green, and see the mountains move nearer—an illusion which cloudless early summer and the magnifying air of the mile-high altitude creates.

When the second summer came, the beauty and the seeming nearness of these familiar mountains made me sad, as though from a sense of guilt. I felt that the great hills knew that I meant to leave them soon for another love, a city far away.

CHAPTER

2

Went I wide in this world,

wonders to hear.

—Piers Plowman

IN MAY of 1918 Major General George Morton Randall (U.S.A., retired) took to his bed. The old officer had been cited for bravery in numerous campaigns, from the bridge at Antietam long ago down to the Apache action at Turret Mountain in March of 1873. The general had the broadest shoulders since those of Atlas, and bore a world of dignity upon them. Despite the pernicious anemia which now plagued his hours, he remained large of frame.

I was reporting the illness of the major general—his first in seventy-seven years, and his last. When I chanced to hear his doctor say that the old soldier would die before morning, I telephoned my newspaper. Then I notified Rex B. Yeager, a young undertaker friend of mine, who lived across the street from our house.

Undertakers in Denver—or morticians, as they now called themselves—were an enterprising group. They had to be, else go out of business. True, the local embalmers no longer wrestled one another on the front porch of the recently dead, or played tug-of-war with the long basket, as at an earlier time when a pioneer's body became a trophy to be won in a free-for-all.

The more modern crêpe hangers of our town occasionally let us
see that the old-time tradition of prompt service had not expired.
Some embalmers sent greeting cards whenever a good citizen
seemed in a bad way. My friend Rex was tactful, efficient at all
times, and professionally spry, but much too ethical to send cards
or cup his ear for death rattles. If, however, an unsolicited piece
of business came his way, Mr. Yeager knew where to find his black
hat.

Prompted by me, Yeager was first in line at the general's hospital bed, and was given the body. Attorneys for the estate asked
that he garb the old hero in the dress blues of the Spanish-
American War period. It required more than an ordinary casket's
dimensions to accommodate the general; his broad shoulders were
amplified by gold-fringe epaulets as ornate as the arm rests of an
ante-bellum settee.

Earlier that year my friend Yeager had acquired a railway car-
load of stranded caskets from a receiver in bankruptcy. His rivals
put him down as a bullish speculator, bargain or no bargain, for
having sunk all his working capital in so many boxes. There was
not room enough at Mr. Yeager's funeral parlors for a proper hori-
zontal display of his new stock, so he stood the surplus coffins on
end in sentry-box fashion, here, there, and in the corridors.

A Spanish influenza epidemic found mortician Yeager with a
local corner on caskets. When the broad-shouldered general died,
my friend had to find an outsize piece of merchandise among his
vast inventory. He reverently eased the general and the epaulets
inside the biggest box. It probably was the tightest place the old
hero had been in since the fracas at Turret Mountain.

Many compliments came Mr. Yeager's way because of the skill
and dignity with which he prepared the general for shipment to
Ohio. Word-of-mouth publicity, together with Yeager's Olympian
position in respect to the law of supply and demand, put my
mortician friend at the head of the class. He wished to thank me
in some substantial way for my interest in his behalf. Perhaps
I would like a free trip to New York.

He pointed out that an occasional tourist from the Empire State died while in our midst. The next time a visitor from New York gave up the ghost, he meant to send me East as a traveling custodian of the obliging customer. Until now I had not known that two tickets were required by law for the interstate shipment of a body.

"Jack Dempsey is planning to fight a high-pockets plasterer named Fred Fulton in New Jersey this summer," I informed my friend. "I'd like to see that bout."

"Keep your fingers crossed," said Mr. Yeager. "Next to the Stork, the Grim Reaper has the largest clientele this side of the Pearly Gates."

One day soon afterward Mr. Yeager received the body of an elderly woman, a visitor from Gansevoort, New York, a tiny town in Saratoga County, north of Albany. I began at once to plan my itinerary. I had never been east of the relatively small Western League cities I had visited as a baseball reporter with the Denver Grizzlies. I meant to see these places once more and then inspect Chicago. I began to feel sophisticated, a man of the world.

"It's a little out of the ordinary to do it your way," Mr. Yeager mused. "Let us hope the family of the lamented won't grow impatient."

I had now been married for almost two years to Agnes. Her father, Edgar Hubbard, a bearded Missourian of calm and forthright nature, had advised her against becoming the wife of a newspaperman. He once knew a drunken editor in Sedalia.

Mr. Hubbard was a champion rifle shot in his day; and, for that matter, Agnes herself was an expert with the pistol. Against the opposition of the father—not to mention the risk of gunfire from two sides if I made any false moves—I persevered in my suit. I persuaded Agnes that wives of newspapermen enjoyed rare excitements and adventures denied to other women, who could hope for nothing better than mere diamonds and boredom. Agnes did not know any wives of newspapermen at this time; they might have told her that marriage to a member of our profession was a gypsy initiation.

We now had a year-old son, who from the very first seemed to view me with an air of amused suspicion. The child and his grandfather had much in common. I could not as yet afford to take my new family East. Agnes insisted that I go alone to look at the promised land.

I was twenty-eight years old. I had faith in everyone. I have not changed much in this respect. Arthur "Bugs" Baer has said that I looked at life through rose-colored eyeballs. I believed in myself, although at times I felt a burden of inferiority, and had the biggest guilt complex since Macbeth's. I still have occasional feelings of inadequacy, especially so when I find a blank piece of paper in front of me. It is then that I envy all the cocksure braggarts in the world. But at twenty-eight it is early in the morning, and a young man then thinks that he is as tall as his shadow.

Eastern editors, harried by the cost of war news and by a paper shortage, were not presently hiring Western reporters. I meant to go East, nevertheless, to see what was what.

It soon would be quite warm in New York, I was told, so I bought a pongee suit. Agnes made four silk shirts for me and three light-weight cotton nightshirts. These knee-length garments were to replace the long outing-flannel ones I wore in winter. What a dolt I was, later on, to let the meticulous Alfred Damon Runyon talk me into putting aside my comfortable home-made nightshirts which he called "hick-town togas."

For my great journey I purchased a pair of wool spats, and a flowing tie like Lord Byron's. To appear older and more worldly-wise, I acquired a pair of Oxford eyeglasses—something I did not need. Optician Weiss put weak-powered lenses in the tortoise-shell rims. These eyeglasses had a springy gold crossbar for the nose; a black silk-braid ribbon dangled at the right side. Optician Weiss said that I reminded him of James Whitcomb Riley, his favorite poet. He then recited a stanza from "Little Orphan Annie."

I got out a walking stick with which I once had sought to impress a sweetheart. It was a Malacca cane with a silver knob and a leather thong for the wrist. I still have it; the leather wrist strap is missing, the silver knob tarnished and dented. I might see in this a revealing symbol of my several disappointments as a ladies' man were I not mindful of Dr. Samuel Johnson's advice that a writer should under no circumstances disparage himself, lest a reader leap upon an admitted fault and multiply the evidence by ten.

As I prepared for the journey I decided that I didn't look like Byron or Riley, but more like the late war correspondent Richard Harding Davis. It was said that Mr. Davis had often been seen on Park Row with an English bulldog on a leash. I could not take a dog.

To my dismay, Otto Floto received a telegram from his friend, promoter Jack Curley, that papers for the Dempsey-Fulton fight had not yet been signed. I reported this to Rex Yeager. He saw that my spirit was near the breaking point. Accustomed as he was to the consoling of widows and orphans, he put his hand on my shoulder. "We shall do something about this," and he smiled. "You see, I shall never forget what you did in tipping me off about the general."

I was heartened by his next remarks: "I shall send a wire to the bereaved that I am providing a special escort for their mother; that my chosen delegate is ill, but soon will be on the mend."

"Do you think they'll agree?"

"Motherhood is sacred in America," he said. "Even New Yorkers want their mothers to have every attention."

The family consented to wait a "reasonable time." The Dempsey-Fulton fight twice again was delayed. The weeks went by; my editors seemed on the point of ruling out my leave of absence. Otto Floto interceded for me, and so did Dempsey, in a telegram sent to Mr. Tammen. If Dempsey were to win this fight, he would be in line to meet Champion Jess Willard. Floto had been the first writer to predict that Dempsey would be champion one day.

I wondered if Mr. Yeager's embalming efforts would stand the test of waiting for the fighters to sign the papers. "I have even surpassed the technique of ancient Egypt," he assured me. "This one will last till Judgment Day."

A night letter from a family spokesman reached Mr. Yeager's parlors. Would he please speed up the shipment of Mother? Due to a mixup of signals, the clan had already assembled on two consecutive Saturdays at the Gansevoort burial ground.

Jack Curley wired that the fighters had signed up and gone into training. Late in June my wife and infant son, and a delegation from the Denver Press Club, went with me to the Union Depot at the foot of Seventeenth Street. We found Mr. Yeager already there. He took me aside for some instructions. We stood beneath a large sign that had the word "Welcome" spelled out on one face of it and "Mizpah" on the other. A scholarly friend, Lee T. Casey, a reporter for the *News*, interrupted our conference to say that Mizpah was a sacred spot in Gilead.

He gave me a quart of Old Crow. "This," he said, "is to refute the claim that there is no balm in Gilead."

Our town had gone dry soon after Evangelist Billy Sunday made his Denver crusade against sin and rum. Sin had regained some of its popularity, but good liquor was hard to come by, and quite expensive.

Mr. Yeager eyed my bottle and seemed worried. "If by any chance you get separated from the . . ."

He left off speaking whatever thought he may have had in mind. We walked over to the loading platform, where our box rested upon a high-wheeled truck. Mr. Yeager gave me two tickets and a baggage claim check. He pointed out a metal holder tacked to one end of the pine box.

"When you get to Chicago, or wherever else you plan to stop over," he said, "be sure and put this claim check in that little slot. Understand? In case of a, well, a mishap—and of course there *won't* be—the remains will go on through to Albany, and be transshipped to Gansevoort. And, oh, yes, I almost forgot; turn in the Gansevoort portion of the tickets at Albany. Everything clear? Well now, Mizpah to you."

There were good-bys by one and all. Courtney Ryley Cooper, Sells-Floto press agent in the summer, magazine writer, and a reporter for the *Post* in the other months, said, "You'll just love Chicago." I saw no significance in this remark until some days afterward. The waggish Cooper once had been a circus clown.

Otto Floto said to remember him to his old-time pal "Sandy" Griswold, an elderly Omaha sports editor. He promised that Jack Curley would give me a ringside press pass, and arrange for wire facilities for me to write a feature story of the match.

I felt sad but important as I kissed my wife and our baby. Mr. Casey said good-by to me in Latin. A porter took my Gladstone bag, and a train took me into the future.

By the time I reached Omaha for a stop-over, I realized that much of my money had been spent in the dining car. I would have to be more economical. At Omaha I first saw to it that the box was unloaded and placed in a shaded spot for reshipment at my discretion. Then I set out to find Sandy Griswold.

It was a Sunday and, besides, Mr. Griswold was on vacation, fishing somewhere near the Great Lakes. I returned to the depot, reflected on my lack of funds, and then decided to take the next train to Chicago.

Omaha is very hot in July, even in the shade. I felt thirsty and unsure as I sat on the box. I took off my coat and loosened the Byronic necktie. As I sat there in my damp shirtsleeves, I wondered if the heavyweight pugilist James J. Corbett had been right when, not long ago, he had said in Floto's office, "Son, a champion always gets off the floor."

While I was sitting there in the shadow cast by the loading shed, a middle-aged traveler in a broad-brim straw hat and wrinkled linen suit, the coat of which he carried over one arm, walked past me two or three times. Eventually he stopped beside the box. He took off his hat and blessed himself, the coat shifting as he did so, then said, "Don't take it so hard, neighbor. It comes to everybody sometime, one and all. Finis, as they say."

I looked up at him. "I know. But it shouldn't happen to me."

The sweating gentleman fanned himself with his straw hat, then said in a tone of polite inquiry, "I assume it's your darling mother?"

I was too tired and thirsty to reply. He construed my silence as a "yes," then drew from his hip pocket a handkerchief as large as a parachute. He dried his brow and almost dropped his coat as he swabbed the sweat band of his hat, which he then put on with an "Excuse me, neighbor. No disrespect intended." Now he ventured an almost whispered query, as though he were about to bribe a constable. "Would a little drink of something help you?"

"Sir," I said, "you speak like the good Samaritan!"

The Samaritan looked up and down the platform somewhat furtively. "I am led to believe they have certain liquor laws in this state." He thought a while in silence, again peered around and about, then explored the inside pocket of the coat.

"I got fixed up for the train," he said, "but you need it worse than I do, neighbor. Yes, finis is the word. Gotta face it. You see, I too lost a mother once. God rest her soul." He paused a moment. "Of course, it *is* your darling mother? I can see it is, because we all bear up when we lose our father."

I had read that philosophers were terribly absent-minded, so I ventured to prompt him. "My throat is parched."

"Yes, yes, indeed," he said. "Finis! Everything is finis."

He brought a pint bottle from the coat. "Keep it stashed, neighbor."

In a trice the bottle was in my own inside pocket. As I boarded the train I made a little prayer for the man in the wrinkled linen suit.

There were other stops along the way. When I at last reached Chicago I heard my name called by a Western Union boy in Northwestern Station. A telegram from Mr. Yeager suggested that

I was spending too much time along the road. The family at Gansevoort now was making demands instead of mere inquiries; they wished to get on with the funeral.

By this time I was referring to my silent partner as "Nellie," for I was always slow to remember names. I wired Yeager that I would be seeing Nellie home as soon as possible.

It was a hot July day in 1918. I had never been in a big city before. The crowds, the traffic, the movement of men on their way to war, the clamor of it all scrambled the brain. I bought a newspaper and turned to the sports section to see if the White Sox were in town. I chanced to read that Duke Kahanamoku, the Hawaiian swimmer, was to give an exhibition at the Jackson Park pool. I decided to go there instead of to Comiskey Park.

There I found something more exciting than a swimming meet in progress. I saw police wagons along the gravel paths. Sturdy fellows in civilian clothes were asking young men of military age to show their draft cards. When a man was unable to produce a card the officers put him into a police van. Unknown to me at the time, Washington had ordered a nation-wide crackdown on enemy aliens and draft dodgers. A special deputy United States Marshal asked for my card. I had left it at home. When the deputy asked to see my other credentials, I demanded to see his.

I had an unfortunate manner of saying some things. By now I have almost corrected this trait, but occasionally revert to old ways. Just recently a lady backed her car out of a parking place and dented my fender. As I was trying, as politely as you please, to remind her that a parked motorist should make sure that no one is astern before moving a car, she asked did I think she had eyes in the back of her head.

To which I replied with some of my old-time gallantry, "No, madam, nor did I think, until now, that you had your brains in your hind end."

On that afternoon in Chicago long ago, I might have convinced the deputy that I was in the clear, had I but answered his questions in a submissive way. Instead, when he asked my destination and

what was the purpose of my journey, I replied that I was on my
way to fire upon Fort Sumter.

"Oh, a wise guy, eh?" he said. "You are going downtown to
the clinkeroo!"

Word of my plight somehow reached the Chicago Press Club.
I was not at that time acquainted with any of its members, but so
strong was the fellowship of newspapermen everywhere in America
that any stranded journalist could expect the courtesy of the port.

I was wondering just how to send up smoke signals from the
bull pen of the Harrison Street jail, when three young newsmen,
strangers to me, but later on my close friends, appeared at the brig.
They were the Messrs. Harry Hochstadter of the Chicago *Journal*,
Ben Hecht of the *Daily News*, and Charles MacArthur of Mr.
Hearst's Chicago *Examiner*.

Mr. Hochstadter was the first of my champions to arrive. In
appraising my problem, he chanced to mention—somewhat self-
consciously, I thought—that he was a silent partner in a South
Side pawnshop. His extramural connection, he went on to say,
would enable him to arrange a loan at most reasonable terms on
my gold watch.

He seemed almost startled, as well as incredulous, when I said
that I had no watch, gold or otherwise. I tried to explain that I
looked upon all timepieces, including the sun dial and the hour
glass, as symbols of mankind's surrender of both body and soul.

While I was enlarging upon this view, my other rescuers, Charley
MacArthur and Ben Hecht, entered the bull pen. These young
gentlemen, if I may use the word loosely, were friends, pals.

Charley MacArthur was the liveliest Scotsman I ever knew, and
among the brightest. He was but twenty-two years old at the time
of our first meeting; indeed, I always thought of him in terms of
twenty-two until the day he died. Even now I find it hard to believe
that he actually was sixty when he died. To me it seemed that
Charley and Ben and Damon and the rest would stay young until
the time of their farewell.

Dark, slender, tall, and born with the spirit of a wild colt, Mac-

Arthur had no sham or pretense about him. He was a specialist in exposing these faults in others. He has been styled "a cynical prankster" by persons who could not have known him well. I thought him anything but cynical; he was merely skeptical when in the presence of pompous bigwigs. As the saying was, he knew the score. Beneath it all—and he would know much tragedy and pain—he had great compassion and understanding.

In his shining youthful years MacArthur looked upon each day as a time of festival and the gathering of the clans, with pipes skirling. Among his many gifts, MacArthur was one of the nimblest rewrite men of the newspaper world, and could say much in a few words. When an antique privy was destroyed by fire, he wrote but a single line: "The last one in Chicago burned down yesterday."

Not long before I met him, Charley had been ousted from an Illinois National Guard regiment which had seen service in the Mexican Border campaign of 1916. While in a Texas military camp he became editor of the Army newspaper, was placed in the guardhouse with a pal for demonstrating his belief in the freedom of the press, and then smuggled out reports of mistreatment of Chicago's soldier boys. After these stories appeared, a committee of wroth civilians called at the military camp in Texas.

The commandant was showing the committeemen through the prison, assuring them that his wards actually were being coddled, when MacArthur off-scene began to call out hoarsely, "Water! Water! Just one drop!" and "Don't beat me again, sergeant! Have mercy!"

Private MacArthur was released from custody at once, and fed like a Thanksgiving Day turkey. He had grown a black beard while in the guardhouse. No sooner had he been freed than he trimmed the beard to resemble that of General Frederick Funston. He persuaded a pal to "borrow" the general's automobile for a joy ride. They traveled many miles, received salutes, wrecked the car, and only MacArthur's tremendous charm and his newspaper's influence saved him from severe penalties. He was *asked* to leave the regiment.

MacArthur had a way of making his pals feel that life was a highland fling. His friend Hecht called him "Angus," and said to watch out whenever the young Caledonian tugged at his forelock; it meant that he was planning some hilarious scheme. At the time of our meeting Charley MacArthur was trying to enlist for the war overseas. Eventually he succeeded, became an artilleryman, proved capable and brave, but once again got fouled up with a general, "Black Jack" Pershing.

It appears that a group of MacArthur's fellow members of the Rainbow Division, while returning to the rear somewhere in France, had come upon a stallion and a mare enjoying a courtship in a field. A German prisoner of war began to play on a concertina. A member of General Pershing's staff asked Private MacArthur what was going on here. Private MacArthur said that it was the dress rehearsal for a play, in which a stud horse named "Black Jack" would do the thing he now was doing to a mare named "Rainbow"—the same thing that General Pershing had been doing all the time to the Rainbow Division.

Private MacArthur immediately was given credit—or, rather, discredit—for this display and denied promotion. He made up for past military mistakes by enlisting in the Second World War, and became a colonel in the chemical-warfare division. He did not, however, permit himself to lose his zestful spirit, or depart entirely from his gay though skeptical outlook on the ways of men puffed with self-esteem.

As Ben Hecht has pointed out in his book about our late friend, Charles MacArthur had his moments of deep melancholy. But he hid from the world his miseries and his sufferings. He did not wish to see life through a stained-glass window, and to the sound of holy bells.

MacArthur was the son of an evangelical preacher not often in funds. As a mere lad Charley had preached from church pulpits or in tents. During his teens he made up his mind to shun the sawdust trails, whether as a persuader or as a suppliant. His clash with a carbuncle decided him. He had a king-sized specimen of this malady on the nape of his neck. His father believed prayer more powerful and much less expensive than medical aid. The carbuncle burst after several weeks of prayer and the laying on of hands. This experience left MacArthur with a life-long distaste for religious therapy.

Charley said that his father was a great optimist. The Reverend MacArthur moved the family to a desolate farming community with the intention to work the soil to make up for the meagerness of evangelical income. He bought a second-hand harvesting machine on time. Toward evening of their first day in an almost bare farmhouse, the Reverend MacArthur called his brood to the front door to see "God's own glorious sunset."

"It wasn't a sunset at all," Charley told me. "The harvester was on fire. It burned to the ground."

When asked for his philosophy of life, Charley one day replied in the words of a condemned man whose hanging he had witnessed as a reporter. The doomed fellow paused at the steps of the gallows to inquire, "Is this thing safe?"

MacArthur's crony Ben Hecht also was very young at the time I met him at the Harrison Street jail in Chicago. And as I sit thinking of these and other friends of the long ago, I try to recall who among that company had an abler mind and a readier talent for words than Ben Hecht. I cannot think of one.

When I first met him, the young Benjamin already had won more than local recognition as a journalist. I saw in him a muscular fellow (he had been a trapeze artist with a small circus) who had a manner quite friendly yet analytical. He was wearing a porkpie felt hat that day, and a smart mustache like that of a perfume salesman or a Mississippi River gambler.

Young Mr. Hecht was writing feature articles for the *Daily News*. Soon he would be the editor and chief contributor of the Chicago *Literary Times*, one of the memorable "small" magazines of the twenties. Moreover, he was working on his first novel, *Erik Dorn*, a work which brought him early fame among the rising Chicago luminaries.

Although Hecht said of me in an aside to MacArthur, "Here is an authentic muzhik, Charley," I saw in him a new friend.

New friends do not always become old friends; and besides, they have a way of dying before you do. And you grow lonesome, and are apt to live in the past, which is one of the things that frightens off your juniors. I believe that Mr. Satchel Paige, the ancient Negro baseball pitcher, was correct in saying, "Never look back, because someone may be catching up with you."

You do not waste time; time wastes you.

My three advocates persuaded the authorities at the Harrison Street jail that I was not a draft dodger. A sergeant, who sneered like a dissatisfied poet, gave me a voucher to show that I had been properly registered to bear arms. Several other gentlemen of the press now joined us. One of them, chubby Sam P. Hall, said that the Dempsey-Fulton fight had been set ahead to July 27, at the Harrison, New Jersey, baseball park.

Was the name "Harrison" a jinx? I had been jugged in the Harrison Street jail; Dempsey's middle name was Harrison; the fight was to be held in Harrison, New Jersey. I would have to go home before the day of the boxing match.

The hearty company invited me to stay on in Chicago. I was beginning to enjoy the city to the full when, a day or so afterward, a gimlet-eyed man in a broad-brimmed Stetson accosted me in the lobby of the Morrison Hotel as I lifted the house telephone to call a prize-fighter manager of my acquaintance, Larney Lichenstein. The gimlet-eyed man displayed a badge. He announced gruffly that he was arresting me for having violated the Mann Act!

"Just hang up that phone," he said. "We don't like white slavers here. Chicago is famous for its decency."

"What the devil are you talking about?"

"Transporting a woman from state to state for immoral purposes is a federal offense," he said. "Come on, Buster!"

For the first time in days I thought of "Nellie" and of the box at the railway station. I had a feeling that I had neglected to place the baggage slip at the head of the box. Indeed, I fumbled in my pocket, and there it was—the slip. Well, as Runyon used to say, life is made up of a lot of this and that.

The man in the Stetson agreed to go with me to the baggage room of the Northwestern Station. The box could not be found there. I then asked the man to take me to the LaSalle Street Station, from which the New York Central trains left for the East. He obliged me. No Nellie there. She had gone to France, for all I knew.

The man in the Stetson agreed not to apply handcuffs if I behaved myself, but refused to let me telephone my friends. As we went outside the station, I saw Larney Lichenstein and Sam P. Hall getting out of a taxicab. Larney and Sam Hall gave me a cordial hello. Larney greeted my enemy in the big Stetson with "Hello, Tom," then asked how the "carnival happened to go broke in Peoria." It was then I learned that Tom was a "carney" barker, an old friend of Courtney Ryley Cooper of Denver, and that Cooper had authored this hoax about the Mann Act. I now remembered what Cooper had said at the time I left Denver: that I would "love Chicago."

I received a telegram from Rex Yeager that evening. From it I found out that Cooper had written a front-page story about my Chicago adventures. Should we sue for libel? Another wire, this one from Agnes, informed me that Rex had come across the street to announce that the scandalous publicity had ruined him and his mortuary business for all time. I thought of the man who had told me in Omaha that everything was "finis." Was he a seer?

"Steady now," Mr. Hecht advised me. "Your undertaker friend actually will benefit by the publicity, once the air is cleared of the yodels and snorts and cries of disaster. As for the body, it will wash ashore with some friendly tide and will reach the town of Gansevoort, if indeed there actually *is* such a place."

I thought it expedient to leave next day for Albany. I kept remembering Gentleman Jim Corbett's adage: "A champion always gets off the floor." But the word "finis" offset Mr. Corbett's philosophy. I telegraphed Yeager that I had *lost* the body. Would he please trace it through official channels?

Just before I left Chicago I heard again from my wife. Agnes said that Mr. Yeager had paid her still another visit upon receiving word of the lost body. He had seemed desperate. "This is curtains!" he had said. He had kept on muttering something which sounded to Agnes like "Mrs. Paw," or "Mizpah." And what did it mean? I telegraphed her, collect, not to worry, and to tell Rex to keep his shroud on.

At Albany, while I was strolling outside the railway station, and eating peanuts and just wondering, a Western Union boy called my name. He delivered a telegram: "Where is mother?" It was signed by a spokesman for "Nellie's" family at Gansevoort. In self-defense Mr. Yeager had advised them of my whereabouts.

I sent a wire to Gansevoort: "Mother is well. Will be with you soon."

On the wall behind the Western Union counter a poster advertised the sailings of the Hudson River Day Line. I decided to make the last leg of my journey to New York by water. The excursion down-river served to quiet my frustrations. Washington Irving had introduced this stream and this countryside to my imagination. It seemed the most beautiful valley in the world. And of all the craft I would sail upon in the years to come, none would appear as water-worthy as the old white-hull side-wheeler *Hendrick Hudson*.

The river boat's engine beat like the heart of an Irish queen. Gray clouds moved slowly overhead but the sun kept breaking through. The Hudson then became a silver sash across the July-green breast of the storied land. Three hundred years of history sailed with me from the portals of the Catskills to the rise of the Jersey Palisades, and between banks of wondrous imaginings in the valley of the Dutch. Downstream we passed moored vessels camouflaged for war. They seemed cubistic exhibits from a gallery of modern art. Hemp-bearded rugs, with strings of lighters in tow, and ferry boats crisscrossed our course.

Toward evening we came alongside the landing at the foot of Desbrosses Street. The waterfront smelled stale and briny, like the inside of a sauerkraut barrel. Beyond the piers and ferry slips the buildings reached up like a petrified forest of mighty trees.

Here Washington Irving's Hudson was called the North River. It washed the western flank of the islands of Manhattan. Why it is known as the North River has never been explained to me; it plainly serves the western margin of the borough.

I claimed my Gladstone bag, held my cane as though to begin a duel, then got into a decrepit taxicab. I asked the brisk gnome at the wheel to drive me to the Hotel McAlpin. A widely traveled Denver editor (he had even been to Bermuda) had told me that the McAlpin was "strictly the class."

"Always go first class," he had said. "If you can't ride the cushions, stay home."

At the hotel I found the telephone number of Damon Runyon in a book as thick as a pulpit Bible.

Damon's wife Ellen, formerly a society reporter in Denver, answered my ring. "Alfred's out of town," she said. "He's expected back tomorrow."

This seemed a bad omen, perhaps another "finis."

The rumbling of the Sixth Avenue "El" became a hostile din. I decided to look for something to read. The hotel-room library consisted of a Gideon Bible and a cast-off copy of the New York *Sun*. Inside that newspaper I came upon the report of a Tammany Hall picnic. The unsigned story was written with extraordinary liveliness and charm. How was the young stranger to gain a place among men who could write in this splendid way?

I learned afterward that Frank Ward O'Malley was the author of this article. O'Malley frequently "covered" Tammany outings for the *Sun*. Accomplished reporters of the Big Town needed no signatures to identify their articles to other masters of Park Row. These recording angels had style and stature. They had looked long upon life and its perishable actors, yet stayed on more or less good terms with mankind, and seldom coveted the fame or the estates of the mighty. The seasoned reporter finds that the only thing which money actually can buy is people.

A bellboy brought a telegram to the door. It was from Agnes. Rex Yeager had called upon her a third time. He said that my conduct did not make it too easy for him to live on in a community where his customers always died.

"Besides," he had asked, "why did Gene have to send an insulting wire to the family after losing their mother?"

It so happened that the town was delighted with Courtney Ryley Cooper's story of my misadventure. Mr. Yeager's prestige grew because of this publicity. He soon afterward built a large mortuary in Denver. Eventually he "expanded" to the Pacific Coast, where he owned a whole cemetery, and where at last he himself kept a date with the Digger.

As for Nellie, she was buried in the little town of Gansevoort, a place which I shall never see. How the box eventually reached Gansevoort, as if of its own accord, was a circumstance never fully explained to me or to Mr. Yeager. Rex did learn, however, that it had been shipped from Chicago to Montreal, and then to some place in Maine. It reached Albany late that month on its belated way to Gansevoort.

As the fellow said, everything is "finis."

CHAPTER

3

The Fates sit darkling in the
fog with thread and scissors.

—MAURICE HEWLETT

ON A July afternoon of the war year 1918, I went with Damon
Runyon to the Polo Grounds to see the New York Yankees play
the Chicago White Sox. The flag in center field draped the mast
with slow-swaying folds. There was not enough wind to spread
the banner or change the course of balls hit high away. Today
the colors lazed at half staff; John Purroy Mitchel, ex-mayor of
the city's five million, was dead.

On January first of that year, Mr. Mitchel yielded office to
William Randolph Hearst's drab political protégé John F. Hylan.
Mr. Mitchel thereupon had enlisted in the aviation section of
the Army Signal Corps. He was given the rank of major. During
a solo flight in a scout plane at Lake Charles, Louisiana, he
neglected to buckle his safety belt. Searchers found the body in
the marsh grass half a mile south of Gerstner Field.

Runyon said that the ex-mayor's coffin right now was on its way
from the uptown home of Mitchel's mother to City Hall in
lower Manhattan. Tomorrow, with former President Theodore
Roosevelt, Governor Charles S. Whitman, and other men of state

and the military attending, there would be a Requiem Mass at St. Patrick's gray cathedral. As we sat at the Polo Grounds below Coogan's Bluff, Runyon remarked that nothing was as dead as a dead politician. He went on to say that nothing, except war, was as brutal as politics; this was especially so in the City of New York.

The grandstand shadow moved like an eclipse toward the mound where Reb Russell was winding up for his next pitch to Eddie Collins of the Sox. Like many other ballplayers, Mr. Collins was superstitious. When at bat, he would put his wad of chewing gum on the button of his cloth cap. When a pitcher had two strikes on him, Collins would restore the gum to his mouth, then chew vigorously. In those days the batsmen wore no head protectors. The pitchers had more freedom of delivery. A hitter had to take care.

The grandstand shadow seemed a band of mourning for the ex-mayor, and for all the others who had died, or were dying, or would die in battle. The newspapers were speaking of peace. The Austrians were retreating. The Germans, however, were poised for a blow along the Marne.

Skeins of mist drifted in from the Harlem River. The wedge of sky as seen from the press box became Confederate gray. Joe Vila of the *Evening Sun* asked Damon how soon he expected to go overseas as a war correspondent. Runyon wasn't sure; reading Mr. Hearst's mind, he said, was like "trying to make four the hard way with the dice."

Runyon said that Mr. Vila had been mentioned in a letter from Grantland Rice of the *Tribune*. Henry Grantland Rice was now an Army lieutenant with the 15th Field Artillery in northwestern France. I would meet Rice the next February. Tennessee-born, soft-spoken, kindly, athletic, this man was our beau ideal. George M. Cohan called him "a virile saint." Granny died in 1954 at the age of seventy-five, the dean of sports writers.

In 1918 Rice turned down an offer by *Collier's* to send him overseas as a war correspondent at a dollar a word. Instead he volunteered for active service in the Army. Rice had saved $75,000 during his eighteen years on the newspapers. He entrusted this nest egg to his lawyer, to take care of his wife "Miss Kitty" in the event he did not return from the battlefields of France. The lawyer at once proceeded to waste this money, all of it, then committed suicide.

When he heard of this, Rice had three drinks, then said, "It was my own fault, mine entirely. I should not have put so much temptation in the man's way."

During the many years I would know Grantland Rice, I would hear him speak against but two persons with any show of bitterness or contempt. One was a motion-picture personality whose heart was as big as a mustard seed, the other a writer who, in Rice's opinion, had mistreated his wife and family and, worse still, had exchanged publicity in his newspaper articles for cash on the line.

Rice's own ethical conduct as a newspaperman was unimpeachable. When promoter Tex Rickard made him a present of a traveling case one Christmas, Rice gave Rickard a golf bag and a set of matched clubs worth three times that of the Rickard present. Grantland Rice traveled with champions, and indeed was regarded by them as the greatest of champions in his own profession.

On the day when Runyon mentioned Rice's letter, he remarked that the press box was not the same with so many friends overseas. Nor was anything else the same, he went on to say, including Broadway, a street sometimes called "the Rue Regret."

The baseball writers of long ago worked at two built-in benches, one behind the other, in a wire-screened enclosure at ground level back of home plate. The press accommodations then at the Polo Grounds, as at other athletic centers, indoors or out, would seem primitive today. Now the newspaper gallery at the sports parks sit like members of the board. At the Los Angeles Coliseum the football reporters have a private elevator, swivel chairs, elbow room, and eagle's-nest privacy above the playing field. They also enjoy free refreshments more varied than the hot dogs that Harry

Stevens, pioneer sports-park caterer, used to provide for the scribes.

Sports writers of my time had gargantuan appetites (excepting Runyon, who was very choosy, as the saying is, about his food, and would balk at frankfurters and similar rations). The athletes also had tremendous capacities for food. Wrestlers were among the heartiest eaters. But I suppose that Babe Ruth could put away more groceries than any of his fellow trenchermen.

Babe Ruth would eat a frankfurter and a bun each time he would waddle in from right field to the dugout, and then gulp a bottle of Coca-Cola as a chaser. Were the game to go into extra innings, say twelve, the Bambino's belly would rumble like Mt. Stromboli. After he had left the ball park, he would enjoy an extra-thick steak, five or six potatoes, and a whole apple pie, then complain about the belly ache and take bicarbonate of soda. In 1918 Ruth was with the Boston Red Sox—a left-handed pitcher, one of the best.

The press box at the Polo Grounds frequently became overrun by members of the Lambs, actor pals of John J. McGraw, manager of the Giants. These thespians got in the way of reporters and telegraphers; eventually they were barred after the writers threatened to boycott the home games.

During football season the working press sat halfway up in a then unsheltered section of the stands at the third-base side of the Polo Grounds. Whenever they would feel cold they would pass the flasks. Sports reporters of today are protected from the elements as well as from kibitzers. Fans used to look over a writer's shoulder, examine his prose, and make constructive criticisms. One time at Sportsman's Park in St. Louis, when reporter W. O. McGeehan was writing about an unruly fan who had cracked the skull of center-fielder Whitey Witt of the Yankees with a pop bottle, a St. Louis partisan read McGeehan's criticism over Bill's shoulder. He then pushed a hot-dog sandwich in the reporter's face and shouted, "Send *that* to New York!"

The jerry-built benches for the working press at the outdoor prize fights of my time were not smoothed expertly. I still seem to feel the splinter I picked up with a restless backside the day Jack Dempsey knocked out Georges Carpentier at Boyle's Thirty Acres in New Jersey.

The New York Yankees had no playing field of their own until 1923. In 1918 they were coming to the fag end of a slipshod season which had been a migraine headache to major-league bosses, in terms both of poor attendance and of the wartime draft of the younger players. The regular schedule of 154 games had been curtailed to 140. In August the sport would take a recess till the war's end, except for the forthcoming World Series in September. Other athletic ventures had been ruled out by President Woodrow Wilson's wartime work-or-fight decree. The race tracks had closed.

My first day as Runyon's guest at the Polo Grounds became a memorable introduction to New York and its wonders. That night I wrote a long letter to Agnes. In it I told of all that I had seen and heard and felt. I wrote that almost every journalist in New York seemed to know my newspaper stories, and that several editors were competing for my services. Agnes was the only person I ever boasted to so outrageously. It would be many years before I would realize that she had been wise to me all the time. She was her father's daughter, as the saying is, willing to believe that the whale swallowed Jonah, but refusing to allow that Jonah could swallow the whale.

Runyon and I left the baseball park an inning or so before the game ended. He said he had a date to see "a certain party" downtown. The Yankees had been determined, or so it would appear, to make a present of the game to the World Series winners of 1917. There was nothing crooked in their lackadaisical manner of play; no gamblers had bribed the players to throw away the game, as would happen the next year when the Chicago team would become the "Black Sox."

We drove away from the park in a taxicab. Runyon sat back, chain-smoked in silence for a while, then said as though to himself, "Just listen to it roar!"

At first I thought he meant the roar of the baseball fans. But that could not be, for they had sat on their hands all afternoon and kept their voices down, except when "The Star-Spangled Banner" had been played. My friend was speaking of the everlasting noise of the city. He had the solemn look of a child that holds a conch shell to its ear.

"Just listen to it roar!" he said once again.

Forty years and more have gone since that day; gone to whatever place the years go in the momentum of time, and wherever the hopes, the fears, the longings, the joys, the griefs go. I cannot, of course, recollect in context Damon's every remark of that or of any other day; but I remember the words, "Just listen to it roar!"

Somewhere uptown we got out of the cab at a subway kiosk to board a West Side express train. We left the subway at the Park Place station. I recollect my sense of anticipation as we came out of the tiled catacombs beneath the Woolworth Building, at that time the tallest of the skyscrapers. We left the cave smells of the underground to cut across the ancient green acres of City Hall Park. I saw the home-bound workers swarming out of the office buildings at the borders of the park triangle. Here at this hour was the greatest pedestrian traffic of all the cities in the world.

I tried to see the various faces, but saw them as a composite face, apparitional, as if looked at through banners of chiffon. That face wore no smile. The city's voice that cast a spell on Runyon sounded to me like the throatings of an asthmatic Titan. The face and the voice troubled me, I knew not why.

The home-goers moved in swift-paced streams of migration, a massive prison break, a gold rush in reverse, to the various subway burrows or to the Brooklyn Bridge terminal, a shed as ugly as the shaft house of a coal mine. That shed is gone now, and so is old Park Row. And the years have gone, and friends, and the bright adventures. But love and memory last, and will so endure till the game is called because of darkness.

CHAPTER

4

*There is no harm done to
saints if their faults are shown
as well as their virtues.*

　　—SAINT FRANCIS DE SALES

RUNYON was a tight-lipped man, a listener, a watcher. He had occasional periods of garrulity, however, especially if he had in hand someone as wonder-struck as I. Bits of his conversation drift back to me, things he said as we came upon the bilious-green lawns of historic City Hall Park. This tongue-shaped common lay among buildings which had erupted like great irregular teeth, some old and low, others new and very high. In an effort to cover my astonishment, my fear really, at this dragon's jaw, I mentioned that the grass here was not July grass, if grass at all.

To which Runyon said, "The bravest thing in New York is a blade of grass. This is not prize grass, but it has moxie. You need plenty of moxie in this man's town, or you'll soon find yourself dispersed hither and yon."

As we walked along, my friend singled out some of the spires and domes and towers and gave their pedigrees. He said that the brownstone walls of the Pulitzer Building, where the New York *World* published both morning and evening editions, were almost ten feet thick, and no steel in the structure. Built like the pyramids, he said. The *World* had a restaurant for staff members beneath the gilded dome; but anyone with the time and wherewithal dined elsewhere.

He called my attention to a gray stone building with bold wings and a central arcade where Chambers Street pierced it. The tall pile, fella, was the new Municipal Building. It had cost twelve million modern dollars. And to think of it—he pointed out a dingy stone structure, one corner of which I could see at the rear of City Hall—that sorry old heap also had cost twelve million, soon after the Civil War! It was the county courthouse, built by Boss Tweed and his "Forty Thieves."

"There's always a payoff for everything in this man's town," Runyon said. "Twelve million smackers was more than somewhat in the days when a dollar was enough to buy an eight-course dinner at Delmonico's and a thousand dollars win the favor of aldermanic philanthropists."

The Tweed ring had allowed for a short lane between City Hall and the courthouse. Several generations of politicians had strolled there to exchange views about "civic betterment." Damon called it "Handshake Alley."

The roar of the city bullied the ears of the outlander. Runyon described it as a cheer for the winners, a jeer for the losers. "The city is yours," he said in effect. "Not for you or anyone else to take as Grant did Richmond, but to earn by hard work, plus luck. Without luck a reporter is as out of place as a door buzzer in a tomb."

He was sorry for having taken me to the worst-played game since A. G. Spalding had quit throwing baseballs and had chosen to manufacture them instead. We now were approaching the main entrance of City Hall, where General George Washington had heard the Declaration of Independence read. A bell somewhere south of the park was ringing with much resonance—the bourdon bell of St. Paul's Chapel, the oldest church building in Manhattan.

At thirty-second intervals a bell much nearer to us, an old bell in the cupola of City Hall, beat a single solemn note. The clock which this bell served had been overhauled just recently. The cupola of the post-Colonial building had been destroyed by fire a year ago, Damon informed me, but the clock had kept time all the while. Repair men had left behind them a tinker's pot of live coals on the ancient roof. It was the second time this tower had burned; fireworks set it ablaze during the celebration of the laying of the Atlantic cable in 1858.

As the solo beat of the clock-tower bell hummed down, a detail of police officers of Traffic-A held their sticks at salute. Soldiers acting as bearers brought a coffin up the stone steps of City Hall. In it lay the body of former Mayor Mitchel. The soldiers carried the flag-draped coffin across the marble threshold, above which was hung a service flag with a solitary gold star upon it.

The mahogany coffin—draped with the flag, the dead officer's cap upon its field—was set upon black trestles. A strip of purple carpet beneath the bier lay upon the floor stones above which the coffins of Abraham Lincoln, Horace Greeley, and Ulysses S. Grant successively had rested long ago.

Candles were lighted. There was a guard mount. The passing bell tolled again. It would ring at one-minute intervals all that night. The clamor of the living city became somewhat muted by the thick masonry of the Hall. But one was still mindful of the rumblings of elevated trains and of the trolleys which served the Manhattan terminus of Brooklyn Bridge. One could hear, as though from far away, the Broadway streetcar gongs, taxicab horns, police whistles, the bronchitic cries of newsboys.

We stood with our hats off and apart from the thin line of comers and goers inside the City Hall. I thought it strange that so few of the tens of thousands I had just seen outside this building had left the mainstreams of traffic on Park Row, Nassau, and Broadway, to spend a little time beside the closed coffin in the rotunda.

I said as much to Runyon. He drummed the crown of his hat with his fingers, somewhat impatiently, I thought. "I wouldn't be here myself," he said, "if I hadn't promised Bill Mizner to do a favor for that certain party I'm to meet." He nudged me. "Here's one of your heroes."

Colonel Theodore Roosevelt, former President of the United States, appeared on the scene. He spoke for a few moments with Mayor Hylan's handsome young secretary, Grover A. Whalen, just outside Room 9, where the City Hall reporters had their press headquarters. Mr. Whalen had a black mustache and very white teeth. Mr. Roosevelt now shook hands with the merchant-financier Cleveland H. Dodge, then left with a bespectacled Army colonel of the Medical Corps whom Runyon could not name.

The next morning the sixty-year-old ex-president would walk from City Hall to St. Patrick's Cathedral, a march of four and one-half miles uptown, behind a gun carriage provided by the Army for the dead mayor's last ride. Somehow I had expected to see in Colonel Roosevelt a man of heroic stature, an American Hercules, for his legend was a mighty one, his gospel strenuous. Instead I saw the Rough Rider in close view as a person of but medium height. I thought that he appeared trail-weary at sixty notwithstanding the don't-tread-on-me thrust of his jaw.

Like other hero-worshipers of my generation, I had believed T.R. to be ageless and industructible. I had not actually seen him during his three whirlwind visits to Colorado and Wyoming, the last in 1910. But I had read almost everything our newspapers had said of his holidays among us, and studied the press photographs. Only a true Westerner, I used to think, could have ridden horseback each day from dawn till dark over Senator Francis E. Warren's Wyoming cattle range. On one occasion he remarked, "My horse is breathing some—and then some." Each sundown he appeared fit, the reporters had said, as he sat with the cowboys in the bunk house to eat black bread and bully beef. But today he looked tired.

Theodore Roosevelt had seemed as Western to me as anyone Frederic Remington had painted, although I knew that he had been born in New York. Today, dressed in black coat and pin-stripe trousers, a black felt hat in his left hand (he would wear a silk topper on the morrow), he was indeed the New Yorker.

A good friend of mine, Dudley Field Malone, disclosed to me at a later time that Woodrow Wilson had privately begrudged Roosevelt his hearty manner with one and all. Malone had been Governor Wilson's protégé during the presidential campaign of 1912, when Roosevelt as a Bull Moose split the Republican vote for Taft.

Young Malone traveled with Governor Wilson during that campaign, and occupied the same hotel rooms with the future President. Malone afterward became Collector of the Port of New York, and then an assistant Secretary of State. He might have risen to higher places had he not resigned with hot words because Mr. Wilson put off keeping his pledge to give the women of America the right to vote.

Malone once told me that Mr. Wilson actually was a warm and sentimental man behind his austere façade. Few newspapermen could see that aspect of his personality. The reporters heard that he privately recited limericks and did an occasional jig; and it was evident that he liked vaudeville shows; but they felt that he had a refrigerated contempt for journalists. He saw the press, if at all, from Mt. Everest.

Mr. Wilson actually was a shy man, Malone said. He spoke of a day when Governor Wilson and he were in the waiting room of the Philadelphia railway station as the campaigning Colonel Roosevelt chanced to arrive, a throng following him. The colonel was shaking hands and clapping backs, and even calling out first names. He was showing his piano-keyboard teeth in a smile for everyone. He was delighted. He felt bully.

No one, however, paid much attention to Woodrow Wilson. "Dudley," said the scholarly candidate, "I'd give my right arm if I could meet people the way that fellow does."

Later in that campaign Colonel Roosevelt's train stopped at a wayside station. The colonel addressed the townspeople from the observation platform of his private car. A drunken man interrupted from time to time with "I love you, Teddy Roosevelt!"

As the locomotive whistle summoned the train crew aboard,

the colonel's admirer acted as though the signal were for him. A brakeman sought to keep him off the train, but the hearty colonel said that any warm-blooded American had the right to shake the hand of a fellow patriot.

At this there were more cries of, "I love you, Teddy!"

When the boozy enthusiast embraced the candidate too long, he was pried loose, then fell headlong down the car steps. The train was pulling out. The colonel was waving his campaign hat and displaying his dental masterpieces.

His bruised admirer sat up on the roadbed to call out, "I love you, Teddy Roosevelt!" Then, making use of his constitutional right of freedom of speech, he announced, "But I'm going to vote for Woodrow Wilson!"

On the day when I closely observed Colonel Roosevelt at New York's City Hall, he seemed careworn and much older than in his published photographs. Perhaps he had a premonition of a tragedy impending in France, where, a few days from now, his son Quentin would die. Colonel Roosevelt himself would die within a few months of this day.

Likely enough the hardships of the South American jungle, where he discovered the River of Doubt, had been too strenuous even for him. Runyon thought otherwise. He said that the political miscalculations the colonel had made, the rebuffs he encountered in the evening of his career, had subdued the exuberant statesman. Colonel Roosevelt had been snubbed by President Wilson when he offered to recruit and lead his own regiment against the Kaiser. Runyon told me that Mr. Wilson had called the colonel a show-off and had said that the best way to break an exhibitionist's heart was to keep him from showing off.

My well-informed friend looked at his wrist watch, and whispered to me, "Let's go."

We went outside the place of mourning to see an early-evening mist, moody and miasmic as a Whistler nocturne, drifting in from the harbor. The jaundiced veil muffled some of the city's bluster and screened off the downtown towers. From far away a foghorn moaned, hoarse and disconsolate, like the farewell solo of a tuba player contemplating suicide.

I was about to ask my guide if he ever got homesick for the West, but just then he called out, "Jimmy!" and was greeted on a first-name basis by a dapper man of slight build who was coming as though mounted on springs up the old marble steps. Maybe this was the "certain party." Runyon and the newcomer shook hands and whispered and nodded and gesticulated. I saw in Runyon's friend a know-the-score person, cocksure though cordial of manner, a surrogate for a faun. I noticed his small expressive hands, his smart boots. He wore a soft-brim straw hat at a jaunty angle. I observed that the little dandy stood with his weight on the balls of his feet, as though awaiting the orchestral downbeat at the beginning of a soft-shoe dance. In fact I thought him a song-and-dance crony of Runyon's from Broadway, perhaps the Palace Theatre.

The gentlemen now had ended their whispered conversation. To my amazement, Runyon introduced me to Senator James J. Walker. My friend told him, with a touch of irony I thought, that I was a Western journalist "casing New York."

Senator Walker evidently saw that I was ill at ease. He went out of his way to be kind. He explained that he was only a state senator, then repeated my full name, as though he meant to remember it for all time. I thought his voice unusually deep for such a small-size man. He made me feel that I was most welcome to the City of New York, where he had been born, a place which he loved next best to the United States of America, or so he said. Were I to decide to go to work here, both the city and I would benefit no end by that fortunate arrangement. He could make blarney sound like the Gettysburg Address.

I had no way then of knowing that Mr. Walker made everyone whom he met feel important and confident. For that matter, I had no way of foreseeing that I was to become the managing editor of Mr. Hearst's New York *American* at the very time when this jaunty state senator would be elected mayor. These events were to occur within the next eight years.

Nor did the young senator (he was then thirty-seven) know that one day he would be regarded as the symbol and the chief celebrant of the grand fete; or that, at the sad quick close of the escapade, he would be marked off as the most conspicuous victim of an age which created him in its own image. James J. Walker was his own worst friend.

He had not wanted to enter politics at all, I afterward learned (when I wrote his life story, *Beau James*) but had done so to please his father. He had wanted most of all to be a lyricist of popular songs. What happiness might he have found, had he stayed in Tin-Pan Alley? He sometimes asked that question.

Senator Walker was saying that the death of ex-Mayor Mitchel was a tremendous loss. He pronounced the word as "tremenjuss," and glanced this way and that, as though to challenge anyone to flout his opinion. Damon replied somewhat casually, "Oh, he'd do a fellow a favor." Then Runyon remarked as one "in the know," "They say he liked a little fun on the side. A little this-and-that, but on the Q.T."

The senator was slow to answer. "He was human," he said. As though anxious to change the subject, he said to Runyon, "Now about that matter you were speaking of a while ago . . ." He cast a glance my way and hesitated; but Damon nodded with a go-ahead signal, and Mr. Walker continued. "It's this way, Damon. I'll drop a word in his favor, but it's really out of my jurisdiction. Red Mike and I don't sleep in the same barn. But tell Bill Mizner any friend of his is a friend of mine. I'll do my level best. Hope you understand."

"I understand, Jimmy, and thanks," Damon said.

The dapper little man said good-by to us and went on his way with the manner of one who has not a care in the world.

"Who is Red Mike?" I asked Damon.

"He's the mayor. Mayor Hylan. Used to drive an engine on the

El. Got fired, and hates anything that has wheels, or the people who own wheels on public conveyances. It was his nickname on the El, Red Mike. Has a head thicker than the wall of China. But he's Mr. Hearst's man. As soon as I get through with this business with that certain party, we'll drop in on Tad Dorgan at the *Journal*."

I knew of course that Mr. Dorgan was one of the most popular cartoonists of the day, originator of slang phrases, and friend of sportsmen and theatrical figures whom I had met in Otto Floto's office in Denver.

On our way to Park Row Runyon told me that the late ex-Mayor Mitchel and Senator Walker had looked enough alike to have been brothers. Mr. Mitchel also had resembled the jaunty state senator in that he liked to stay up late with spirited companions. All this may have been true, but now it is to be seen that he had been much more discreet than the record shows Mr. Walker to have been. The Mitchel playtime activities were off-the-record events. The day had not yet arrived for men of mark to kick up their heels to the applause of the Big Town.

Walker was seldom discreet. He lasted for some years in public favor because of his immense wit, his warm personality, and because his days of wine and roses coincided with a postwar time which cast off the moral restraints our elders had decreed. He had a heart as big as Pagliacci's drum.

Jimmy Walker had real abilities, too, as an orator and a law-maker. He was quick of mind when on his feet; but, as the sagacious Robert Moses has said of him, "Jimmy Walker lacked staying powers." He tired of many things, and eventually seemed to tire of life itself.

As its mayor, Walker charmed the city, just as he charmed almost everyone he met along the way. Mr. Mitchel also had pleasing social faculties, but avoided scandal and the hazards of hasty romances. Mr. Walker never undertook to hide his heart's caprice. As for official mistakes, he all but invited political betrayal by ill-chosen playmates. He learned at last, when in self-imposed exile, that fame and happiness are total strangers.

As Runyon and I walked along Park Row on our way to meet that "certain party," my friend pointed out the few buildings that still housed publications in what once had been the journalistic nerve center of the town. The *World* and the *Tribune* and the war-harried *Staats Zeitung* were the only newspaper plants that remained here, although New York reporters and editors who worked uptown always referred to themselves as men of Park Row.

Through a street-front window of the *Tribune* I could make out an oil painting in a massive gilded frame of Victorian flavor. It showed the full figure of an old man with a high forehead, steel-rimmed spectacles, a fringe of whiskers, and wrinkled trousers which seemed to lack proper means of suspension. He seemed to be standing halfway between hope and dread.

"Horace Greeley," Runyon said of the picture. "His pants were about all he had left after he sold the *Tribune* to Whitelaw Reid. He's shown here protecting 'em with his last bit of strength."

The *Tribune* building, Runyon said, was the first-built of New York's tall structures. I glanced back to see, high up on the northern side of the masonry, a large painted sign that amazed me. Within its black borders there was displayed a fearsome serpent ready to strike. Beneath it was this legend:

"Coiled in the Flag! Hears-s-s-ss-sss-t!"

CHAPTER

5

*As leaves on trees do with the
  turning year*

*The former fall, and others
  will appear;*

*Just so it is in words, one
  word will rise,*

Look green, and flourish,
  when another dies.

—HORACE

AS WE approached New Chambers Street, I was wondering
about that snake legend on the north flank of the *Tribune* tower.
It contained fighting words, and I said as much to Runyon. Editors
out West would not take an insult such as this lying down—or
give one, unless prepared to break out the horsewhips and the six-
shooters. Did Damon remember the time W. W. ("Plug Hat")
Anderson, attorney for Packer the man-eater, shot the owners of
the Denver *Post* for having written of him as a low-down thief?

Yes, Runyon recalled it as well as several other flurries of guns
and fists, even a touch of dynamite in Western editorial rooms.
This was New York, however, he admonished me, a more civilized
place. I was not to expect Wild West displays by metropolitan
editors. And by the way, how long had I been wearing "those fancy
cheaters"? My eyeglasses. And that "nifty crutch"? My walking
stick. I sensed his strong disapproval of these accessories.

The bell of City Hall was heard again above the roar of Runyon's
town. A street organ somewhere in the neighborhood was playing
an epileptic version of the "Merry Widow Waltz." We had come

to a low old building, and above its doorway I saw a pock-marked gilt sign. This was a restaurant, if one believed the sign: "Max's Busy Bee."

"Here's where I'm to see that certain party," Runyon said.

It became apparent that Runyon did not mean to take me inside Max's hive. Beyond the open door, I could see the patrons moving about like drones. For one thin dime, Runyon explained, a person of slender means might obtain a hot meal of sorts here at Max's, and a mug of so-called coffee.

Mr. Runyon was a prodigious coffee drinker, but a bit particular as to its quality, as he was about many other things which had to do with food or dress or the proprieties. He said that it was very hard indeed to come upon a genuinely bad cup of coffee in all the City of New York, what with the soft clear water borne by the great aqueduct reaching southward from the Catskill Mountains. However, said Damon, Max had been able, by means of a closely guarded recipe handed down by the three witches of *Macbeth*, to brew coffee which dissolved the tonsils and started a five-alarm fire in the gullet.

Damon probably would have continued his tribute to Max's coffee, for he liked to improvise upon any topic which chanced to suit his sense of comic irony. But now a small, elderly fellow, by no means poorly dressed, except that his heavy tweed suit suggested several winters before last, came out of Max's hive and gravely approached us.

"Did I keep you waiting, Mr. Runyon?" he asked.

His voice was hoarse, a croaking whisper really. He seemed hungry for air. I observed that he was sallow of skin, thin-stemmed, and I hoped that Runyon would give him whatever it might be he wanted. He had the look of one who wanted something, and always had wanted something.

"Doctor," Runyon was saying, "meet Mr. Fowler. Mr. Fowler, this is Doctor DeGarmo. Fowler works for Otto Floto out West, Doctor."

"Oh, yes," said the hoarse fellow. "My pleasure."

I don't know why, but some impulse caused me to palm a dollar bill as I shook hands with Dr. DeGarmo. He never batted an eye. I hoped that Runyon had not observed this business. Upon shaking hands, I was aware that the forefinger of the doctor's right hand lacked the first and second joints.

"Doctor," Runyon said in a matter-of-fact way, "you'll be fixed up solid before cold weather sets in."

"Thank you," said Dr. DeGarmo, and he turned to go. "Thank you very much, Mr. Runyon."

That was all. Runyon and I walked around the corner of Park Row at New Chambers Street. I was quite mystified by the brevity of the meeting with the "certain party." I felt that so much importance had been implied prior to the meeting itself as to have made it seem an anticlimax. However curious I may have been, I thought it best to say nothing, but wait, as it were, for the other shoe to drop.

As we turned to our right we abruptly came upon a world-in-little, much older, it seemed, than the one we had just left behind us. I did not know that the island of Manhattan was a jig-saw puzzle of contrasting settlements.

In Colonial times this neighborhood lay at the northerly side of a district known as "the swamp." Long ago it had been reclaimed from the tadpoles and water bugs. Here the early-day tanners of hides had set down their soaking-pits and pickling vats. The shabby environs just east of Park Row still remained a trading center for wholesale leather merchants, although the tanners had been gone these many years. The land was low and damp; the foundations of the buildings rested on piles, Runyon said. The neighborhood still had a rancid smell reminiscent of the gall-nut refuse and half-cured pelts of its earlier time.

We walked past a pawnshop, then a second-hand clothes store, where the bearded proprietor stood outside his door to play catch-as-catch-can with passers-by. The trains on the iron-stilted "El" that reached in from Chatham Square and Chinatown and the Bowery to the north harangued the murky evening. The street lamps came on to fight a losing battle with the darkness. The scene had the quality of a Horatio Alger story background; and, indeed, Runyon said that the rags-to-riches author had often frequented this part of town.

The narrow streets formed a maze of colliding angles that might have puzzled Euclid. The old thoroughfares were paved with stone blocks brought from Belgium as ballast in the hulls of sailing vessels. The traffic here was slow; horse-drawn trucks and vans usurped the strictured ways.

This labyrinth is gone with the glacial flow of time.

Runyon's Broadway-styled clothes, a fawn-colored gabardine suit and a Panama hat, as I recall his attire, made him seem all the more the dude as we moved among printers and press men of the district, many of whom wore improvised square hats of paper. Meandering bums, whose chins needed razors, were among the pedestrians. The air smelled stale, as though the redcoats of George III had forgotten to take it with them upon their evacuation of New York.

I was still thinking of Dr. DeGarmo when a blue-chinned fellow in a dirty blue shirt asked Runyon to stake him to coffee and crullers. Damon gave him a coin. The moocher promised to burn a candle for his benefactor at the Church of St. Andrew in nearby Duane Street.

"You never can tell," Runyon said. "He might be a Hearst editor in disguise. Speaking of *Macbeth*, as we were a little while ago, reminds me of something that happened in this same neighborhood."

Sports writer William "Bunk" Macbeth, Damon went on to say, had come out of Mike Iorio's saloon one evening, right about here, on his way to the *Journal* office to write a piece about "Big Six," pitcher Christy Mathewson of the Giants. Mr. Macbeth heard a groan that sounded from the gutter. He saw a fallen fellow there at his feet, called him a no-good drunken bum, and then went on his way to the Rhinelander Building.

Soon after Mr. Macbeth left the scene, Runyon continued, another *Journal* man came out of the saloon. This was Runyon's mentor and friend Charles E. Van Loan, a huge, amiable writer of magazine fiction and of newspaper stories for the Hearst newspapers. When Van Loan heard moans from the gutter, he investigated. He saw there a man with a broken leg. Van Loan called an ambulance and accompanied the victim to Bellevue Hospital.

Macbeth had no luck thenceforward as a staff member of the *Journal*, said Runyon. In fact, he became as ill-starred as the Shakespearean king whose name he bore. As for the compassionate Van Loan, he could do no wrong from that time on at the *Journal*. The man he had rescued was Solomon S. Carvalho, not a drunkard but a teetotaler, and one of Mr. Hearst's mightiest executives.

After his gutter accident, Mr. Carvalho spent the rest of his years with one leg shorter than the other. Sometimes, as he cross-examined editors in his museum-like office, he would limp about the room and flourish a pair of long-billed scissors with which he occasionally snipped stray hairs of his gray goatee. He collected rare old china, and also grudges. I am still wondering how it came about in the twenties that this remarkable old man, whom many Hearst executives regarded as a brilliant spider, was partial to me. He patiently sought to teach me how to win the kind of success which I did not covet, and did not attain.

Runyon and I went up the stone steps of the Hearst newspaper plant at 238 William Street. The building in which Mr. Hearst published his two New York newspapers, the *Morning American* and the *Evening Journal*, occupied the site of the old Rhinelander Sugar House. The original building had been used by the British as a prison during their occupancy of New York in Revolutionary times.

The elevator in the gloomy foyer of this place may well have been the original patent model of Elisha Graves Otis. It carried us with jerking reluctance to the seventh floor. The operator seemed unable to bring the cage to its proper level at any of the landings; he halted it a foot or so above or below the right spots. The passengers announced their respective floors and hoped for the best. One of

Runyon's friends, sports editor Wilton S. Farnsworth, amused everyone but the operator when he called out his floor as "Six and three-quarters, please."

The *Journal* editorial department occupied about one-half the seventh floor of the old Rhinelander Building. Mr. Hearst's morning newspaper, the New York *American*, took up the rest of that floor space. The *American* was Mr. Hearst's official mouthpiece. The Sunday edition had the largest circulation in the United States until the New York *Daily News*, a tabloid founded in 1919 by Captain Joseph Medill Patterson of the Chicago *Tribune*, outdistanced it and all others in this respect. The Sunday *American* made a great deal of money, but the profits were lost on the elaborate upkeep of the daily *American*.

The composing room was on the eighth floor. Dante would have loved the purgatorial aspects of that region of the newspaper plant. Sometimes molten lead from the linotype pots seeped through crevices in the floor, turned into pellets of hot hail, as from a shot tower, then fell upon the desk below, where the imperturbable Martin Dunn of Denver sat as night city editor.

Runyon asked a copy boy where Tad Dorgan might be. The boy said that the artist had gone inside the editor-in-chief's office of the *Journal*. Damon told the lad that we would meet Tad at the elevator. Runyon informed me that Mr. Dorgan had business with "Double Dome," alias "Big George." He winked knowingly as he said this.

In attempting to piece together the circumstances and the words of that day, I do not pretend to remember them in every detail. But of the many times afterward when I used this elevator, I remember best the first day when I stood with Runyon beside it. Unless a man has kept a log book of his voyage, he cannot seize upon each accent of a distant day. Anyone who says to the contrary may not be a liar, but assuredly is the greatest inventor since the time of Archimedes.

I cannot find among my attic hoardings any stand-pat record of that first visit with Damon Runyon to Park Row. Other than a long letter, which I wrote to Agnes that night, I have no prompters except distant voices crying in the wilderness of time. And fickle winds are blowing all day long.

It should be remarked that in 1918 Runyon's celebrity rested mainly upon newspaper work, and not upon his talent as a writer of fiction. True, he had sold several short stories, but his was not a magazine name at this early time. Had I but known that I was standing beside the future Aesop of Broadway, you may be sure that I would have set down everything he said. Now, with the benefit of a long backward glance, and in the light of his subsequent renown, it becomes clear to me that Runyon foresaw even then the day when fame would come to him.

As I piece together as best I can the things said that day, it seems to me that he knew the goal he meant to reach, and how to prepare himself for his mission. He had great natural ability, but he also was a hard worker, a careful planner—not one to let anyone or anything stay his intentions.

Runyon wagged his tongue when with newspapermen of his liking, or with Broadway cronies. If some passing circumstance caught his imagination, he would invent pleasing stories, drink black coffee, and smoke cigarettes, and frown when the waiter served whisky to one of his favorite disciples, and not go home until everyone else had gone. His wife once remarked to Agnes that Alfred, as she invariably called him, came home only to change his clothes—a stint which he performed twice a day.

Dr. DeGarmo set Runyon's tongue in motion when we went down to Park Row. "You slipped him some dough, eh?" Damon said after we had left that gentleman.

"Only a buck," I said. "Thought he could use it."

"Yeah? He can also use you. Lots of guys fall for his hankering look. They give him something to remember them by."

I shall now try to recapture the many other things he said, and attempt to set down these matters in sequence, without pausing to note the interruptions when Runyon's friends got out of the old elevator.

One of his remarks puzzled me: "I have deposited Doctor De-Garmo here." And he tapped his brow with a well-manicured forefinger. "Locked up tight, right here. Money in the bank. The Runyon Savings and No-Loan Bank."

"Fella," he went on to say, "you invested one dollar in a most peculiar firm known as Doctor DeGarmo. The Runyon bank does not approve. The Runyon bank does business on a much different basis. You will lose your dollar, just as a lot of other suckers lose every time they pass the time of day with this DeGarmo party. I do not wish to shock your faith in human nature, but the doctor is a one-hundred-proof bum, a con man, a hophead. And he is likewise as of right now on the lam from a little job of snatch-pretties in Council Bluffs. He is a beggar, and he has done time, with encores; and he is not a doctor of medicine at all, but got his degree while posing as a vet."

He then continued in substance. "Before you put in an oar to ask how and why the Runyon Savings Bank is interested in the doctor, let me give you a biographical sketch that somehow is overlooked by *Who's Who*. He is one time a vet, or somesuch, around the horse barns at Belmont Park. And one fine morning he is applying stimulants to a filly that is to run that afternoon against a passel of selling-platers. The doctor is using on this filly a syringe the size of a seltzer bottle. He is too charged up himself with dope to notice that a gentleman belonging to the Pinkertons is coming his way. And even if he does see this track detective, the doc is likely to take him for the same Lieutenant Pinkerton that is in the opera *Madame Butterfly*; and has come here only to hear the doc sing 'One Fine Morning,' or whatever it is that the Jap dame sings when she gets the whiskbroom. And the next thing you know, the doc is practicing medicine on the warden's dog up at Great Meadows prison."

I was, of course, wondering all this time why Runyon had gone to such obvious pains to do some kind of favor for Dr. DeGarmo.

"Before his days of eminence as a sawbones," Runyon resumed, "the doctor is a piano player at Spider Kelly's knockout-drops establishment and café at the corner of Mason and Eddy, out San

Francisco way. That is a long time ago. And our resourceful friend
Wilson Mizner, the apostle of easy living without work, is singing
in this same café. One night a great society dame, the Widow
Yerkes, is doing some slumming thereabouts. Mr. Mizner's pipes,
which are more loud than charming, begin to sound the mating
call."

As Runyon told it, Mizner was not in love at first sight, but Mrs.
Yerkes was. When the widow of traction magnate Charles Yerkes
left San Francisco, Mizner had promised to become her husband.
He insisted upon taking with him Professor DeGarmo (he was not
yet a doctor) as his gentleman's gentleman. Mrs. Yerkes demurred,
but yielded when Mr. Mizner threatened to go back to Spider
Kelly's.

"In New York," Runyon went on to say, "the bride and groom,
and Mr. Mizner's new valet, hole up for a very short time indeed
in the mansion the very recent Charley Yerkes has built up there
on the corner of Sixty-eighth and Fifth. In a few days Mr. Mizner
decides to get rid of his ever-loving, but he waits until an artist pal
of his can copy some of the masterpieces that hang on the Yerkes
wall, and sends DeGarmo out to peddle these phonies to rich suckers from the sticks."

When word of the art forgeries spread, there was a slump in the
Mizner market. He consigned six or seven unsold copies to an auctioneer. Among them was a picture of the Last Supper. Mizner himself appeared at the auction rooms one day when the bidders were
hesitant about acquiring the paintings. The auctioneer could not
get a bid of more than six dollars for the Last Supper.

Mizner leaped onto the rostrum to bellow, "Six dollars! This is an
outrage!" Then he asked of his audience, "Can't I at least get one
dollar a plate for this banquet?"

Runyon went on to say that Mizner and Dr. DeGarmo left the
Yerkes mansion and its chatelaine. They next appeared as card
sharps aboard transatlantic liners. I interrupted to ask how
DeGarmo could have manipulated cards, in that one of his fingers

was missing. Damon decided to tell me an anecdote which he intended to use for a short story, or so he said. (He never got around to the writing of it.)

"Doctor DeGarmo is a talented man," Runyon said. "In his prime, if you give the doctor a box of soda crackers he can deal you four queens. He has all his fingers when he works the boats with Mizner. Their home base is the Rand Hotel. Maybe Floto told you about this hotel. Mizner runs it. The Rand is a very special place indeed in midtown Manhattan. Mr. Mizner partakes of the opium fumes himself now and then, and he wants someplace where he and his pals can get on the hip and play their Hong Kong flutes without saying, 'By your leave,' or, 'Pardon me while I take a concert tour to Singapore.' The tenants of the Rand Hotel all like Canton caramels, and use nose candy of various flavors. They decide one Christmas season—a time when all hopheads, hookers, grifters, and actors on the loose get mighty homesick—to have a Yuletide tree in the lobby of the Rand Hotel. And there is gladness all around."

Mr. Mizner appointed Dr. DeGarmo, Runyon said, as chairman of the committee of arrangements and décor.

"The doc is climbing up on a chair to pin the Star of Bethlehem on the topmost twig of the tree," Damon continued, "and he loses his footing, which is none of the best whenever he is charged up with three or four nosegays of the poppy. And his luck is the kind that when he obeys Sir Isaac's law—the only one he ever obeys—and takes a Brodie, he lands on an open shiv, or cutlass, that somebody has left there while pruning a lower branch of the lovely tree. And the doctor's first finger of his best mitt is cut bad. And he has to let a real doctor snip it off."

Dr. DeGarmo's piano-playing days, Runyon went on to say, and his card-dealing days, and certain other days suitable to his various talents, were cut off simultaneously with his forefinger.

"The doc is now retired from games of skill," Runyon continued. "But Wilson Mizner is not the one to let a pal down. He appoints Doctor DeGarmo house physician of the Rand Hotel. Many of his patients thereupon and soon get free transportation to the morgue, for Doctor DeGarmo is almost always full of the happy-happy. And the monkey on his back interferes with a true diagnosis.

"One day there is a scarcity of hop," Runyon went on, "what with one of those crackdowns which a district attorney orders when he needs publicity before election time. Doctor DeGarmo, however, has enough Oriental goodies in his satchel to stoke himself with happiness till the polls close."

During their abstention from drugs, the tenants of the Rand decided to look for someone they might "take" in a card game. They came upon a "mark" in the person of a fat Philadelphia playboy, now in town for a bit of heigh-ho and hey-nonny-nonny. They lured him from the apartment of a chorus-girl friend of Mizner's, and escorted him to the Rand.

"It is a fine game indeed," said Runyon, "that Mr. Mizner cooks up for this tubby fellow from Philly. The stranger has at least four chins, one folded over the top of the other, like in that ad for Michelin tires. They let him win a few pots, and everyone is drinking plenty.

"The play lasts three days and three nights. And the sucker now has gone to the South Pole with a bundle. He happens to ask if they got a new deck of cards, if you please. And one of the players gets it into his head that this is a terrible insult to the honest deal. And he thereupon picks up a bottle of Old Taylor and lets the fat boy have it right on the melon. The citizen of Philly is cut up something fearful, and there is more blood let than at Waterloo. Mizner is frantic. He sends for his house doctor to come quicker than at once.

"They have a hard time getting the doctor off his hip," Runyon went on to say. "But he finally comes down with his black bag. He almost falls across the patient, whose blood now is pouring in the channels between his various and sundry chins. Doctor DeGarmo diagnoses it as a multiple cut throat. One of the drunks threads a needle, and the doc sews all four chins together. And then they take the victim in a cab to Central Park, and stretch him out on the bridle path."

The Philadelphian was very well known, Runyon said, his family as prominent as that of Harry Thaw. He would likely enough remember the Rand as the place of his misadventure. Mizner ordered an employee to take Dr. DeGarmo to Grand Central, and put him on a train, any train. Then Mizner called a meeting of the card players to decide on alibis and other emergency measures against a raid by the police.

"They are sitting there by the front door," Runyon continued, "and making plans, when in comes, of all people, the wounded sucker! His looks have taken a big turn toward the grotesque. He is all hunched over, with his head very low indeed, what with Dr. DeGarmo having basted his many chins together. He can look only at the floor, which, you can lay a hundred to one, by now is mopped up of blood, and the rug put back all nicely and neat. And the card players make a bolt towards the door. But Mizner has nerves of absolute zero, and he tells his colleagues to desist and halt. And he acts surprised to see his dear sucker again. He says a friendly hello to him, and so glad to see you, and what in the world happened to you, sir? And then everybody is rocked back on their heels when the bent-over fat boy, who looks like he is saying a long prayer to St. Luke, pipes up. He says, so help me, he says he has come back here to *thank* Mr. Mizner and that wonderful doctor *for saving his life!*"

Damon left off speaking for some time, and looked very serious. "You invested a dollar in this fellow," he then said in substance. "And you'll never get it back in any form, except to feel like Lady Bountiful. Well, Mizner telephoned me only yesterday. And what do you think he says it is that Doctor DeGarmo wants? He wants a peddler's license for selling roast chestnuts this fall in the vicinity of Max's Busy Bee. And you say is that an easy thing to arrange? And I say it is not. For everybody competes in the Big Town; and lots of fellows want to sell chestnuts right here, where the gentleman who had an oven dropped dead last winter. And with the doctor's record he can't get a license unless somebody puts in the right word. And that's what I was talking about to Senator Jimmy

Walker. I went to this trouble because it is an investment, as I said. And there is a story in Doctor DeGarmo, maybe several, and I am always looking for stories, for characters mostly.

"For it is characters that I remember from the things I have read," he went on to say. "I never got beyond the fourth grade. I learned geography by traveling hither and yon, and as a soldier. The best geography there is is the map of a man's life; not just anyone's life, but a special life like Doctor DeGarmo's. His life has latitude and longitude; and it has islands, like the ones that come up and then disappear when there is an earthquake under the sea. And the stories I mean to write later on will be good, because they'll have to be good, or I'll not send them along. I'll cash in on my investment in Doctor DeGarmo, and on my investment in a lot of other mugs of the Big Town.

"I invite you to do the same," he said. "And to hell with plots, because nobody ever remembers much about the plots of Dickens or Mark Twain. They remember the characters. . . . And I hope Tad won't keep us waiting much longer. I want to get out on the town, and look for some other sound investments."

When, in the course of my story, I speak again and again of Alfred Damon Runyon, it is because our lives in the yon years were closely drawn. It is possible that I knew him longer and better than does any other writing man now alive. The stories told of him by various chroniclers mostly concern his later days. None of them—except the sad and searching book written by his son Damon, Jr.—reveals the nature of this gifted man, his great longing to reach out and love, and be loved, and his inability to do so.

A courageous man, Runyon seldom complained of personal woes. His son saw him weep but once, and that near the close of the voiceless years of cancer and domestic grief. Sports writer Bill Corum, in a posthumous autobiography (*Off and Running*), said that a few days before Runyon's last trip to the hospital Damon turned his back to him to hide his tears. He had looked, secretly, upon a photograph of his second wife Patrice, from whom he had been separated. Corum said that Runyon had kept her picture hidden beneath an old-fashioned scarf on the night table near his bed.

I never saw him weep, but did hear him cry out in anguish upon a few occasions which were most revealing of the man's loneliness and frustration.

6

I have many times spread my
lodging when the evening has
promised well, yet have been
forced to withdraw before
day. —Dampier's Voyages

SEVERAL important journalists got out of the elevator the day when Runyon and I stood there, among them Kenneth C. Beaton, writer of *Ye Towne Gossip*, and Winsor McCay, the jockey-size artist who created the comic-page character Little Nemo. Runyon told me that McCay was sixty years old; he appeared much younger.

Just as I was about to ask Runyon who "Double Dome" was, the elevator door opened and several men got out of it. One solidly built gentleman of perhaps fifty years tripped against the poorly nego- tiated floor edge, but ignored this slight mishap. The self-assured party wore a dark gray alpaca suit and horn-rim spectacles on a short nose, and had a shallow chin, with tightly set lips. He cradled a fat briefcase in football fashion with one arm. In the other he carried a bale of papers and pamphlets, as well as a soft-brim hat which ap- parently had outlasted several summers. His head made his other features seem subordinate; it was as big as a soccer ball, though not quite as bare. A series of wrinkles made an insect's ladder on his brow. Were he to drop his ballast of papers and the fat briefcase, there might well be a balloon ascension.

This fast-talking man had an air of proprietorship, as though he owned not only the seventh floor but the seventh heaven as well. He swept past us, dictating on the run to a tall young man who moved in his wake. This sprinting amanuensis had a melancholy air. He held an open notebook with one hand and managed a pencil stub with the other.

It occurred to me that the man with the captive-balloon head was editor Arthur Brisbane. Runyon confirmed my guess. Mr. Brisbane fired his words in machine-gun tempo. The editor regarded himself as an orator of the first class, as I afterward learned, the peer of the Hon. Chauncey M. Depew, or Senator William E. Borah. Phrases such as "The first thing a child does is to give pain to its mother at birth" and "Don't sell America short" were among the salvos fired by the gentleman in the alpaca suit.

Mr. Brisbane plunged past us like Diogenes playing halfback for Holy Cross. Then Runyon said of him, "A.B. is the greatest newspaperman of all time, bar none." Runyon added that Brisbane's late father, Albert, a radical socialist, had been a columnist for Horace Greeley. Damon showed his large teeth in a smile of admiration, then said that the shrewd Arthur drew $275,000 a year as an editorial wizard and God only knew how much more in real-estate deals. Originally Mr. Brisbane had been a socialist, as was his father —but not *now*.

Damon explained that neither he nor Tad meant anything of a derogatory sort when they referred to the master as "Double Dome" or "Big George." Almost every important Hearst man had a nickname—spoken behind his back, of course. One executive, Bradford Merrill, was "the Silver Fox." Brisbane's lean-limbed secretary Emil was "the Moose." The council that governed the Hearst enterprises had been dubbed by Runyon "the Great Sanhedrin."

The Moose, Ramon said, had to stay in the best health, and sound of wind and leg, to keep within earshot of the ever-bustling Brisbane. Sometimes A.B. dictated his "Today" column to the recording cylinder of a battery-activated machine as he motored to New York from his estate at Lakewood, New Jersey.

"A.B. lives very high on the hog," Damon Runyon said, "as is right and proper for a man of parts."

After the cyclonic coming and going of A.B., Runyon expressed a doubt that Tad would make out very well today—that is, were he planning to ask for a bigger salary. Runyon implied that Big George was as tight-fisted as a pipe wrench.

Tad had been trying for some time to get a new contract, Runyon said. A.B. had a remarkable bag of tricks to thwart any salary increases other than his own. In Tad's case Mr. Brisbane had managed to offset the artist's demands by using cartoonist Rube Goldberg as a pawn. Whenever Dorgan asked for a raise Brisbane would get in touch with Goldberg. Rube was the *Evening Mail* comic artist. A.B. would ask that he bring samples of his work to the *Journal*. Dorgan became suspicious of Goldberg's several visits. He thought—as Brisbane meant him to—that Rube was trying to get his job. Tad consequently was afraid to ask for a raise; he quit speaking to Goldberg for some time.

Goldberg and Tad had been boyhood friends in their native San Francisco. That city sent many outstanding artists and writers to New York—Jimmy Swinnerton, Harrison Fisher, Robert Edgren, Herbert ("Hype") Igoe, Sophie Treadwell, W. O. McGeehan, Robert Ripley, and Will and Wallace Irwin.

The Irwins had attended the same high school in Denver as I had. Our Latin teacher, Sarah M. Graham, tutored them for entrance to Stanford University. Will Irwin revisited his old high school in 1908. Miss Graham asked the now successful man to advise me on how to become a writer.

"First of all," he said to me, "be sure that you *can't* do anything else. Grave-digging, for example."

Irwin got his first newspaper fame for having written the story of the San Francisco earthquake and fire, and without having been on the scene. He had gone to New York in 1906 to work on the *Sun*. The *Sun* had but one wire service, the Laffan Bureau. Its correspondent could not get his earthquake copy through to the *Sun*. Because Will Irwin knew San Francisco so well, he was able to write what seemed an eye-witness story on "the city that was." For the next eight days he wrote one hundred and twenty columns in all on the disaster and its aftermath—a journalistic feat which still commands admiration.

Runyon said of Irwin that he had great ability and much luck. "You must have both skill and luck," he went on to say. "Some men are born to get the breaks." Others never could find a four-leaf clover, or come upon a horseshoe, or have an earthquake fall into their laps.

Runyon abruptly asked why I was wearing spats in the summertime. Why did I wear them at all? Once again I felt ill at ease. Before I could reply, Tad arrived from the editorial rooms of the *Journal*. He seemed chastened. Big George, he said, had a hermetically sealed pocketbook. Tad liked his shillings and his pence. He had a morbid fear that he would die a pauper.

That evening, during the dinner-table conversation at Whyte's restaurant, Tad brought from his pocket a smooth silver disk. He fondled it with the fingers of his left hand. In his boyhood he had lost all but a part of the forefinger and the thumb of his right hand in an accidental encounter with a block and tackle during a housemoving job. He eventually learned to draw with his left hand.

Runyon alleged that the silver disk was the first dime that Thomas Aloysius Dorgan ever earned. It was not until 1956 that I learned from the veteran comic artist Jimmy Swinnerton that he indeed had given this dime as a luck piece to Tad in the early 1890s. Tad and his friend Hype Igoe had been office boys for cartoonists Swinnerton and Homer Davenport on Mr. Hearst's San Francisco *Examiner*. Swinnerton brought them to New York in 1905. Brisbane had wanted to hire Tad only, but Dorgan would not come East without Hype.

Igoe's feet were of the same size as Runyon's; he "broke in" Damon's bench-made shoes by wearing them a few days.

Runyon and I went with Tad to the Long Island waiting room of Pennsylvania Station (Runyon paid the cabbie). We stayed with him until the departure of the last commuters' train to Great

Neck, where Tad lived with Mrs. Dorgan and two adopted Chinese boys, Wong Ho and Wong Hong Kee.

Tad said that when he had asked for a raise A.B. replied, "Do you know that a baby is born every ninety seconds in America?" and, "One gorilla can whip any three prize-fight champions."

This prompted me to inquire if Mr. Brisbane disliked boxers. Tad said that Big George liked only the pictures of dead Presidents engraved on folding money. Runyon interrupted to say that Brisbane at nineteen had been a foreign correspondent for Dana's *Sun*. Heavyweight champion John L. Sullivan had taken a liking to the young journalist. When the sports writer for the *Sun* became drunk, Brisbane substituted for him, and brilliantly reported the Boston Strong Boy's fight with English champion Charley Mitchell at Chantilly, France, in March of 1888. The men fought in spiked shoes on the turf, and with bare knuckles, to a thirty-nine-round draw, for a side bet of $2500.

Brisbane told me, some years afterward, that Mitchell purposely trampled Mr. Sullivan's left instep and drew blood with the half-inch spikes. Mr. Sullivan thereupon had said, "Let's fight like gentlemen, you son of a bitch!"

Sullivan invited Brisbane to go with him to England, where John L. was to box in private for the future King Edward VII. The prince sent John L. a walking stick as a mark of his favor. John L. threw it at the prince's equerry with a roar: "Give this back to His Nobs, and tell him I'm no cripple!"

When the prince invited Sullivan to call upon him, the champion took Brisbane along as a matter of course. The prince's secretary admonished John L. that his Royal Highness would receive only Mr. Sullivan in private audience. The gruff athlete replied that, unless his young pal was allowed in, the prince could do something most undignified with his crown.

When his Royal Highness received both the pugilist and the young newspaper correspondent, Sullivan said, "Prince, if you ever come to Boston, look me up."

A day or so after our dinner at Whyte's, Runyon invited me to be his guest at Jack Dunston's all-night restaurant on Sixth Avenue. I saw many celebrities there: actors, artists, song composers, writers, pugilists, politicians, and playboy stayer-uppers of the Broadway cult. Everyone seemed so well-disposed toward me that my tongue became quite loose. Such journalists as Edwin C. Hill, Frank Ward O'Malley, Ben De Cassares, and Hype Igoe made a point of treating me as though I were an important fellow, and I began to think that I was. I also met playwright Augustus Thomas, Victor Herbert, and press agent Jack Francis, whom Runyon called "the Janitor of Broadway."

Just before dawn, I went with Runyon in a taxicab to my hotel at Broadway and 34th Street. On the way I remarked that New York newspapermen seemed hospitable. It did not occur to me that most of these journalists were not natives of the big city.

It was still dark as we drove past the *Herald* building, a Stanford White creation which Runyon called "the Doge's palace." Two bronze figures, smiths of heroic size that obeyed the *Herald* clock's mechanism, beat the pre-dawn hour with sledges on a huge bell. Bronze owls with electric eyes stared down at us from the cornice of the low building.

The owl, said my friend, had been the trademark of James Gordon Bennett the younger, owner of the *Herald*. His father had founded the newspaper in 1835. The elder Bennett, an enterprising Scot, had but $10,000 when he began publication of this journal. His first editorial desk was a rude plank supported by two flour barrels.

When the younger Bennett was made editor, he would set a bad example by leaving the newspaper office before press time. His father reprimanded him. "Young man, your future career depends upon night work and eternal vigilance. Otherwise, after my death, the *Herald* will soon belong to someone else. Bear in mind, that as long as you live, the owl—the bird of Minerva—should be your fetish, and not the eagle, or anything else."

"Since that time," Runyon told me, "the younger Bennett stayed on the job, made millions, and plastered the owl on everything he owned: his yacht, his stationery, his carriages, the masthead of his papers; and there is a rumor that one of his girl friends had owls tattooed on both her knees."

I thought that Damon sometimes looked like an owl. He kept night hours, too. And occasionally he hooted.

Bennett the younger had died this May at his home on the French Riviera. His will now was being probated. In it he left his millions for the building of a memorial home for aged newspapermen. The home never was built. The late Mr. Bennett's assets were not as extensive as had been supposed.

One of Mr. Bennett's reporters, the scholarly Eugene K. Campbell, once told me that among the several fictions spread during the career of the expatriate publisher there was a solemn prediction that he would return from Europe any moment, and appear at his long-unused office in New York. An old "copy boy" sharpened two dozen new pencils each morning, and placed them on the owl-ornamented desk. The "copy boy" gave these pencils each night to a pal, who became "blind" at that hour, and sold them in Herald Square.

Lucius Beebe, collector of Fourth Estate oddments, tells me that Mr. Bennett did return quite unexpectedly to New York one morning aboard his steam yacht *Namouna* (irreverently known as "Pneumonia"). That was a long time ago. Mr. Bennett had as his guest on the yacht a Captain Candy of the 9th Lancers. Bennett and the captain were said to have introduced into the United States the ancient Oriental game of polo.

A waterfront reporter learned of the presence of the Bennett yacht off Ambrose lightship and notified the city desk. The frantic editor ordered the members of his staff, as well as the men of the mechanical department, to sober up instantly, to shave, put on clean garments, and stand ready for inspection. One old printer dissented; he refused to spruce up or to jettison his bottle. The plant foreman hid the boozy printer behind some rolls of newsprint.

Commodore Bennett, accompanied by Captain Candy (known to the Newport set as "Sugar Candy"), went up and down the ranks of his employees. He said nothing until he chanced to see the drunken printer.

"Who is this man?" the publisher asked.

"It's only old Elmer," said the plant boss. "A loyal employee of your great father; and very loyal to you, sir."

Mr. Bennett remarked that old Elmer was the only one present who looked as though he had been doing any work. He thereupon fired the foreman and promoted old Elmer to that job.

As Damon Runyon and I went southward in the cab and along the Broadway side of Greeley Square, he said that he had been meaning to tell me something these last days—something for my own good. I was wondering at his words when we drew alongside the McAlpin. Damon instructed the driver to give us a moment or so to talk inside the cab.

The street of that early morning was deserted except for a placid white horse hitched to a milk wagon, a water-tank crew flushing the street, and some loiterer, obviously under the influence, singing "Smiles."

My friend lighted a cigarette from the one he had been smoking, then began to speak in a stern but coolly polite way. "Take this or leave it," he said. "You are getting off on the wrong foot in this man's town."

I tried to pretend that I did not care what he or anyone else said or thought of me. He went on with the reprimand. He said that he had put great store in me, had advertised my presence among the first-rank reporters, actors, and other Broadwayites; in short, he had announced to one and all that I was of big-league timber, and that I was his protégé. But what had I done to deserve this build-up?

I asked him just *what* I had done. He replied that I had come East with eyeglasses which I obviously did not need, a walking stick which I handled like an oar out of water, a flowing tie, which he called a "Greenwich Village bib," and, besides all that, I talked out of turn. . . .

When I tried to enter a defense, he said that a successful reporter could dress in a robe of ancient Greece, and go barefoot, or even ride a hippopotamus to work, but *not* until he had earned a solid reputation. A reporter at the beginning of his career should be a spectator, not a spectacle. I was a spectacle, he said, and much too fresh with celebrated strangers. Men were not born equal, notwithstanding the words of the Founding Fathers. They only died equal.

Then he said something that I remember quite well. "Those guys tonight were laughing *at* you, not at what you *said*. I'd think you'd get wise to yourself. Victor Herbert probably has a rupture this minute. What in hell do *you* know about music?"

"All right," I said. "There are only two kinds of people who dislike me: the ones who don't know me, and the ones who do. Let Mr. Herbert go buy a truss!"

In a somewhat less sardonic tone he said, "Well, good night. We all have to live and learn. Looks like you'll have to reach ninety to do it."

I was much too sensitive in those years. I felt most unhappy over Runyon's criticism. And I felt very much alone. The night clerk gave me my key and a letter. As I let myself into my room I wondered how many others were lonely in this slow dawn, how many were not. As I turned on the wall light the shadows it cast formed patterns of loneliness; the room itself smelled of loneliness and frustration.

The letter was from Agnes. She had written not to hurry home; everything was all right. I snapped off all but the night lamp. I sat looking out the window to see the new morning glide in like a solemn Gray Friar on his way to help the poor. I had little self-pity then or at any other time; still I longed to be home, where one could see a much brighter sunrise, and be among Western friends.

The banging of trash cans on the sidewalk announced that the city's scavengers were moving in like artillerymen on a binge. The Sixth Avenue "El" trains joined the fray. It was time, I thought, to get rid of my trouble-making symbols. I flung the eyeglasses and the spats under the bed. I did not part with my cane. And I had but the one necktie, the Byronic bib.

I sat down to write a telegram to Agnes. In it I sought to hide my real opinion of New York. I told her that New York seemed the friendliest place in all the world. "You'd fall in love with it, just as I have. Nothing like it."

I was so in love with New York that I couldn't get out of it soon enough! I did manage to fall asleep for an hour or so. Then I got up, showered, and had coffee in my room. Then I packed my Gladstone bag. I left for Grand Central Station without saying good-by to Runyon or to anyone else—except to the city. I never wanted to see New York again, or hear its evil dissonance, or breathe its antique dust with my Western nose.

So many excellent newspapermen of my acquaintance, I since have learned, have felt that way: Nunnally Johnson of Georgia; Stanley Walker of Texas; Dudley Nichols of Ohio; Don Clarke of Massachusetts; Warren Brown of California; John Hutchens of Montana; Barry Faris of Missouri. . . . Even the cocksure Tad Dorgan wanted to go back to San Francisco after his first day in town. Hoodlums chased him across City Hall Park, seized his straw hat, and broke it to bits. Mr. Dorgan did not know that after Labor Day a straw hat was fair game for metropolitan roughnecks.

On the way crosstown to the railway station, and as my cab reached Fifth Avenue at the street corner where the old Waldorf stood, I heard the slow cadence of drums, and then the blare of massed bands playing Chopin's funeral march.

I saw them coming toward me: the mounted police, the plumed Knights of Columbus, the soldiers, the men in high silk hats, the black-draped gun carriage, the flags—the funeral procession for the late Mayor Mitchel. Three airplanes, flying low over the avenue, were dropping flowers on the marchers. Were I to remain a few moments too long at the west side of the avenue I surely would miss my train. A traffic officer let the cab cross the street.

It seemed as though my entire journey had been an adventure in association with the dead.

I never wanted to see New York again or hear it—that is, until I had arrived home.

I then could hear it two thousand miles away, or so it seemed. The distant chant seemed both repellent and alluring, a siren's chorus that even now I seem to hear. I listen to it once again across the many miles and the many years, not with the pathos of yearning for gone days but with the gladness of having known the springtime.

CHAPTER

7

From the fire flees not he who
over it leaps.

    —The Younger Edda

I HAD been home a month or less when Damon Runyon sent word that he had been assigned by Colonel Caleb Van Hamm, his editor, to go overseas. Obviously he could not attend the September baseball series between the Boston Red Sox and the Chicago Cubs. Would I like to report the games in his stead as a sports staff member of the New York *American?*

My Aunt Etta Wheeler promised to look after my grandparents, and Agnes's mother said she would take care of our infant son until we could make a home in New York. I borrowed some money and then made ready to leave the scene of my apprenticeship. It was not easy to say good-by to the places and the persons of my upbringing, but by the time I had stepped on the heels of tomorrow it was yesterday.

On Sunday, August 25, 1918, Agnes and I registered at an old hotel on West 48th Street, New York. This behind-the-times place was a halfway house for show folk on their precarious journey to stage careers, as well as for the saddened casualties of the Rue Regret.

The lobby gave off a musty odor. The premises seemed to be awaiting the sheriff and his documents of foreclosure. The desk clerk perfectly suited this environment; he too was in need of repairs, or, better still, the embalmer's needle. The bellboy who saw us to our room had thinning white hair and the complexion of a banana. He nickered like an old horse as he pried open a window. I asked if I might have some coffee.

As Agnes unpacked our luggage, I sat down to read the newspapers. The Sunday editions were thin because of the wartime shortage of newsprint. Surely this was an untoward season for a stranger to enter into metropolitan journalism. I read in the *Times* that the morale of the German armies was running low; but even correspondent Philip Gibbs would not say outright that the war had reached its last innings. The British were advancing on a broad front north of the Somme. President Woodrow Wilson soon would sign the Manpower Bill, to extend the draft to all American men between the ages of eighteen and forty-five. . . . Banana Boy delivered the coffee in a cardboard container. I can still taste it. The stuff that killed Socrates.

Runyon had gone to Washington to see someone in the State Department. He had left word with Ellen that on my arrival I should call William Randolph Hearst's confidential secretary, Joseph Willicombe. Mr. Willicombe, I learned to my dismay, was in Staten Island. It seemed that of a Sunday all New Yorkers obeyed a quarantine that kept them out of circulation.

We had about seventy dollars left of our borrowed money. I seldom concerned myself about such things, but Agnes was a realistic person. She wondered why the hotel room should cost three dollars a day; the décor was that of an almshouse. Neither of us then knew that in summer New Yorkers took down their window drapes, rolled up the rugs, placed slip covers or bed sheets over the larger pieces of furniture, and left things in that morgue-like array until early fall.

Agnes said the place looked tired and untalented. She suggested that I telephone the cadaverous clerk downstairs to inquire if he had not made a mistake. When I did so, the sardonic fellow gave me the address of the Hotel Astor and suggested that I take my business there. I told him that I hoped he would get to heaven on a base on balls, but not to wait much longer.

The next day Agnes called upon Ellen Runyon to discuss our housing prospects. Meanwhile, I kept my appointment with Mr. Willicombe at the Hotel Claridge. I was delighted to find Runyon there. He introduced me to Mr. Hearst's secretary, a native New Yorker of Welsh extraction. I judged that Mr. Willicombe was in his mid-thirties, a man of solid character, and as solemn as a composer of alma-mater hymns. He was economical of speech. Mr. Willicombe at a later time became executive assistant to Mr. Hearst, a job which he managed with great tact for thirty-three years, and never once had to consult a psychiatrist.

Runyon seemed to think me suddenly daft when I asked for a salary of one hundred dollars a week. When I addressed Mr. Willicombe as "Joe," my sponsor winced. Mr. Hearst's negotiator asked where I was staying. Runyon had an aversion to second-rate addresses; he hastened to say that I planned to move to an uptown apartment as soon as my furniture arrived from the West. Mr. Willicombe said that he would let Mr. Hearst know how matters stood.

Outside the Claridge, Damon advised me not to go around and about calling important persons by their first names. New Yorkers, he said, were not chaw-bacon rubes. He let me know that I was putting him in a most embarrassing position, asking for one hundred dollars a week. Was I an extortionist? He pointed out that he himself had been content to begin his New York career at only forty dollars. Grantland Rice had started at a reasonable sixty fish. Who in hell did I think I was? Irvin S. Cobb? Herbert Bayard Swope? What did I want of life?

I did not know precisely what I wanted of life (nor do I now), but was quite sure of two or three things I didn't want. Runyon said that he had taken the almost unheard-of liberty of asking Mr. Hearst himself to employ me. Mr. Hearst's editors usually did the hiring and firing of lesser journalists. For that matter, there were several veteran editors who had never set eyes upon Mr. Hearst, nor he upon them. The Chief observed only their mistakes, then rolled what New York newspapermen awesomely referred to as "the iron ball."

"Fella," said Damon, "cool off your soup before you burn your tongue."

Nor was Runyon pleased when his friend William "Slim" Farnsworth, sports editor of the *American*, chanced to meet us on the street and to say that I was dead right in asking for the hundred.

"If you start at the sixty the Demon recommends," said he, "you'll *never* get a raise. Mr. Hearst hates bargains."

"The Demon," as his Eastern newspaper cronies called Runyon, promised to quit tossing up the pigeons unless I lowered my sights. Slim Farnsworth and I then went to the Knickerbocker bar. Prohibition laws had not yet fallen upon civilized man, and the draft beer was excellent at the Knickerbocker. The Demon by now had gone to his tailor's for a fitting of a custom-built war correspondent's uniform.

"The Demon"—and Mr. Farnsworth gazed at the Maxfield Parrish mural of Old King Cole above the bar—"is like all reformed drinkers. Wants to run the lives of his friends."

I asked Slim how it happened that a glass of beer at the Knickerbocker cost ten cents. He replied that the owner, Mr. James Bernard Regan, disliked newspapermen; he had raised the price on beer to discourage the patronage of journalists.

Mr. Regan was known as "the General," not because of his military record, but for his battlefield manner of issuing orders. The only person he allowed to break any of the house rules was Enrico Caruso. The great tenor occupied almost half a floor of the hotel. He was even permitted to have a typewriter (his social secretary's) and a piano in his suite.

The next day I heard nothing from Mr. Willicombe. At Runyon's apartment that evening, Ellen said she had found a suitable place for us to live. This was a piece of luck, she explained, because apartment-house leases were not up until October 1, when tenants moved in or out. However, a friend of hers wished to sublet a ground-floor apartment in West 112th Street, one block south of the Runyons'. Several newspapermen resided in this neighborhood, near the uncompleted cathedral of St. John the Divine.

Ellen Egan Runyon was a slender, vivacious person in those days, and extremely generous. She liked very much to solve the problems of others, whether or not they wanted her to do so. It so happened that we appreciated her interest in our welfare, except that she agreed with Alfred that I should go slow with my hundred-dollar ultimatum about salary. Agnes replied, in all truth, that I seldom went slow. You see, I didn't believe that I would grow old, ever. Or that a time would come for swan songs or for sighs when yellowed diary leaves drift out of the past.

Ellen said, somewhat plaintively I thought, that she sometimes disagreed with Alfred—for example, when he chose to stay up all night at Jack's with underworld gamblers, chorus girls, playboys, and Broadway racketeers. But in this instance, the salary matter, she believed that he was as right as the key of C; Runyon asked his wife to stay out of it, if you please. He then inquired whether I meant to take his advice or that of Farnsworth, a gifted newspaper editor to be sure, especially at the making up of the sports pages, but careless about other practical concerns.

I replied by saying that I had asked automobile racer Barney Oldfield one day why he was such an extraordinarily bad driver when in street traffic. Among his recent mishaps, and while driving his wife to the beauty parlor, Barney collided with a road-grading machine. Mrs. Oldfield survived the accident with a broken jaw. Oldfield had told me he couldn't think clearly under one hundred miles an hour. The Demon asked what in hell Oldfield had to do with his question. I said that I could not think clearly at less than a hundred dollars a week.

I gave Ellen the better part of our dwindled funds as a down payment on the apartment she had earmarked for us. I assured Agnes on our way back to the flea-bag hotel that we soon would be living at Number One Easy Street. I believed that. So did she.

The next day I had one of my rare resolves to economize. I ate free lunch at a saloon adjoining the Gaiety Theatre, where Billy LaHiff was the chief bartender. Mr. LaHiff saw to it that I had several miniature welsh rabbits, a specialty of the place. Some years afterward, Mr. LaHiff operated the Tavern on West 48th Street, where sportsmen and stage folk met to eat and drink and plan great jests. Billy LaHiff was a fine man, a quiet little man, a friend of young scribes, among them—much later on—Arthur "Bugs" Baer, Ed Sullivan, Walter Winchell, Leonard Lyons, and Louis Sobol.

In the after years I wrote much of my first novel in the basement of the Tavern. Billy would send his jovial headwaiter, Jack Spooner, downstairs with food and drink to bolster me. LaHiff's one-time bouncer, "Silent" Toots Shor, still upholds this tradition of grub-staking likely lads.

I returned from LaHiff's saloon to the hotel to find a message there from Mr. Willicombe. Why had I not telephoned? I replied that the sixty dollars which he and Runyon seemed to have in mind affected me the same way a dog would receive word that there were no trees in Death Valley. I said that I had decided not to bother him further, but to go back to Denver. I neglected to say that I was broke; worse still, I had burned my home-town bridges. No bands played in Denver when a beaten native son returned home.

Runyon telephoned to say that I was behaving like a holdup man. Besides that, I was ungrateful. I replied that I wasn't living on gratitude at the moment; it was a hundred dollars or nothing. He hung up the receiver.

Early next afternoon, a blustery day as I remember it, Mr. Willicombe once again telephoned. Mr. Hearst himself wished to see me. Some years afterward I learned that Mr. Hearst had told his secretary that a young man who placed a high price upon his talents likely would be of value to the Hearst service. I did not know that this publisher paid no attention to subordinates who tried to save

him an expense whenever it suited his fancy to hire someone, or to
do anything else of his desire, such as buying an old castle in Wales
or spending thousands of dollars to move a tree at San Simeon a few
feet.

I believe that Mr. Hearst had less regard for money, as such, than
anyone else of his financial size. Arthur Brisbane once said that his
chief was the only man he ever knew who could not get along on
less than ten million dollars a year.

Mr. Hearst's indifference to money was indicated when Henry
Ford was his guest one day in 1921, a time of postwar inflation. The
automobile magnate had just recently managed to keep his empire
from passing to the control of the big banks. His dealers had raised
the millions needed to re-finance the Ford corporation. They had
to do so, else lose their Ford franchises. Mr. Ford consequently was
angry at Wall Street. Nor did Mr. Hearst regard the traders in
stocks and bonds at his kissing cousins.

"Mr. Hearst," Ford inquired, "have you got any money?"

"I never have any money, Mr. Ford. I always spend any money
that I am to receive before I get it."

"That's a darned shame," Mr. Ford said. "You ought to get yourself two or three hundred million dollars together and tuck it away;
because if you don't those bankers are going to get you one day."

My source of this prophetic anecdote is Richard E. Berlin, head
man of the Hearst Corporation. I mention this because the things I
mean to write are drawn not from stories written of William
Randolph Hearst but from my own first-hand observations, or from
recollections supplied me by my colleagues of old Park Row. I first
met Dick Berlin when he got out of the Navy in 1919 and went to
work for the Hearst magazines. It has been a long friendship.

Mr. Hearst owned the Clarendon apartment house at West 86th
Street and Riverside Drive, three blocks south of the Soldiers and
Sailors monument. Originally he had leased the ninth floor of the
place, then expanded his quarters to three other floors, and built a
ballroom on the roof. He bought the property outright, not because
the rental came to tens of thousands of dollars a year but because

the landlord objected to Mr. Hearst's passion for remodeling the premises on a large scale, day or night.

Mr. Hearst kept many art objects at the Clarendon: paintings by the masters, a collection of armor, a library of rare books and manuscripts. Ben Hecht once said that Mr. Hearst had gathered more European works than Napoleon had, and without firing a shot.

One day Mr. Hearst invited a curator of armor of the Metropolitan Museum of Art to inspect his collection of knightly hardware. Upon examining a complete suit of fifteenth-century plate armor, of which Mr. Hearst was especially proud, the visitor pointed out a lance rest, saying that it was counterfeit, a restored piece. Mr. Hearst challenged the expert to prove this charge. The man explained that some years ago he was commissioned to make this very piece for a one-time owner of the specimen. Mr. Hearst thereupon hired the curator to take care of the collection.

Many items of the Hearst library had not been unwrapped since the time the newspaper publisher or his agents had obtained them. When I asked to see some of Sir Walter Scott's correspondence, Mr. Willicombe shook his head, somewhat sadly I thought. He said he was damned if he knew offhand which of the boxes or bales contained the letters.

"Would you care to look at some of the Chief's Bibles?" he asked. "Mr. Hearst likes old Bibles. He knows eighteen Psalms by heart."

On this occasion I met a remarkable old fellow who had charge of the Hearst household. In a sense he also had charge of Mr. Hearst. George Thompson was a solidly built Irishman, five feet short. He had protruding blue eyes. Thompson had been a baggage smasher at either the old Hoffman House or the Albermarle Hotel. (Dick Berlin thinks it was the Albermarle.) Mr. Hearst and certain of his bachelor friends had lived at both hotels.

W.R. had taken an immediate liking to Thompson, whose appraisals of men impressed the publisher. George's way of speech amused Mr. Hearst, especially his habit of saying "although" at the close of a sentence. Early in this century Mr. Hearst moved from his bachelor apartments to the Chester A. Arthur residence on Lexington Avenue, where in 1881 Mr. Arthur had been sworn in as President. George Thompson became Mr. Hearst's factotum there and thereafter.

When the publisher bought material for neckties he would have bolts of silk brought to wherever it was he happened to be in residence. From these bolts he would select patterns. For many years an old friend of his mother made all his cravats. She lived near Mrs. Phoebe Hearst in Pleasanton, California. The tie maker would not accept money from Mr. Hearst without performing some service in return.

W.R. preferred "loud" neckwear. One day he spread some bolts of silk across the bed. "George," he asked, "what do you think of these?"

"Well," Thompson replied, "they're no worse than some of those you've got, although."

Mr. Hearst drank no hard liquor. He ate candy instead. On occasion he would sip a glass of Tokay at his dinner, or a glass of beer with a midnight sandwich or a welsh rabbit prepared by him in the butler's pantry. Nor did he approve of heavy drinking by anyone, although some of his best men leaned against the bars. Several Hearst lieutenants, however, were abstainers, among them Arthur Brisbane, Morrill Goddard, Bradford Merrill, and S. S. Carvalho.

George Thompson drank too much at times—not too much for him, perhaps, but too much for Mr. Hearst. The boss occasionally fired George but regularly took him back. One time, however, W.R. gave George the sack and said that he hoped never to set eyes on him again. After a week had gone, Mr. Hearst seemed offended. George had taken him at his word.

It was sometimes difficult to fix upon the exact dimensions of a Hearstian request, to know just how far to proceed—when it was wise to handle one of his hints with the bare hands or with fire tongs. A successful editor had to be a mind reader, a Chinese diplomat, a high-wire walker. It was like living in the eye of a hurricane.

One of Mr. Hearst's most able seers was Bradford Merrill. Among other things, "the Silver Fox" had spent twenty-five years developing an "unbreakable" telegraphic code. There were two major telegraph and cable companies in those days. The Merrill code was keyed to the use of split telegrams, or split cables; a message was recast in the form of two telegrams. Alternate words of the original message were filed over separate wires, one on the Western Union, the other via Postal.

Several newsbeats were had by the Hearst newspapers during the early part of the First World War by means of messages cast in the Merrill code. The code temporarily cleared the zones of restriction. The fact that some words were missing from a message was interpreted by the censors (*before* America got into the war) as a device to save toll charges. After the United States declared war, no Hearst messages, in cipher or otherwise, were sanctioned by the British.

When away from New York, Mr. Hearst would use this same code to communicate with editors. He would sign these split telegrams with the code word "Doctor."

One day the Silver Fox reported to Mr. Hearst to discuss a reconciliation with Mr. Murphy, boss of Tammany Hall. Mr. Hearst would have none of this business until a more important matter was resolved: the disappearance of George Thompson. Mr. Hearst was the kind of man who would call upon the north wind to snuff a candle. Surely a brain able to devise an unbreakable code could suggest a way to bring the butler out of hiding.

Mr. Merrill consulted Police Commissioner Richard E. Enright. He in turn assigned Captain Ayres of the Bureau of Missing Persons to the job. A mere rookie patrolman, however, found George Thompson happily driving an ice wagon in Brooklyn. The alcoholic butler went back to work for W.R. So far as anyone knows, the incident never again was mentioned by the Chief.

George Thompson had a considerable say-so as to which callers were to see the publisher. Mr. Hearst made a practice of summoning his executives to headquarters, whether in New York or his palace at San Simeon, California, then letting them wait at his own convenience. They quite often would come a long way. Sometimes they would stay over for days, or even weeks, before they would have an audience with the Great Mogul. If George Thompson approved of you, he would immediately place you near the head of the queue. Otherwise you would cool your heels.

Mr. Hearst occasionally would receive a current favorite in his private suite at the Clarendon, where he slept or worked above the reception room and the private art gallery. One time he kept Mr. Moses Koenigsberg, his syndicate manager, waiting all afternoon while the Chief, behind the scenes, was learning a buck-and-wing dance routine taught him by his father-in-law, George H. Willson, a one-time vaudeville performer.

The Chief ordinarily would get out of bed in the late forenoon, have a light breakfast, then spend an hour or so studying the morning newspapers. He would spread these on the floor of his bedroom and turn the pages with his toes. After this "bird's-eye" view of the newspapers, he would sit, tailor-fashion, on the rug to scribble criticisms in the margins. He used heavy-lead pencils, and wrote with a hasty but legible scrawl. Ordinarily he would phrase his comments in polite terms, such as "Don't you think we should?" or "Wouldn't it be a good idea to?" Sometimes he would put a word of praise at the top of a page, but lower down make an ironical query, such as "Was our staff working yesterday?"

I once was overheard to describe Mr. Hearst's morning survey of the newspapers as "the daily urinalysis." I was then an editor; mine had been but a chance remark. A few days afterward he sent me a marked newspaper with the notation, "Today's urinalysis indicates an acid condition in the editorial page."

If George Thompson did not like somone among the Pooh-Bahs waiting in the reception hall, he might say to Mr. Hearst, "Boss, that terrible Mr. So-and-so is sittin' down there, botherin' the life out of us. What should we do? Would you be seein' him? Or would you like me to tell him to go away?"

Mr. Hearst was apt to respond, "Tell him to go away."

But if George liked a caller he might say, "You know, Boss, that awfully nice fellow, Mr. Who-or-whom, is sittin' down there. Would you be seein' him now, although?"

And then Mr. Hearst would be likely to reply, "Have him come right up."

Among the executives whom George Thompson disliked, Arthur Brisbane headed the list. Thompson thought that the many-sided editor was misleading W.R. in certain property investments. He had overheard Mr. Brisbane boasting, "Mr. Hearst is a great big safe, and I am the only one who has the combination."

A.B. built a handsome midtown hotel but had sought to save money on materials by lowering the ceilings a few inches from the norm. This practice is now quite common, but in a day of more lofty ceilings the shrunken inchage did not appeal to tall tourists, especially Texans, who liked to wear their hats indoors.

Mr. Hearst's real-estate expert, Martin F. Huberth, once asked the Chief why he allowed Brisbane to unload this hotel on him. He replied, "Oh, Artie has been dreadfully worried. I don't want him to worry. When he's happy he writes better, and that's a good thing for the paper."

Brisbane called upon the Chief one evening to find him in the butler's pantry. Mr. Hearst was having a sandwich and a small glass of beer. A.B. began at once to urge his employer to buy a Detroit newspaper. He did not tell Mr. Hearst that he himself had already taken an option on this property, and might look for a cozy profit were he to sell it to W.R.

Mr. Hearst listened attentively, then said in his high-pitched voice, "Artie, why do you always take advantage of me when I'm drinking?"

My first meeting with W. R. Hearst was brief. He said that he liked to have young men in his service. He went on to say that the most remarkable newspaperman of Queen Victoria's time was John Delane, who had made the London *Times* great. He asked me how old would I say Delane was when appointed editor-in-chief of the

Times. I not only did not know how old, but never had heard of anyone named Delane except a red-nosed police sergeant in Denver. Mr. Hearst said that editor Delane was but twenty-four years of age at the time when he took charge of the *Times* of London, and made of it a guardian of good government.

Mr. Hearst was quite unlike the person I had expected to see. Until now I had imagined him to be a fire-snorting ogre; he was constantly attacking or being attacked by big men who portrayed him as the mouthpiece of the damned. And that snake I had seen painted on the side of the *Tribune* building!

Instead, I found this large-bodied man (he was six feet two inches tall at that time and weighed two hundred and ten pounds) to be a person of extraordinary charm. He was then fifty-five years old and robust, although fussy about his health. He kept his telephones sterilized. A mere sniffle would send him to bed for the day, the doors and windows closed, and a croup kettle steaming nearby. Yet he rode horseback, played tennis, swam, tap-danced, and took long walks till he was seventy-five years old, and lived on till he was eighty-eight. His bagpipe voice seemed a contradiction, not only of his physical size, but also of the tiger tones of his newspaper crusades. The falsetto voice quite likely had something to do with his frustrations; surely it was a handicap to him as a political orator.

Mr. Hearst greeted me as though I were an ambassador (not from England, of course) and at once put me at ease.

Whatever anyone has said in disparagement of this man—and his faults and his prejudices were not puny ones—and no matter the mistakes he made in either his public or his private life, I can remember him only with affection. He in turn, for reasons never disclosed to me, again and again befriended me. He usually referred to me as "that young man from Denver." He refused to fire me, as he should have on the several occasions when I had the youthful effrontery to defy my superiors.

I believe that he had a great deal of whimsical humor, a side which none of his biographers seems to have found. A few of his

familiar friends, among them artist Jimmy Swinnerton and publisher Dick Berlin, support this view. Perhaps I was one of his pet
jokes. Or possibly he favored me because I never tried to deceive
him to serve my own fortunes. I was either too lazy or too smart
to lie to him. A man should never lie to anyone except his wife.

Years after I had left the newspapers, a guest at San Simeon
asked Mr. Hearst if he remembered Fowler. To which he replied,
"How can I ever forget him?"

I shall only set down that which I saw in him, or thought I
saw during the years. His taboos were of interest to me: his insis-
tence on never being the first to go through a doorway; his dislike
of tale bearers, even when his own best interest was involved; his
playing the banjo, an art learned from the late Ashton Stevens; his
refusal to kill any living thing (except editors, of course), although
he was a crack shot.

Even the mice were safe at the San Simeon estate. W.R. devised
traps that would capture but not injure them. He would send the
filled traps to the seashore, eight miles away, and there have the
captives set free. Eccentric, you might say, but quite in keeping
with his crusades against cruelty to animals and his attacks on
vivisectionists. Were he to learn that one of his doctors ever had
experimented on living animals, he would dismiss the man, no
matter how eminent in medicine.

His editors for the most part were very able journalists. Hearst
executives—with the exception of a sycophantic minority, who
capitalized on the ever-present intrigues in the organization—were
men of probity and skill. Of course, even the most upright of these
executives had to act in self-defense against office politicians, else
go by the board.

Their salaries were the largest on Park Row. Many of them became rich. Some of them lasted a long time. Others bogged down
early, had ulcers or strokes; and three of them jumped out of
windows.

The editorial empire underwent many changes of premiers.
New cabinets were formed overnight. Mr. Hearst seemed to en-

courage, even to prefer dissension among his editors. Indeed, he appears to have done so in the belief that trouble in the hive kept the bees awake. He regarded failure as a much worse sin than disloyalty.

It has been said that a vindictive Hearst took the view that anyone who made friends among his enemies must immediately forfeit his favor. I did not find it so. I never allowed Mr. Hearst or anyone else to choose my friends or—more important than that —to select my enemies. Everyone needs a warm personal enemy or two to keep him free of rust in the movable parts of the mind.

Mr. Hearst did not take offense when informed that I had a friendly regard for his number-one foe Alfred E. Smith. I also liked several other men who thought, as I frequently did, that some of the publisher's views were ill-advised, and many of his attacks unwarranted and perverse. It was the man himself whom I liked from the first. I could like him without being unduly dazzled by his virtues, or without finding it necessary to be stone blind to his blemishes.

Whatever his public show of getting even with his antagonists, Mr. Hearst in private would make wry comments—as when a news magazine published an adverse criticism together with a most unflattering cartoon of him. "I do not know why the gentleman should do this to me," he said. "To the best of my knowledge I have met him but once; furthermore, I have never done him a favor."

Whether or not his thirst for power was of a more sordid intensity than that of his jungle-minded contemporaries I do not pretend to know. The era was one of ruthless men. Nor have I anything of moment to add to or to subtract from the indictments of those who have said that Mr. Hearst egged on the authorities to declare war on Spain, or that his editorials incited anarchist Czolgosz to shoot down President McKinley. When critics sit in judgment it is hard to tell where justice leaves off and vengeance begins. The adverse testimony has been offered mostly by Mr. Hearst's declared foes, few of whom seemed to have had open minds and none of whom, so far as I know, has been nominated for sainthood.

Few writers—or readers, for that matter—measure a man in relationship to his own times rather than theirs. Mr. Hearst lived in an age of corsairs. His ambitions and the means he took to further them were no better and no worse than those of his contemporaries. When it became apparent—even to him—that he could not be President, he decided to become an emperor. He was the last of his kind, uncrowned but absolute in his domain. When—as almost always happened—he could not for long impose his will upon the electorate, he exercised the press power of the veto, as witness the defeat of Mr. Wilson's League of Nations.

He has been portrayed, and with much documentation, as one who changed his course with every wind. I think that the man himself, calm and detached as he seemed on the surface, had great storms of contradiction and cross-purpose raging within him. For example, he was extraordinarily modest in private conversation. So far as I know, he never referred to his wealth or boasted about his art treasures, his castles, or his other assets. But in *print* his editorial blusterings, trumpetings, crowings, struttings, and journalistic swaggerings outdid the gasconades of Terence's Thraso. Brilliant and able though he was in recognizing news values, he sometimes "fell" for documentary forgeries. At such times he semed unable to tell the difference between a fistful of gravel and the beads of a rosary.

During my brief visit at the Clarendon, George Thompson brought Mr. Hearst a yellow apple and a paring knife on a pie-crust salver which Mr. Willicombe, in an aside, said had belonged to Dolly Madison. As though reminded of something, Mr. Hearst told George that he meant to attend an old-silver sale. He would walk part of the way, he said. Anyone waiting to see him must come back tomorrow. He then shook my hand, and said he hoped I would be happy in the Hearst service.

Somehow I felt that he was a very lonely person.

After his chief had gone to the bedroom, Mr. Willicombe said that I had made a good impression. He offered nothing in evidence to sustain this view. He said in parting that he would notify Colonel Van Hamm that I was now on the payroll of the sports staff of the New York *American*, and at one hundred dollars a week. A dollar in 1918 meant what it said; one hundred dollars was an oration.

Although Runyon had spoken warmly of Colonel Caleb Van Hamm, the celebrated managing editor, I had no personal knowledge of his journalistic size. I would know it soon enough, and under circumstances not of the happier sort. The colonel enjoyed a reputation comparable to that of the mighty though self-effacing Carr V. Van Anda, managing editor of the New York *Times*. Mr. Van Anda was the most accomplished editor since Dana's time, a scholar and a fine gentleman.

Mr. Van Hamm, born in Cincinnati in 1861, had given up the practice of law to go into newspaper work. He went to New York in 1892 as city editor of the *Journal*, then an unsuccessful newspaper controlled by John R. McLean, owner of the Cincinnati *Enquirer*. When Mr. Hearst bought the *Journal* for $180,000 in cash, Colonel Van Hamm joined Joseph Pulitzer's *World*. In 1903 he became managing editor of the *World*, and showed executive ability. He moved to the Hearst offices in 1910.

The colonel was an outstanding judge of the news, a specialist in politics, both local and national. Dignified, somewhat portly, and with the complexion of a Sandy Hook pilot, he had an iron will with a few flecks of rust on it, and an insulated manner. Colonel Van Hamm was thrifty of words. More often than not he would grunt his replies. One grunt meant "Yes." Two meant "No." Three grunts meant "Get the hell out of here!" The colonel's subordinates held him in high regard, and accounted him a just man. Occasionally he had been known to misjudge talent, as when O. Henry contributed Sunday stories to the *World*. According to the late Bob Davis, friend of O. Henry and veteran discoverer of writers, Colonel Van Hamm took a dim view of the abilities of Mr. Henry.

"I don't like those stories that fellow is writing," the colonel said to Davis. "He never writes about anything important."

"Colonel Van Hamm," Davis exclaimed, "God heard you say that!"

"I still don't like O. Henry *or* his stories," the colonel said. "He's fired!" And he grunted three times.

Damon Runyon seemed pleased that I had joined the staff, but somewhat ruffled by my having demanded, and *got*, the one hundred dollars a week. From that day on, no one could persuade the Demon that I was not a sharp businessman. He wrote a column, years afterward, in which he said he had grown tired of hearing that Fowler should have a guardian for his purse.

I now set out for Chicago on my first assignment, the World Series, the last games until the war would come to its close. It was called the "Straw Hat Series" because of the earliness of its occurrence as compared to the usual October meetings of the baseball champions.

This first assignment almost became my "finis," as the fellow in Omaha might have said; and I learned how success can be born, then die the same day.

CHAPTER

8

O *saddle me the black, the black*

Or *saddle me the brown;*

O *saddle me the swiftest steed*

That *ever rade frae a town.*

—"Ballad of Lady Maisry"

THE hearty old rogue seems forthright enough when he says over his glass that life owes him nothing, nothing at all, sir; and that he is ready, as he puts it, to go this minute without regrets. He looks you in the eye, as though daring you to question his indifference to the Reaper's whims. You nod politely, of course, and by so doing become an accessory to the falsehood.

No one, other than a saint or two, or some pain-gaffed invalid, wants to leave this place of earth and sky until the day after tomorrow of the year after next. Among the men I have seen die—several by appointment in prison—none seemed eager to go out of a world which had pounded the wrongdoer so hard that even hell would seem an improvement.

I called upon a murderer in the Sing Sing death house one day long ago—Bull Cassidy, an ex-pugilist of the fourth class. The Bull was brooding over the recent loss of a fellow member of the death-house glee club. No. 687524 was the finest basso profundo ever to sit in the Sing Sing electric chair. When he sang "The Bell in the Lighthouse" during his last meal, even the head screw sniffled. The Bull, however, had an even more personal concern: because of the seasonal change-over from daylight saving time to standard, he was to be deprived of an hour of his life. To use his own words, he claimed foul.

When told of the Bull's grievance, Warden Lewis E. Lawes postponed the execution of the sentence one whole day. The overseer of Sing Sing opposed capital punishment. He frequently sought reprieves for condemned felons. If the governor said no, and a man had to go to the chair, Warden Lawes would attend the electrocution, as the law directed, but at the final moment turn his back. He had never actually seen a man die in the chair.

To what moral purpose the Bull devoted his bonus day, I was not informed. It seems a paradox that men who covet just a little more time to live have wasted so much of it. If I had my own life to relive, as the elders sometimes say, I most likely would do no better a second time; perhaps even worse.

In some respects I was as unreliable as an automobile clock. I managed to learn something from the defeats, hardly anything from the victories. I now wish that I had been somewhat less impetuous, or at least able to have applied an ounce of prevention to my inch of time. Whenever I chanced to exercise my considerable vitality I behaved like a panther doing the hoedown. Still and all, I am glad that I paid so little attention to good advice; had I abided by it I might have been saved from some of my most valuable mistakes.

There were days which I would like to forget. There were days that I would like to remember, each glad moment returning from the misty dunes of time and circumstance. Memory, however, is a Coney Island mirror. Its distortions reflect a mistake in a thinner form than that in which it originally appeared, and a good deed in a wider aspect than it deserves. A man may strive to beat down his vanities, as some of us do, but anyone who writes about himself is apt to fall into the card sharp's habit of peeking at the deck to find out where the aces lie.

I should like to forget some aspects of the Straw Hat Series of

1918. An avalanche of recent mishaps has at last convinced me that it takes more effort to climb a mountain than it does to fall off it, and that, of the troubles that come to a man, he causes most of them himself. Fortunately, I never thought that mankind was against me. Men are not against you; they are merely *for* themselves.

On Wednesday, September 4, a drizzling rain began to fall on Chicago. A sullen wind blew in from Lake Michigan. The increasing storm lasted all morning. By noon Comiskey field was awash. The first game of the series between the Cubs and the Red Sox was set forward to the next afternoon.

Only a few drenched fans had waited overnight at the park gates to buy general-admission tickets. There was a feeling of depression among the sportsmen in the Loop. The baseball players, for the most part, seemed disgruntled. They lounged about the hotel lobbies, or played cards in their rooms. Except for this series, the wartime curfew on sports had been invoked, as I have mentioned. The ballplayers heard that their share of the world-series money was to be less than last year's award. They threatened to strike. The gamblers were slow to quote odds on the outcome of the games. Men's thoughts were on that greater series overseas.

I was cold and wet-through that day. I had with me only a summer suit of clothes, and no raincoat. I was lonely. I had a touch of buck fever, an ailment known to actors as stage fright, and to aviators who make a first parachute jump as "having the such-and-such scared out of you." My congenial Chicago friends were out of town, or out of the country for the most part. Charles MacArthur was shooting off a cannon somewhere in France. Ben Hecht was away on a lecture tour with the albino poet Max Bodenheim, who always smoked catnip with his tobacco. However, I had three friends on the scene: Larney Lichenstein, the manager of pugilists; Harry Hochstadter, the sports reporter; and Jack Coffey.

Coffey and I had been friends in Denver, where he had managed the baseball team. Just recently he had gone to the Boston Red Sox as an infielder. Coffey had prematurely gray hair and the face of an altar boy. Among his other talents, he was able to remember your birth date, once he had heard it. Whenever I met him, he would say, "Hello, March 8, 1890." Of course he never spoke to the ladies in this manner. Nor did he ever mention Damon Runyon's birthday to him, for the Demon was sensitive about his age.

Jack was a tolerant man, although there springs to mind an incident which challenged his friendly regard of me. It happened in Wichita, Kansas, a place that was not the bustling city it is today. One evening I asked Coffey if I might take the members of the Denver club's pitching corps to the amusement park. He gave me permission to do this if I promised not to let his six hurlers ride on the aged roller-coaster, and to have them back at the hotel by ten o'clock.

At the amusement park I spied one of those games at which, for five cents, you were given three boy's-size baseballs to throw at a pyramid of six dummy milk bottles. Each time you knocked over all six wooden "bottles," the concessionaire gave you ten cents. My friends were delighted to try their skill. I don't think anyone failed to bowl over six bottles at each throw. We collected eight or nine dollars in prize money. The dumfounded concessionaire shouted, "Crooks!" and closed up shop. One would have thought that we had broken the Bank of Monte Carlo.

Next afternoon at the baseball park, Coffey was astounded when all six pitchers successively were knocked out of the box. We lost the game by a disgracefully lop-sided score. You see, the athletes had thrown their arms out, as the expression is, because they had not warmed up before hurling the light-weight balls at the milk bottles.

On the rainy day when I wrote my pre-series story for the *American*, Mr. Coffey was occupied with baseball matters. Mr. Lichenstein had gone to Evanston to post bail for a fellow manager who had blackened the eyes of his best girl during a game of hearts. A third friend, Mr. Hochstadter, was very much on the town with a young Red Sox athlete, George Herman Ruth. The Babe had been assigned by the Boston manager Ed Barrow to pitch the opening game. Other members of the two clubs had gone to bed, as all good athletes were supposed to do on the eve of the big tournament.

Mr. Ruth always made his own rules. Rather, he had but one rule: never to go halfway in anything, on or off the baseball diamond. During his homeric moments at home plate, he used a forty-two-ounce bat. It weighed almost half a pound more than the weapons of other batsmen. He gripped the bat at the handle end, and swung it from way back there. Once committed to the swing, he could not check its mission. He would either drive the ball out of the park or strike out in a manner of itself spectacular.

The Babe had the personality of an overgrown adolescent— buoyant in spirit, unmindful of yesterday, indifferent to tomorrow.

Unable to find my cronies that rainy day in Chicago, I decided to visit Otto Floto's long-time friend Charles A. Comiskey, founder and first president of the Chicago White Sox. He had little to do with the Straw Hat Series, other than to have leased his park to the participants. Mr. Comiskey was known as "the Noblest Roman of Them All." No one seems to remember how he came by that title (especially since he was on the slow side when asked to increase the salaries of his ballplayers). White Sox historian Warren Brown thinks that Mr. Comiskey once saw an ancient coin bearing the likeness of Julius Caesar, and erroneously thought he was seeing his own likeness in a mirror.

Mr. Comiskey was not frugal when entertaining his sports-writer friends or his duck-hunting pals. He supplied them with food and drink in his private quarters at Comiskey Park. This was a tavern-like place for "the Woodland Bards," and from it one could look down upon the baseball diamond. On the day I called upon the Roman, a tarpaulin covered the infield area to protect it from the rain.

Now in his sixties, Mr. Comiskey told me of the days when he had driven a brick wagon, and how his father "Honest John" had been an alderman. He then drew upon his baseball memories, spoke of his association with the pioneers of baseball: "Cap" Anson, Patsy Tebeau, Connie Mack, John McGraw, Ban Johnson, Clark Griffith, and the rest. I wrote of this, and sent it as my first story to the *American*. I received a telegram of congratulation from Runyon, and another one from Agnes.

My joy over this response was marred by a telegram from the West. It said that my grandmother was dying. Until now she had been in robust health all her life. I wanted to be with her. She had been the closest one to me since I was four years old, and had reared me. What was I to do? I had in my pocket less than sixty of the two hundred dollars that sports editor Farnsworth had advanced for expense money.

A wire from my Aunt Etta Wheeler now arrived. She would take care of Granny. I sent Aunt Etta most of the money I had. Then I set out, sad and confused, to tell my troubles to Harry Hochstadter.

It required no frontiersman's skill to follow his well-blazed trail. I came upon him in the hotel suite of a three-hundred-pound wine agent, John "Doc" Krone. There I saw a galvanized metal washtub in the middle of the floor, and in it a mound of cracked ice and an ammunition dump of wine bottles. Sports writers, gamblers, and other students of human nature were gathered about the tub, some of them drinking the wine, others the stronger stuff. Mr. Hochstadter was addressing the guests, few of whom paid much attention to his speech, which had to do, as I recall it, with the behavior of lovesick tortoises. The orator leaned over too far, then collapsed across Doc Krone's huge knees.

Babe Ruth lifted Mr. Hochstadter to a couch, and advised him to switch to beer. Ruth seemed as fresh as a cornflower, although he had taken aboard many helpings of the sauce. I inquired of an Ohio journalist, "Wild Bill" Phelan (who used to carry a pet lizard in his coat pocket), if the Babe would be in shape to pitch tomorrow's game. Mr. Phelan suggested that I put the question to the athlete himself.

The hale young man gave me a bone-rattling slap on the back. "I'll pitch 'em all if they say the word!" The Babe then announced that he was leaving us to keep a date with someone who wore skirts. On his way out he urged that Mr. Hochstadter be given a Christian burial.

Ruth was young and strong; he managed to stay up all that night, and then shut out the Cubs, 1 to 0, the next day. At the close of the series, which the Red Sox won, four out of six games, Ruth had established a pitching record of twenty-nine and two-thirds consecutive scoreless innings for combined World Series play (against Brooklyn in 1916, and the Chicago Cubs in 1918).

I was young and strong, too, but the all-night escapade at Doc Krone's left me somewhat less effective than the Babe the next afternoon. Also, I was down to my last button. I had failed to mend my fortunes at dice. Along with a makeshift story of the ball game, I had wired Farnsworth to send me one hundred dollars. Colonel Van Hamm vetoed the request.

Runyon telegraphed to ask who, if anyone, had written my story. A wire from Agnes had in it an implication of concern. I went to the room of my friend Jack Coffey to think things over. Mr. Coffey said that persons born under the zodiacal sign of Pisces should ride herd on their impulses at all times.

I heard a song again and again that afternoon. It somehow became associated with my spirit of unrest. In those days song pluggers introduced Tin-Pan Alley ballads in public places. At the ball park I heard one of those ditties that even now, forty years afterward, distresses me—"I'm Always Chasing Rainbows." The theme had been borrowed from the middle section of Chopin's *Fantasie Impromptu*. Whenever I hear Chopin's original melody, or the song derived from it, the tune brings to mind my troubles of the afternoon when men with voices like sea captains sang "Rainbows" through their megaphones at Comiskey Park.

Upon learning that Colonel Van Hamm had turned thumbs

down on my request, I sent him a telegram over our leased wire. In it I said that I wanted no more money. Instead, would the colonel favor me with a photograph of himself—a profile view if that was possible. I explained that I had been troubled with intestinal sluggishness. I proposed to hang his picture on the lavatory wall.

The telegram was delivered by mistake to sports editor Farnsworth. He promptly pigeonholed it. When the colonel got wind of the "God-awful message," he asked that Mr. Farnsworth produce it. Mr. F. was not the sort to betray anyone, high or low. He said that the wire had been mislaid, that it wasn't important anyway, just routine.

Although Farnsworth liked gossip of all sorts (his fellow workers called him "the Ear"), he never turned anyone in, as the saying is. One time in the twenties, for example, he testified in the defense of Tex Rickard. The boxing promotor had been charged with the molestation of two teen-age girls. Farnsworth took the witness stand to say that he had seen Mr. Rickard at a football game on the afternoon of the alleged offense.

The prosecuting attorney sought to impeach the witness. "Mr. Farnsworth, what was the color of Mr. Rickard's suit that day?"

"I don't know," replied Farnsworth. "I'm a sports editor, not a tailor."

Rickard was acquitted.

When Colonel Van Hamm obtained a copy of my message at the telegraphers' room, he became a candidate for an apoplectic seizure. Unmindful of his historic loss of O. Henry, he advanced on Farnsworth with the demand, "Fire the bastard!"

Farnsworth replied that he couldn't. The colonel asked why the hell not. The sports editor reminded him that Mr. Hearst himself had hired me. The colonel telephoned Mr. Hearst.

Years later I learned that Mr. Hearst had listened patiently to Colonel Van Hamm's recital of my misdeeds, then had said, "No, colonel. Let's keep that young man from Denver."

In an aside to his secretary Mr. Hearst then voiced one of his truisms, "Joe, for a man who does not drink, I suffer more from alcohol than anyone else in the entire newspaper world."

I had a return railway ticket to New York, but only ten cents. I could have borrowed from my Chicago friends, of course, but did not wish to reveal my plight. When I got off the train at Pennsylvania Station, I had no tip for the porter. I have overtipped everyone since that day.

I used a nickel of my last dime to telephone Agnes at the Runyons'. Then I got on the wrong subway train. It took me to the Lenox Avenue side of town, instead of the Broadway station at 116th Street. I had to walk in the rain across Morningside Park to reach Runyon's apartment. My Gladstone bag seemed loaded with iron ore, almost as heavy as my heart.

There was not a word of recrimination by anyone at the Runyons', although I sensed that Ellen would have liked me to say something about the Chicago fiasco. Agnes seemed concerned mainly about my exposure to the elements. As for Damon, I seldom have known a more polite man, almost a Victorian.

He always had a large supply of clothing in his wardrobe, but none of his garments was large enough for me to exchange for my wet suit. He managed to find a dressing gown which a house guest had failed to take with him.

Perhaps I originated a slang saying that evening. I did not intend to have my words go down in Broadway history, but Runyon subsequently used the phrase, and it became popular.

"What's cooking?" I asked.

"We are having chicken," said Ellen. "Would you like some?"

I was hungry enough to eat a typewriter cover, but tried not to show my feeling. "Oh, I guess I'll just nibble at some white meat."

During the meal, Agnes said she had subleased and partly furnished that apartment which Ellen had found for us on West 112th Street.

When I had finished eating, the Demon could no longer

suppress his feelings. "Well, all I've got to say," he blurted out, "is that I wish Ellen would overlook *my* mistakes, like Agnes does *yours!*"

Damon and I then went to his bedroom. I put on my own half-dried clothing. He said that I of course would go downtown the next afternoon early and apologize to Colonel Van Hamm. When I replied that I wasn't going to do anything of the kind, he said, as nearly as I can remember his words, "Now look, fella! There are two strikes on you. First off, anyone hired over the head of an editor has a big handicap. Newspaper owners are always putting somebody on the payroll to please a friend, or square a favor, or keep a wife's mouth shut. Most of these parties are just no-good bums or nitwits that clutter up the place. Dead weight on the budget. So editors let them sit on their fannies, or else put them on tough assignments to show them up. Once in a blue moon a man makes good. But here you come, and you are hired over Colonel Van Hamm's head, and then you haul off and insult him." He paused a moment, then said grimly, "It's going to be hard sledding for you from here in. I hope you can keep your chin up."

"I'll keep my chin up," I said, "till they cut the tendons of my neck."

Brave words, indeed. Inwardly I felt (as my friend Lena Brogan once said of me) like one of those Chekhov characters: always going to Moscow, but of course never getting there.

It was still raining at midnight. Ellen Runyon called a cab. The driver was none too happy about taking us just around the corner and a block south to our new home. Agnes was not a large tipper. This circumstance did not make for good labor relations.

Inside our new quarters, Agnes said, "This is it."

We thought ourselves most fortunate to have ground-floor rooms in this walk-up apartment, not knowing that the upper floors were the choice locations. We did not know many things, then.

Next day I learned that my boyhood friend Jack Dempsey was

in town. He was stopping at the Hotel Ansonia, a place where opera singers resided and visiting baseball clubs and pugilists sometimes stayed; an odd assortment of artists, one might say.

Dempsey now was a year this side of the heavyweight championship of the world. At the moment the Manassa Mauler, as Runyon had nicknamed Jack, was in trouble. At the age of twenty-three upon the advice of his handlers he was to try for Jess Willard's title first and afterward enlist for the war. For this he was being referred to as a slacker. I knew then, as the world afterward would know, that this man had the courage of Spartacus. I felt certain that he would survive this storm—as eventually he did, to become the best-liked pugilist since John L. Sullivan's time.

On the occasion of that visit with Jack, I asked a question, and got from him an answer which I shall not forget: "Jack, when a fighter is caught in a corner, how is the best way to get out?"

"There are two ways, pardner," he said. "One is to quit. The other is to fight your way out."

CHAPTER

9

When I'm determined, I always listen to reason, because it can then do no harm.

—OLIVER GOLDSMITH

THE day General Pershing led the American Army on the Saint-Mihiel salient; the day men registered for the new draft; that same day when Eugene V. Debs, four times Socialist candidate for President, was found guilty of violation of the Espionage Act; on that cool September Thursday, Runyon said that Colonel Caleb Van Hamm expected to see me in his office at one o'clock. And no fooling!

Downtown, as I waited to see the head man, I forgot some of my apprehensions as I looked upon the early afternoon scene: the reporters receiving their assignments at the city desk; the coming and going of editors; these gentlemen of the press behaving in an orderly manner, quite unlike the lunatic heigh-ho of journalists on the motion-picture screens.

Toward deadline, to be sure, the tempo would quicken. The press would stir, then resound like the saber din of a cavalry charge. The thrill of that minute is something that never leaves one's memory. Perhaps an actor has a like feeling as the applause comes on the opening night of a play. The great press in a

114

metropolitan plant would shake the building, and sometimes shake the world.

As I sat in the sports department, which looked upon, and indeed was a functional part of the editorial setup of the New York *American*, I wondered why several small offices of haphazard design opened on, and in some instances extended into, the city room. Some of these compartments were mere booths, glassed in halfway down from the ceiling; others had painted board walls.

The makeshift aspect of these retreats would make it seem that the apprentice architects of shanty town had received their schooling here. I would learn at a later day that this editorial labyrinth had sprung up because of feuds among Hearst executives. Whenever a quarrel would arise between occupants of an editorial office, carpenters would arrive as though on cue to put up partitions which served as spite fences.

A new editor likely would find himself quartered in a hutch which some disgruntled predecessor had designed. One tall gentleman, Mr. Than V. Ranck, found himself newly cloistered as night editor in one of these cells. The shallow doorway had not been revised since the exile of another editor who resembled Napoleon in stature, if not in ability. The absent-minded Mr. Ranck used to bash his skull against the lintel but eventually learned, by means of trial and error, to do a low-bridge lest he become punch-drunk.

The thin and handsome Mr. Ranck had the culture and social charm of an exiled duke, but the copyreaders disliked him. For one thing, he was constantly on the move. Whenever he would sprint past the huge, kidney-shaped copy desk, the breeze set up by his coattails would disarrange the Associated Press "flimsy" as well as all other papers not skewered firmly on the long steel spindles.

Early one morning, when a store of Army munitions blew up at Black Tom Island, Mr. Ranck leaped from his chair with cries of "What is it? Where is it? How many are dead?" Before the on-the-spot news flashes could identify and properly orient the series of booming sounds, Mr. Ranck summarily decided that the

World building had been dynamited; then (after knocking his head against the low transom bar of his office) announced that a ship, loading ammunition in Gravesend Bay, had exploded. Still later on, he became temporarily positive that the town house of John D. Rockefeller, Sr., had been blown sky-high, taking the University Club with it.

Mr. Ranck was sustained in these contradictory impressions by the opinions of a "character" known as "Johnny Uptown." Johnny Uptown was a newsboy of middle age. His side job (at a good fee) was to give a special and somewhat furtive service to the mercurial Mr. Ranck; Johnny was to snatch early editions of opposition newspapers from the respective press rooms each evening, then hasten like a pony-express rider to the *American*. After his delivery of the red-hot *Worlds* and *Tribunes*, he would leave on the run to raid the more distant press rooms. When asked where he was going, he would shout over his shoulder, "Uptown!"

Mr. Ranck had two nicknames—"Replate Joe," because of his obsession for eleventh-hour revisions of the front page, and "Headlong Harry." Each night he would make a hasty survey of the fresh editions of rival newspapers. Then, while the presses were rolling, he would order story changes and new headlines. This meant an interruption of the press run until new page plates could be clamped in place. Sometimes he would stand on one long leg, storklike, the foot of his other leg hoist on a desk or a chair, and would peer over the shoulder of some resentful headline writer and make clucking noises.

The copyreaders unjustly said that Mr. Ranck's brains resided in the exact center of his spare buttocks, and that his body should sue his mind for separate maintenance. Actually he was a very bright person.

Mr. Ranck's given name was Nathaniel, but he apparently disliked it, and insisted upon the "Than" label. His reluctance to make up his mind while making up the newspaper and his many journeyings up the circular iron stairway to the composing room, there to issue conflicting orders, prompted the strongly unionized typographers to bar him from their precincts.

The chapel, as the fellowship of compositors is known, stood for no nonsense from editors. A union rule stipulates that a non-union member must not so much as touch the type about to be locked in the page forms. Mr. Ranck, in his anxiety, would toy with galleys of type, or else with the trays of "leads." These rectangles of wafer-thin metal were kept at hand to space out the columns evenly in the forms. In those days, the so-called "leads" were of brass and after press time were salvaged from the "hell-box" into which used type had been thrown.

Another fiddler with leads was the capable Fred Eldridge, a Los Angeles editor deputized on occasion by Mr. Hearst to go from one paper to another as a "trouble-shooter." Both Eldridge and Ranck had worked as young men on the Philadelphia *North American*. Mr. Eldridge, irreverently known as "Nervous Nellie," was cured of his lead-fiddling ways one night as the front page was being locked in the steel chase. A member of the chapel had heated a galley of the brass shims, then set the tray within the reach of "Nervous Nellie." He absently picked up a sheaf of these blistering plates, squealed like a castrated mink, and added *le grand jeté* to the dance of St. Vitus.

On the day I was waiting to report to Colonel Van Hamm, I became interested in a box stall behind the city desk in the *American* city room. It had the appearance of a makeshift hot-house with grimed opaque glass in its flanks. In it there sat the new city editor, Victor Watson. This short-waisted gentleman was said to be the most mysterious of all Mr. Hearst's seven thousand employes. He was known on Park Row as a "hatchet man." A sprightly assistant city editor, Royal Daniel, nicknamed him "the Hetman." Mr. Watson seldom smiled, but when he did so looked as though rigor mortis were setting in.

Watson was of early middle age, was sphinxlike in manner, and wore spectacles, the lenses as thick as perfume-bottle stoppers. He smoked three packages of Piedmont cigarettes a day, ate rich food, was a black-coffee addict, but did not drink hard liquor. He was one of that minority of metropolitan editors who work in shirtsleeves. The others wore regular coats, or in summer put on dust jackets, and addressed staff members as "Mister."

Mr. Hearst just recently had moved the mysterious Mr. Watson from his uptown office, where he had been in charge of theatrical advertising. To the amazement of almost everyone, W.R. had put him in charge of the city desk. Mr. Watson commenced at once to harass his colleagues. Later on in his career, when Mr. Hearst was considering Watson for an even higher position, the Chief consulted one of his most successful veterans, editor Edmond D. Coblentz of the San Francisco *Examiner*.

Mr. Hearst asked a leading question, as sometimes was his way. "You do not like Mr. Watson, do you, Mr. Coblentz?"

"I don't know him well enough to have an opinion for or against him, Mr. Hearst."

"But you have heard of him?"

"I have heard that he is a red rag to everyone in the organization."

"He's not as red as he has been painted," said Mr. Hearst. "My only objection to Mr. Watson is that his mind travels on one track. He's a one-story man."

"From what I have heard," said Coblentz, "he's more of a second-story man."

Mr. Hearst showed great displeasure at this remark. When he was angry, his face would become even more pale than it usually was. He might not admire certain of his men, but seldom permitted adverse criticism. For example, he once testified in court to the "good character" of a one-time henchman who had sold him a paper factory which had gone out of business. A personal attack upon anyone in his employ seemed only to heighten Mr. Hearst's regard for that man.

Nor did he permit reporters to poke fun at his friends. One day long ago the late Rex Smith (afterward an authority on bullfighting) wrote a flippant article about an astronomer who had made a speech on what, if anything, the inhabitants of Mars looked like. At that time armchair-matador Smith was a reporter for the San Francisco *Examiner*.

Mr. Hearst warned Smith, "Young man, the next time you do a story about *any* of my friends, please take your tongue out of your cheek."

Mr. Hearst seemed to have extraordinary patience with spirited subordinates. One of them, the late John Campbell ("Cactus Jack"), became a noted Western editor. He had been a rough-and-ready pal of Jack London, who worked on an opposition newspaper in San Francisco. During an uprising in Guatemala, London's insurgent friends put Cactus Jack in jail. They kept him there until London had filed an exclusive report of the revolution to his own newspaper.

When Campbell's contract as editor of the Los Angeles *Herald Express* was being discussed by Mr. Hearst and publisher Dr. Frank Barham, the doctor dissented. "Mr. Hearst," he said, "Jack Campbell is a bull in a china shop."

"Perhaps so," replied Mr. Hearst, "but he never breaks our *best* china."

"I know that," Dr. Barham persisted, "but he's not in harmony with the organization."

"Dr. Barham," Mr. Hearst said, "too much harmony is deadly."

Another high-spirited Hearst man was the late Samuel S. Chamberlain. He had been secretary to James Gordon Bennett the Younger on the New York *Herald*, and had helped found *Le Matin* in Paris. Tall, gray-templed, well tailored, Chamberlain was regarded by his friends as one of the aristocrats of the newspaper business, and by his enemies as an unprincipled cynic. He served as editor in the 1890s on the young Hearst's San Francisco *Examiner*. Chamberlain first met Mr. Hearst in 1888 at the bar of the old Hoffman House in New York. At that memorable hotel seventeen drink dispensers stood duty at a bar seventy-five feet long. Mr. Chamberlain knew them all. Perhaps no other editor became as intimate with W.R. as Chamberlain; not even Brisbane.

In the nineties, Sam Chamberlain was one of two journalists of the Golden Gate to wear English tweeds. Mr. Hearst was the other; the young publisher had his suits made by Poole's of London. Young Hearst was of the same size as Chamberlain. Sam inherited the Hearst tweeds. Somehow Chamberlain wore the handed-down suits more impressively than did his employer, who never managed to look like Beau Brummel.

After he had served as a Congressman (1903–1907), Mr. Hearst for a time wore the dark suits and the drooping black felt hats favored by legislators of that period. Even in the garb of a statesman Mr. Hearst looked like the loser of an international sack race. He did not, however, approach the sartorial carelessness of William Jennings Bryan, who resembled an old archery target; or, much later on, that of Heywood Broun, Park Row's all-time example of how to scare a scarecrow. Those of us who seldom looked presentable were grateful to Broun. I can best explain this by an incident taken from my own experience. When the faultlessly groomed Edwin C. Hill of the *Sun* one day asked how I had the nerve to show up in golf knickers, and with no necktie, to meet President Woodrow Wilson upon his return from the Paris Peace Conference, I replied, "Oh, no one noticed *me*. You see, I took the precaution to stand next to Heywood Broun."

Sam Chamberlain was perhaps the best "idea man" Mr. Hearst ever had. The fact that he drank whenever it suited his fancy did not seem to scramble his wits. When the aggressive publisher founded a chain of newspapers, he sent Chamberlain and another lively fellow, Foster Coates, from one city to another as mastermind executives.

Mr. Chamberlain occasionally disappeared from his desk without warning. No one could find him during these absences, which sometimes lasted a week or more. He even strayed as far away as Europe on some of these unforeseen holidays. He kept a passport on his person at all times, just in case. On one occasion he went to Munich, Germany, merely to get some good beer. Chamberlain always came back to work from his junkets, but not until he felt like doing so. After a furlough, he would peel off his gloves, place his stick and his bowler hat on his roll-top desk, and then take up the reins as though nothing at all had happened to him or to the newspaper.

When an efficiency man one day complained of Chamberlain's absences from the bridge, Mr. Hearst replied, "One hour of Sam Chamberlain's time is worth more to me than a month of most other editors'."

On the afternoon when I was waiting to see Colonel Van Hamm, I learned many things about Hearst editors in general, and about Victor Watson in particular. This hearsay evidence was supplied by a vital Irishman, friendly of manner but of fierce visage. His eyes were black. His complexion was that of coffee with too much cream in it. His black hair made him appear much younger than his sixty years. I thought he looked like a dark angel that had fallen out of a Michelangelo fresco.

This squat and swarthy gentleman had come to the city room to confer on matters of editorial policy with Colonel Van Hamm. These editors had a cobra-mongoose feeling one for the other. After the conference, the dark angel saw me. He introduced himself as Philip Francis.

It was hard for me to believe that anyone of his celebrity could be cordial to a mere reporter, especially to one who was but a few strides ahead of the posse. I had heard Runyon say that Francis had been a chum of Bret Harte and of Ambrose Bierce out West. I also knew something of his reputation as a crusader for a free Ireland. I was not then aware that Francis had just recently brought down the wrath of a considerable part of the public on Mr. Hearst's head.

Philip Francis hated England. England felt the same way about him. Violently controversial in print, yet the friendliest of men when in his own personal world, Mr. Francis had managed to outrage everyone who had advocated the war. On the other hand, he had fanned the partisanship of those opposed to it.

Francis was said by the late Moses Koenigsberg, head of the Hearst wire and feature syndicates, to have been of German instead of Irish extraction, and to have been born with the surname "Diefendorf." If this were true, and had it become known that a German was writing Mr. Hearst's editorials attacking England and France, there might well have been more hell to pay than the mere burning of newspapers in suburban communities, or the casting into the sea of Hearst journals delivered to ships at wharf-side, or that snake on the *Tribune* tower.

Koenigsberg, a most genial but outspoken man, a remarkable salesman of Hearst products, looked and acted like a Jewish counterpart of Dr. Samuel Johnson. Notwithstanding his good nature and his friendly bluster, he was somewhat thin-skinned. Like Colonel Van Hamm, he had been worsted on several occasions by Francis in matters of editorial policy. Consequently, he was on the lookout for anything that might give Francis even blacker eyes than nature already had supplied. Koenigsberg conceded, however, that the man whom he called "A German toad in an Irishman's skin" was undeniably brilliant.

It is still difficult for me to think of Francis as a villain. I always have been slow to see flaws in the characters of men of talent. Perhaps I did not want to see them. So long as a man does not show himself to me as one resolved to betray my country, I must assume that he means well.

Perhaps I am out of bounds in this age of clique and claque. Then so be it. I shall not yield to the bush-whackers, or to their likes and dislikes; nor shall I take part in the damnable squabbles that have set so many of my once gay and lovable friends one against the other, and made of them querulous old men, bitter and suspicious, estranged from laughter, and unable even to forgive the dead. I write of men as I have found them; and all in all, I have found them good. Phil Francis was most kind to me till the day of his retirement in 1921. Let God take care of his sins.

On the day of our first meeting, to my pleasant surprise, Francis greeted me by name, and seemed to know all about my Chicago blunder. He asked why I was sitting alone in a far corner of the city room. I replied that I had been praying before the ax was to fall.

He chuckled, then said that if young men were acquainted with the laws of cause and consequence, they would walk backward when in battle.

At this point in our conversation city editor Watson appeared at the doorway of his cubicle. Mr. Watson leaned against a jamb of the door frame, a cigarette in one hand and a pair of long scissors in the other. He seemed as self-assured and as well armed as a leader of the Hip Sing Tong.

"Let's hope you never have the misfortune to be on Vic Watson's staff," said Francis. Before I could ask why, he went on to say, "He is an editorial pole vaulter, in that his butt always precedes his head over the crossbar; but he knows how to get rid of a foe in ways more subtle than those practiced by any emperor of Rome."

The student of Roman history invited me to sit in the more friendly environment of his office until the colonel was ready to give me my medicine. I was glad to leave a room where even the ceiling seemed a mirror of my own confusions. Electric-light cords dangled above the scarred desks. The green shades were suspended at random levels. Pieces of copy paper had been glued to, or clipped onto, many of these shades by reporters who did not want the light to shine in their eyes. I also saw overhead a maze of corroded brass pneumatic tubes, used to convey stories and head-lines from the copy desk to the composing room.

Frequently these brass intestines became clogged, and had to be probed with a long "snake" of flexible steel. Occasionally the air pressure would back up against a stubborn copy container, then, with a loud flatulence, would force out that object upon the copy desk. One day Mr. Fred Eldridge ("Nervous Nellie") was seated in the "slot" of the copy desk as the bobbin landed. He did one of his Ballet Russe leaps and said he wished he were back in Los Angeles.

Philip Francis's office was quite small. It was the headquarters of four editorial writers and a poet. One of these was the elderly Colonel John Temple Graves of Georgia, a spellbinder who had been Hearst's candidate for Vice-President on the Independence League ticket in 1908. It was said that Colonel Graves once had come upon United States Senator Hoar in the toilet of the Senate Office building as that legislator was rehearsing a speech on the tariff and simultaneously occupying himself with a less statesman-like function.

"Senator," Mr. Graves asked, "do you point with pride? Or view with alarm?"

A second editorialist was the modest-mannered Dr. Charles Fleischer, a former Boston rabbi. He brought the staff daily gifts of chocolate candy made by Mrs. Fleischer, and pieces of liver for the office cat "Hypo."

Hypo liked to lie atop a filing cabinet to look down upon the early-morning poker games. This cat had an unorthodox aversion to the outdoors. As he grew older he became quite careless about using his sandbox. Editors and copyreaders regularly complained of the feline odors, and demanded that the decrepit and unsanitary Hypo be sent to the pound. But the cat stayed on to outlast many editors, and deservedly so. He never got the newspaper into libel suits.

Another member of the editorial battery was Frederick B. Landis, brother of Judge Kenesaw Mountain Landis, afterward the so-called "czar" of baseball. It was Mr. Landis's custom to take off his shoes whenever he wrote an editorial. He would pace up and down the corridor in his sock-feet and declaim his editorial in a voice like that of a train announcer at Grand Central. Mr. Landis lived in Port Washington, where as a sideline he operated a stationery store and newsstand. His accounting system was not of the best. Ben Bloom, circulation manager of the *American*, sometimes interrupted one of the Landis readings to ask that he pay his long-overdue bill for copies of the *American* delivered for resale at Port Washington.

The poet and part-time editorial writer was the justly renowned James Jackson Montague. This tiny man from Iowa (via Oregon) also wrote with his shoes off. Some years afterward I, too, wrote editorials for the *American*. I did not work with my shoes off, but some of my contributions seemed to have been written with the feet.

A subscriber wrote in to ask, "When the editor composed yesterday's editorial, did he have his ear or his rear to the ground?"

On the day I entered Mr. Francis's office, poet Montague was the only one on duty. The newspaper bard was leaning back in a swivel chair, his shoeless feet resting upon the decrepit desk. His strong-smelling cigar had dwindled to the size of a burned cork. He said that he was going to France to report the Peace Conference, and would close up shop, come the very next hour. There would be no ode from his pen this night, he said, and let the editors howl their heads off.

"I'm fed up with my own jingles," he went on to say. "And I've got to see about my official papers to get into France."

A freckled copy boy now arrived on the scene. He said through his chewing gum that Colonel Van Hamm wished to see me at once. I followed the lad to the city room. I then entered the managing editor's office to see a three-quarter profile of the colonel at his roll-top desk. His hat pushed back on his large head, he was studying a war map tacked to the wall above the desk. The serene colonel did not greet me either by word or by gesture. I felt like a guest who had stayed one day too long.

Eventually he turned in his chair. "Can you write verses?"

"It's the best thing I do," I replied.

This remark did not enhance my cause, if, indeed, I had one. A young man should keep two things buttoned: his lip and his fly. It always has been my unfortunate practice, when exposed to sudden shifts of fortune, to speak first and think afterward.

After I had self-appraised my abilities as a poet, Colonel Van Hamm said in a matter-of-fact tone, "Mr. Montague is going to Europe. You are to write a daily verse during his absence, beginning as of *now*. Hand in your copy a day ahead. Tonight you'll have till seven."

I seem to remember that he grunted, not three, but *four* times.

I arrived at our apartment to find Agnes gone. I had no key. The superintendent was not in, nor was the landlord, who had an apartment in this four-story building. Mine was a do-or-die situation, what with a locked door between me and Pegasus. I walked up and down the sidewalk in front of the apartment house, and wished that I had a set of burglar tools.

When Agnes returned at about five o'clock, I ran inside the flat and to my typewriter. I composed a poem, the lines of which I do not remember, and hope that no one else does. It had something to do with motherhood and the Flag, two of Mr. Hearst's favorite themes.

During the next days I regularly went downtown to deliver my copy to the colonel's secretary, Gil Laird. Mr. Laird, a gaunt and middle-aged Scot, smoked a corncob pipe. It smelled as though he were using shredded lamp wick for tobacco. He wore a green celluloid visor low on his forehead. This cracked and fly-specked eyeshield gave him the aspect of a pool-hall proprietor. Laird had served six or seven Hearst managing editors as a confidential secretary, but appeared relatively sane. One day he would be *my* secretary. Had he been able to foresee that event it is likely that he would have gone straight off to Scotland, or to heaven, where I am sure he now is.

After some days of tussling with the muse, I arrived at the newspaper office to find Jimmy Montague back at his desk, writing! I mentioned something about his Peace Conference assignment abroad. He merely said that there had been "some snags." Montague and I afterward became good friends; but that day he was none too cordial. He seemed to regard me as a potential claim jumper.

I reported to Colonel Van Hamm that Mr. Montague was back at work. Did he have anything for me to do? He grunted twice, then said with an air of finality that Montague was *not* back. I respectfully said that I had just left Mr. Montague's office; that the poet that very instant was sitting there like Wordsworth. The colonel again snorted his disbelief, but his secretary confirmed my report.

The editor instructed secretary Laird to ask Victor Watson to step into the office. When Mr. Watson appeared, the colonel said, "This man will report to you until further notice."

"Keep in touch with me," said Mr. Watson, somewhat vaguely, I thought. "Telephone me tomorrow."

I kept in touch with Mr. Watson by telephone daily for a week or so. My funds ran low. Agnes suggested that I go downtown to inquire about my pay. I felt sure that I had no pay coming. Finally, to please Agnes, I did go to the cashier's office of the *American*.

Captain Walter Thompson presided at a pay window which had the appearance of something left over from the Wells-Fargo period. The captain long ago had been the skipper of the Hearst tug *Vamoose*, one of several vessels chartered by the publisher during the Spanish-American war. The captain also had been a mate aboard the Hearst yacht *Buccaneer*. The publisher turned it over to the government without cost, and became an honorary ensign in the United States Navy. Later on in the war with Spain the captain served in some capacity aboard the British steamer *Sylvia*. It too had been chartered by Mr. Hearst to carry him and his staff to the scene of war.

I believe it was while Ensign Hearst and Captain Thompson were on a sea-scouting expedition aboard the *Vamoose*, off the coast of Cuba, that they "captured" a band of sixty-five Spaniards. The Spanish soldiers, starved and exhausted, were signaling from shore with a reasonably white flag. Although this "capture" made fine news, it put quite a strain on the galley and living quarters of the *Vamoose*. The captain once told me that he had "a hell of a time getting anyone to take those long-gutted Spaniards off'n our hands."

Payroll bandits occasionally held up the old cashier of the

American at gun-point. The ringing of an electrified gong would announce these outrages to the city room, two floors below. No one would pay much attention to it. The editorial staff seemed to feel that Mr. Hearst would not miss a few dollars now and then. The captain, however, had great respect for Mr. Hearst and his money, as well as a reluctance to be shot. On days when no payroll money would be distributed, the captain would seek to discourage banditry by keeping on hand but a few hundred dollars as petty cash. One evening Mr. Hearst himself appeared at the paymaster's window during one of his infrequent visits downtown. After a pleasant colloquy with the ex-master of the *Vamoose*, Mr. Hearst mentioned that he would like to have some money.

W.R. seldom would carry more than a bit of loose change, and never a checkbook. Whenever in need of cash for an after-theater dinner party, he usually would go to the uptown business offices at Columbus Circle, there to tap the till at the want-ad counter. Captain Thompson said that he would be most happy to oblige the Chief. How much would Mr. Hearst like to have? The newspaper owner said that two or three thousand dollars should cover the expenses of the evening. The captain's sea legs almost gave way. He had but four hundred and forty-odd dollars in the cash-drawer.

Mr. Hearst would seldom upbraid an employee for any fault, real or imagined. A remiss fellow might awaken the next morning without a job, but ordinarily with no reprimand. After his visit with Captain Thompson, Mr. Hearst said a pleasant good evening. He turned at the door. "Would you mind, captain, keeping five thousand dollars in cash here at all times?"

Somehow the bandits got word of this new treasure trove. The gong would ring again and again. Eventually a uniformed watchman was assigned to safeguard the cashier's window, a pistol holstered on his cartridge belt.

On the day when I called upon Captain Thompson I identified myself, then asked if any mail addressed to me had been delivered to him "by mistake." The captain said no, but he had been holding some *pay* envelopes for me. He had been wondering just why I had not collected them.

I found three hundred dollars in the envelopes! "Thank you, captain," I managed to say.

The captain, as I could plainly see, was taken in by my show of unconcern. Somehow he formed the impression that I was a moneyed man, and somehow that impression spread among the staff. Soon I was being asked for loans.

Since then I never would feel so rich. Three "C's," as Mr. Runyon said, was more than somewhat; or, as Jimmy Durante (whom I would know soon) put it, "a king's transom."

The rent was paid. Mr. Von Der Heyde, the grocer, was paid. The neighborhood newsdealer (who to my amazement had never heard of Runyon) was paid. Agnes bought a large second-hand chair, an overstuffed object which became heavier and heavier as I wrestled with it to get it inside our door. It leaked excelsior and horsehair at the seams, so Agnes got some flower-design chintz and made a gay new cover for it. I remember that chair better than I do any of the royal thrones I have seen since that time. It was the best chair I ever sat in; sat in to read, to tell stories to my children and Runyon's children, or to dream.

That chair was not always a place for easy reflections. Some nights, late, when the household would be asleep, and a dim light would shine upon the nearby table of fumed oak where stood a blue bowl of artificial fruit, I would leave off reading to prowl the alleys of my mind. It disturbed me to find so many toppled ashcans lying there.

At such times I would become unmindful of the time I was in, of the night voice of the city that never sleeps. I could not, of course, entirely dismiss the nearer sounds of reality: the kerplunking of the flat-wheel streetcars along Amsterdam Avenue; the yowlings of courtyard cats in violent dalliance; the occasional bomb burst of an electric-light bulb hurled from an upper window to explode among the passionate cats. These noises merely put commas and periods among the paragraphs of my musings, and did not stay the compositions of the lonely mind. My legend to the contrary, most of my adventures have occurred deep within myself. And there only, where none could hear, have I cried out in my defeat and pain.

I would try to measure my twenty-eight years in terms of things done and of things undone, both good and bad. The index of my experience was too slender as yet for me to estimate my stature or to weigh my intentions. Still, I felt that I must believe in myself and in all life; and, no matter what difficulties might arise, I must go the way of faith.

I had many confusions of mind, and had made a bad start on Park Row. I would have to fight my way out of my corner, as the young Dempsey had recommended; or, as the older Corbett had said, get up when knocked down. There were times, however, as I sat in the old chair, when I wondered if I had been created on purpose, or if I was one of nature's slips of the wheel as the clay had been shaping.

One of those early mornings of self-search comes to mind as I sit in another chair, far away in terms of time and miles. I had been wondering if Colonel Van Hamm ever had been young or in trouble. I had been wondering why it was that one of his assistants would always send me to New Jersey on rainy days to cover "one-stick" stories, routine sundries ordinarily assigned to cub reporters. If this man's parents had not gone on their honeymoon, I would have been spared much inconvenience.

I would sometimes sit like a muddled pugilist waiting for the next round, waiting for the bell to sound, wondering just how to block the hooks and jabs that demonstrated whether or not the newcomer to Park Row had a glass jaw.

One early morning in November, when in the chair, after the old steam-radiators had sounded their nightly death rattles, I fancied that two learned visitors appeared out of the past to stand opposite one another beside the fumed-oak table. They did not greet me, but entered upon a colloquy as to my moral fortitude, or the lack of it. My imaginary callers, I was astonished to learn, were Saint Augustine and Monsieur Voltaire.

I remember that they vanished before the matter of their discussion could be resolved. They made some disquieting remarks, however, before they melted away. I did not know which of the wraiths said, "Here is a melancholy man steeped in hilarities," or "To offer him a life of security as the reward of self-discipline would be like giving a rose to a mule."

I wonder what happened to the old chair. In a manner of speaking it was the seat of a giant swing which carried one over into the midst of the carnival age known as the Roaring Twenties. High, high in the sky it went, to the other side of the moon.

I have just left old Fowler, seated and alone, except for his orange and yellow cat, Frank Moran. The author occupies another chair—a love seat, of all things—and it is upholstered in green velvet, a color which, he informs me, matches his insides.

"I live red," he explained, "but inside I remained green."

Actually I did not leave Fowler, as I have just said. I never have left him since we first met seventy years ago—except of course when I had too much to drink, or was listening to the sea. And I suppose that I never shall leave him until the "Sanctus" is rung at his Mass of last repose. Still, it would seem at times that I am a stranger to him, as today, when he told me:

"This time I am writing a book the way I please; a book of remembrance; a love story. I had an ear for music, a nose for news, and an eye for the girls. My love story is not about women, but instead would tell of my love for the newspaper years on Park Row; for my friends there, and for life. Do not set me down, sir, as a Peeping Tom should you find me these winter nights peering into the windows of the past."

CHAPTER

10

Youth is a fine carver and
gilder. —SIR WALTER SCOTT

IN A plain board box which smells of time, I come upon the relic of a calendar, a November leaf of 1918. The page lies half-hidden among a drift of clippings from the old New York *American.* Various marks and notes are scribbled upon the torn-out page. These scrawls, cryptic and long forgotten, now seem as meaningless as the street signs of a ghost town.

One of the days, November 7, is circled with red crayon. This halo, one might suppose, should make the day a time of easy recollection. Offhand I cannot remember its significance, and am unreasonably annoyed by this truancy of mind. I put aside the calendar page and its red-ringed day, first permitting Frank Moran to sniff at it to learn whether or not it is something good to eat.

The box of newspaper clippings contains many stories upon which I worked so eagerly long ago, loving that work with a heart afire, earnestly though gaily embracing it, notwithstanding the precarious position in which I had placed myself at the very beginning of my New York adventure. I was young; so was my world. There were red rings for all those days.

Common sense (of which I have had an occasional flash), as well as my fast-growing reportorial experience, persuaded me that life, human and otherwise, is an ordeal. The way one meets that ordeal marks the size and meaning of a man. Some meet it with pious resignation, others with philosophical stoicism, still others with a desperation which finds the wayfarer somewhere between the poles of terror and heroism, lament and exultation. If life be a tragedy—as many masters say or sing of it—it is touched with mystery and grandeur. No cynic has the moral right or the special wisdom to contend that it is in vain we live; or to hold humanity in contempt, and cast stones of mockery among the footsore pilgrims. If, in my bare-branch years, I still have some sap left, it is because I learned to make a friend of loneliness.

Though wayward at times, I sought to go with faith, to work and live with a measure of gaiety, as opposed to a show of penitential tears. I have had but one fault to find with life: there are too many good-bys.

As I sort the old newspaper clippings, I keep wondering: why the red ring for that day in November? The more I try, the day and its meaning recede, as when one strives to impound the context of a dream. The old cat yawns, revealing his one remaining tooth. He makes a Gothic arch of his back, then once again pads up to me to smell the clippings.

These mementos flake off at the margins, come apart at the folds. The headlines comprise a jumbled catalogue of events: The death of John Murphy Cardinal Farley. . . . The opening of the Fourth Library Loan campaign with an address by Woodrow Wilson at the Metropolitan Opera House. There one heard "The Star-Spangled Banner" sung with seemingly effortless power and essential majesty. Enrico Caruso sang it; and if there be envy among the angels, his voice would be the cause of it. . . . The unveiling by the still vital orator and ex-senator, Chauncey M. Depew, of a bronze bust of himself in Peekskill, where he had been born eighty-four years before this time, and had played on Drum Mountain as a boy, and heard old soldiers of the Revolution tell their tales. . . . The murder by the *Evening World's* sadistic, debt-ridden city editor, Charles E. Chapin, of his tired old wife as she slept beside him. . . . The winning of the amateur golf championship by Charles "Chick" Evans, Jr. . . . Other headlines, other stories, sere testimonials of the three ages of man: I shall be, I am, I was. . . .

The medley of clippings in the old board box—like the men and women they publicized for a day—now are of the dust. And I say to my cat:

"You have seen me rummaging in the debris of my career among printed words. Tell me, Sir Francis Moran—you, who are well into your ninth life, the survivor of hundreds of battles, and no one knows how many wives—tell me, my still sensual friend, do you sometimes have an hour when you seem actually to be living in the past?"

The indifferent Sir Francis is busy washing the inner side of a hind leg with his tongue. This knight of the alley is also a Knight of the Bath. He addresses the leg as though strumming a guitar, poet Carl Sandburg playing "The Blue-Tail Fly." My companion is becoming quite arrogant these days. I hope that no one will further swell his pride by telling him that violinist Eugene Ysaye once played Paganini's *Concerto in D* on the guts of a Moran ancestor.

I put to one side the box and its fragments of ancient history. No sooner done than a full recollection of the red-ringed day, November 7, 1918, pops up in the mind with the minor violence of a window shade whirling to the top of the sash. Elated by this little victory, I slap my knee. It startles Frank Moran from his yogi's posture.

"There now"—I reassure him—"let us stay calm, and I shall tell you about that November seventh. It was the day of the 'False Armistice.' In my opinion, sir, that day marked the true beginning of the age known as the Roaring Twenties. And I will thank your excellency not to make a comfort station of this box. It contains memories."

An older man's memory sometimes is that of a fading opera singer. He must reply upon the prompter in the bubble of the stage apron for his cues, especially when he appears as Figaro in *The Barber of Seville*. My own prompter's box is the dusty bin with its old newspaper clippings, letters, ticket stubs for championship fights and world-series baseball games, police cards, and in particular four small diaries, notebooks which Ellen Runyon gave me, one at each glad Christmastime. I also come upon a beaded watch fob with my initials on it, made by Tse-Quiat the Indian, who did not know that I never carried a watch. He was grateful because I corrected those who called him Tse-ne-Gat (Cry Baby) in print; a lock of a child's hair, Jane's I think; a rusty ox shoe from the Mormon trail out West . . . Whispers from a hidden world long lost . . . Echoes of the strong winds of time. It all seems so long ago.

I have thought that Act II of this century opened on the day of the False Armistice. Other writers say that the rise of curtain came with the advent of Prohibition in July of 1919. It is a matter of historical punctuation just where one should assign the marks which enclose the 1920s in parentheses: Prohibition, if you will, on the one side, and the stock market collapse, if you prefer it as your arbitrary symbol, on the other.

It did seem, however, that the climate of human affairs suddenly changed on the day of the False Armistice, a complete break with the past. The newspapers so testified. The news for four years, especially the last two of them, had come from the areas of battle. Now the emphasis was on peace and the return of the soldiers, the parades of welcome, and then on the strikes, the readjustments of the world's economy, the rise of millionaires, home-grown murders, scandals, and all the rest of the postwar changes in men's lives— and in their hearts.

Hindsight analysts sometimes say that the suddenness of the change which came over us in the 1920s with the sweep of a tidal wave should not have found us unprepared. It is the contention of these wise gentlemen that, had we kept our eyes even half opened, we might have been able to recognize and interpret signs and portents all around us that our moral, social, and economic worlds were not flat. We and our fathers before us, it is now said, had been exposed to prophetic influences ever since Lincoln's day. We should have seen; we should have known.

It is easy enough for one generation to damn the one just preceding it; in fact, it is the rule, as we may see in the history of every nation. Perhaps tomorrow's critics may find that the earth shakers of today will have lacked certain elements of both foresight and insight. Our genius of today, who suddenly has been able to fire a ball bearing or two beyond the air we used to breathe so confidently, may be described by tomorrow's analyst as somewhat less competent as a comet manufacturer than the Maker of all suns, of all space, of all time. We shall see.

Anyone who now remembers that November afternoon, when a bulletin of the United Press prematurely announced the end of World War I, knows where he was that day, and just how he felt when noise and tumult filled the air. After some hours of celebration the official word arrived that the bulletin had been a great mistake. The effect of this was almost terrifying; emotions overrode one's reasoning powers. The desire for peace had built up such a steam-boiler pressure in every breast that when it became quite clear to the street dancers that the bulletin was false a feeling of resentment took hold of them. They had been wasting their joy on a fake. In the first phase of their reaction to the sobering news they appeared to be in a state of mass shock. Then their wrath burst like the fly wheel of some huge machine gone awry. In Times Square they tore up the newspapers which carried the State Department's denial that peace had come. A seismic grumbling became the voice of the town. There was a sound of shattered glass as store windows gave way. The police, until now quite lenient with the disillusioned merrymakers, moved in upon them from all sides.

My sponsor Damon Runyon was with General Pershing in France when the guns cooled on November 11. I had not heard from him except indirectly, when Ellen Runyon read portions of his letters to Agnes. In one of them he said, "Please tell Agnes to hide Eugene's cowboy boots—the ones with the saw-tooth rowels —before he goes to work. And tell Eugene, whatever he is doing, *not* to do it."

The Demon often seemed skeptical of me; but as I look back on the many years I knew him—if anyone actually *knew* him—I have reason to believe that he had a real liking for me. He was seldom demonstrative; so shy in some respects that he would not—perhaps could not—advertise his emotions.

Runyon was by no means the only fellow of stoical appearance among my contemporaries. When among officious persons, Ring Lardner would seem to be stranded on the wet rump of a glacier. W. O. McGeehan, friendly indeed with his intimates, would become stiff-mannered when some Broadway back-slapper caught up with him.

Comic artist F. O. Opper, the creator of Happy Hooligan, was always dour and unsocial. One of Mr. Opper's eyes was artificial. It was an excellent "match." Cartoonist Rube Goldberg was asked one day if he could tell which one of Opper's eyes was of glass. He replied, "The one with the kindly expression."

In our age of Nevertheless we had solemn men as well as gay ones. I believe, however, that the merry ones outnumbered the sad. But even the serious-mannered ones had a special flavor; few of them seemed to be whittling out their respective careers with dull knives.

As for me, I thought that love made the world go round, that life was an adventure, and that the wonder of it and the thunder of it would never die. My definitions were simpler then, because I had fewer things to define. I did not know, nor did the age I lived in seem to know, that whenever there is a greeting there must also be a farewell: sometimes, somehow, somewhere.

11

Outlanders, whence come ye
last?

The snow in the street and
the wind on the door.

Through what green sea and
great have ye passed?

Minstrels and maids, stand
forth on the floor.

—WILLIAM MORRIS

NEWSPAPER work is said to be a "young man's game," and so it is in the main. The power papers were not bide-a-wees for pensioners who had lost their vigor or their enthusiasm. It therefore amazed me as a young man to see the Park Row oldsters keep step with the energetic youths who came to the city rooms of the Big Town in that time of fiddles, fifes, and tambourines.

Our Park Row elders were a hale company, demonstrably capable and button-bright, and as cunning as gray wolves. Perhaps some of them were not quite as old as they then appeared to me. To a boy of twenty-eight it would seem that anyone the other side of fifty should make out his will at once, and stay out of drafts.

I would hear my seniors speak of the things they had written of, and of persons they had known long ago: Black Friday, and the financial panic of 1873; the kidnaping of Charley Ross; the hanging of eleven Molly Maguires; the first telephone; the electric light; the horseless carriage; the financial ruin of Ulysses S. Grant, and then his death from cancer; the marriage of President Grover Cleveland to Miss Frances Folsom in the White House; actors

Joseph Jefferson, Edwin Booth, and Sir Henry Irving; Wagnerian tenor Jean de Reszke; prima donna Adelina Patti and her numerous farewell tours; Queen Victoria's Jubilee and her death; the Klondike Gold Rush; the assassination of President McKinley; the Boer War; the war between Russia and Japan, and the fall of Port Arthur; the San Francisco earthquake and fire; the slaying of architect Stanford White by millionaire Harry Thaw; Commander Robert E. Peary's discover of the North Pole; the sinking of the *Titanic*. . . .

I must suppose that the doughty fellows who lasted on in the newspaper game of the twenties were examples of Darwin's theory of the survival of the fittest, or of the toughest. I am unable offhand to remember that any of them had rheumatism or the palsy. Many of them would not leave the Press Club until three o'clock in the morning; some of them would play billiards well, and all of them would be hard to beat at cards. A few of these gentlemen, however, would take forty winks now and then, especially when they thought no one was looking. My middle-aged friend Kelcey Allen, long-time drama critic of *Women's Wear*, sometimes would fall asleep during the last act of a play.

The ship-news reporters, old or young, did not as a rule stay up late. They kept milkman's hours, for they had to take the revenue cutter, usually before daylight, to go down the Bay to board ocean liners moored off the Quarantine Station. These reporters had much salt, along with printer's ink, in their veins. Their press headquarters was in the Barge Office, a very old building southeast of Battery Park.

The oldest active waterfront reporter at this writing is James Edmund Duffy of the *World Telegram*. The able Jim is a part of the New York skyline. He says of that skyline, "After forty years of basking in its beauty at all hours of the day and night, in storm and calm, in fog and mist, I say that it surpasses anything I have ever seen."

Another ship-news veteran, Ross Duff Whytock, one-time dean of the maritime aces, now resides at a California desert place; but his bones have not dried of the cold sea mists absorbed long ago when Ross rode the tides for the *Evening World.*

Whytock planned in his young years to become an Army officer, but failed to win an appointment to the United States Military Academy. He then took up a brief study of the law, but eventually joined the staff of the Buffalo *Express* in 1903. I have observed that several journalists turned to newspaper work when sidetracked or disappointed in some early venture. In some instances the newspaper profession might be likened to the Foreign Legion as a refuge for men whose emotional flares have been stifled.

Ross Whytock did not of course become a newspaperman because of a lost love. He began his New York career on the staff of the most crabbed city editor of all time, the eccentric Charles E. Chapin of the *Evening World.* This confused cynic might have been likened to the old Duke of Newcastle. According to the eighteenth-century actor and playwright, Samuel Foote, his Grace always appeared as though he had lost an hour in the morning, and was looking for it all day.

At the time when I arrived in the East, Mr. Chapin was in the Tombs, New York's city prison, awaiting trial for having slain his wife. He managed to escape the electric chair, and would die of natural causes some years afterward in Sing Sing prison. There he edited the prison newspaper, the *Star of Hope,* and grew flowers in the recreation yard. A bed of roses planted by Chapin on the sunny side of the death house was admired by the warden.

Perhaps the most memorable of Whytock's news beats was his twenty-thousand-word cable to the *World* at the time he was working out of that newspaper's news bureau in London. He had been assigned to meet James W. Gerard, American Ambassador to Berlin. Mr. Gerard had been recalled on the eve of America's entrance into the First World War. Whytock met Mr. Gerard in Paris, accompanied him to Madrid, then to Coruna, and sailed with the ambassador's party to Havana. During the voyage Whytock obtained what we used to call "a wealth of inside information" from a Naval attaché, and also from an Associated Press bureau chief who had lived in Germany for seventeen years. Ross cabled his newsbeat from Havana. It disclosed in detail, and for the first time, Germany's plan for a submarine campaign.

I remember Whytock as one of the many lively but respected journalists who made Perry's pharmacy their oasis in the Prohibition desert. This tiny drugstore was on the ground floor of the Pulitzer Building in which the *World* published both its evening and its morning editions. It stood to the left of the entrance arch of the newspaper, and was known as the "Pot of Glue" and also as the "Hole in the Wall." Chemist Tim O'Brien served the drinks. A pill-roller named Cahil provided various remedies for the hangover, one of them a pink liquid masterpiece.

Employees of the downtown papers, as well as City Hall district men from the uptown journals, met at the Pot of Glue for a glass of that which we called the Brown Ruin. City Hall lobbyists and other liberal-minded persons of the neighborhood frequented this place. Here one might see reporters of the first class: Martin Green, Frederick Mordaunt Hall, Joseph Jefferson O'Neill, Stanley Walker, Lindsay Denison, Dudley Nichols, Jim Duffy, W. O. McGeehan, George Buchanan Fife (whom Runyon called "George Buchanan Fife *and* Drum"), Don Marquis, Donald Henderson Clarke, Alva Johnston, Edwin C. Hill, Nunnally Johnson, Walter Davenport (afterward editor of *Collier's*), Charles Bayer, Barry Faris, Chester Hope, "Wurra Wurra" McLoughlin, James K. McGuinness, Charles Somerville (O. Henry's protégé), Martin Casey, Frank Ward O'Malley, and oh, so many other fellows of good minds and limber elbows.

Perry's was not, of course, the only downtown resort for the thirsty sons of Poor Richard. We sometimes partook of the creature at Mike Iorio's near the *American*; or at Hesse's all-night saloon a few doors distant from the mail department of the *World*; or at Andy Horn's Bridge Café; or at Lipton's. The bartenders were mostly Irish. They had great respect for the "Charch and clargy," could sing fine chunes; and if a man needed a pick-me-up but had no funds, all he need do was speak slightingly of the Black and Tan, and then have one on the house.

In a rear corner of the Pot of Glue there stood a urinal with room for but one person at a time. Semi-privacy was afforded by a half-door, which left the legs of an occupant exposed from the knees down. The Pulitzer Building stood next to the Manhattan terminus of Brooklyn Bridge. Each weekday, a few minutes past five o'clock in the afternoon, the Perry urinal was in heavy demand on the part of done-with-work Brooklynites heading for the bridge cars. The regular patrons resented this invasion, and so did the Perry management; the leaky transpontine citizens seldom purchased so much as a postage stamp or a bunion pad.

At about five o'clock one rainy afternoon the newspapermen were taking their favorite medicine at Perry's. One of Ross Whytock's good friends arrived, a Mr. Haggerty. He represented an asphalt company which enjoyed sound contractual relations at City Hall.

Mr. Haggerty had with him a pair of hip-length rubber boots. He informed the gentlemen of the press that the boots were the solution to the problem of the urinal. He thereupon set them up right in the booth of convenience, and saw to it that the toes were pointed away from the half-door, to make it appear that some slow-functioning fisherman, or perhaps a strictured employee of the street-cleaning department, was poised inside the latrine.

Soon after five o'clock that evening the Brooklynites began to arrive like a stampede of water buffalo. A glance toward the half-door persuaded the first-comers that their customary port of call had an occupant. A line soon formed. It extended outdoors and along the façade of the *World* to Frankfort Street. The water-logged Brooklynites had to go elsewhere, else succumb to internal drowning. From that day on few intruders—an occasional tourist from Vermont, or a rookie policeman—made free use of Perry's stall.

Just after Prohibition began in 1919, doctors of medicine were permitted by the new law to write a restricted number of liquor prescriptions for bona-fide patients. Two eminent and middle-aged newspapermen who had medical degrees obliged us with these certificates in illegal abundance. One of the merciful scientists was Dr. Esdaile Philip Cohen of the *World*. The other was Dr. Walter B. Peet of the *American*. Neither physician exacted fees for this service; they were men of ethical persuasion.

We were unfamiliar with the respective medical backgrounds of our benefactors, but could see that they knew a great deal about panaceas. Dr. Cohen was a scholarly rewrite man, hired at the direction of Joseph Pulitzer. Although Mr. Pulitzer had gone blind in 1890, and now lived aboard his yacht in foreign waters, he still dictated policy to his executive group of editors. One day, after his secretary had read aloud to him from a copy of the *Morning World*, Mr. Pulitzer said that his writers seemed to have lost the zest for work. He suggested that too much sobriety might be the cause of their lethargy. He dictated a cablegram to his editors to hire a learned but rugged reporter who drank a great deal but could hold his liquor. Dr. Cohen fitted these specifications. Drink never downed him. In fact, it was the other way around, as the saying is. He sometimes became a bit over-stimulated, however, and made speeches against mankind's stupidities, and lashed out with his heavy cane.

Our other medical friend, "Doc" Peet, was the *American's* expert on collegiate water sports. As Columbia's first crew coach, he had laid out the intercollegiate course on the Hudson River off Poughkeepsie. I went with Doc Peet to a regatta early in the twenties to do the "color" story of the annual boat races for the *American*. I remember that we sat next to Heywood Broun that afternoon aboard one of the creaking observation cars. The regatta train had banks of benchlike seats mounted on flatcars. The cars moved along the side of the river opposite the Poughkeepsie shore at the same rate of speed as the shells.

Darkness had come after the varsity race. Broun and some other reporters hired a lobster-trap man to ferry us in an old motorboat across the river to Poughkeepsie, where our wire facilities were "looped in" to our respective offices. The "Doc" had been nipping a bit during the cold afternoon. His vision was not of the best under any circumstance. As our boat put-putted alongside a landing barge, the Doc missed his hand-hold on the gunwales. He went into the river. While using a boathook to fish him out, I also got very wet. It was then I learned that the upper Hudson is quite salty, though many miles north of New York's bays.

While being dried out at the telegraph office, Doc charged that the lobster man had deliberately spilled him overboard. He was too cold to write a stroke-by-stroke analysis of the race. He wondered if I would oblige him by taking dictation on my typewriter.

I was in one of those sophomoric moods. When the doctor would dictate, for example, "And now the coxswain of the Cornell eight raised the stroke from 32 to 36," I mischievously would strike an additional key, one with a fraction on its type face, to make it read "raised the stroke from 32¼ to 36½."

I set down possibly fifty or sixty of these fractional "strokes." Mere scratches of a pencil, of course, would easily cancel out the fractions before the copy was submitted to the telegrapher. But when the dictation was over, and Dr. Peet began to read the pages, he roared like a sacred bull of Egypt. I had to give him some tonic from my own flask.

During the training season, Dr. Peet spent his days at the Columbia boathouse upstream on the Manhattan side of the North River. He owned a silver-plated timing watch of the earliest make, and a pair of big-barreled binoculars said to have belonged to the Mexican general Antonio López de Santa Anna. The ex-Columbia crew coach sometimes dined with the varsity oarsmen at the training table and offered solemn advice.

During the workouts on the river he could be seen on the observation barge, the big watch in hand, the ancient binoculars to his eyes. Sometimes it was thought that he did not have the various eights in focus, but instead was looking farther off across the river to the Jersey Palisades. Perhaps he was trying to make out the progress of amorous couples trysting among the trees atop the bluffs; or, possibly, studying the old dueling ground of Hamilton and Burr.

One cloudy afternoon the doctor was summoned from the barge to answer the telephone at the boathouse. Meanwhile a thunderstorm had set in, followed by heavy rain. Sports editor "Slim" Farnsworth was at the other end of the line. Would Dr. Peet report downtown at once? It was an emergency. And would he take the subway express instead of a taxicab?

Having reached the sports department of the *American,* the rain-soaked Dr. Peet became displeased that the "emergency" consisted of Mr. Farnsworth's need of a pint of spirits. Our house physician got out his pen and prescription pad and began to write the *spiritus frumenti* directions for his patient. Angry voices now sounded across the aisle from the sports department.

A copy editor, Mr. Conrad Miles—one-time press agent for actress Anna Held, and the reputed originator of her milk-bath publicity—had just settled down to his labors at the "rim," or copy desk. A thick-set man in a damp tweed cap and a rain cape came up to the desk to shout at Mr. Miles. The muscular stranger was obviously a taxicab driver. He accused Mr. Miles of having neglected to pay his fare. Furthermore, Mr. Miles had challenged the integrity of the cab driver. Also, he had described the cabbie as "an unmitigated extortionist and a foul niggard."

Not every New York taxicab driver was a student of Webster's unabridged dictionary. Mr. Miles' charioteer, it became apparent, had been unable to plumb the semantic depths of his passenger's epithet. He did, however, think that part of it charged him with African ancestry. As soon as he had figured this out for himself, he decided to follow Mr. Miles to the seventh floor. And here he was now, shaking a big fist at the seated copy editor and swearing.

With a hoarse shout of "My mother is just as good as yours!" the cab driver announced that he was going to thrust the journalist through a meat-grinder, bones and all. Thereupon Mr. Miles—not a puny man by any standard—put down his long-billed shears, pushed aside his paste pot, rose, then planted a left hook on the fellow's jutting chin. The big cabbie went down like a dynamited smokestack.

All this, of course, had absolutely nothing to do with Dr. Peet, who had been writing the prescription for Mr. Farnsworth. Nevertheless, as the taxicab driver sank with a crash, Dr. Peet fell from his own chair. His glasses flew off his nose. His dentures went into a wastebasket. The binoculars of General Santa Anna slid from desk to floor.

Somehow the doctor got it into his head that Mr. Farnsworth had struck him from behind. No one, not even his nearby co-workers, turf writer Ed Curley and Mr. Runyon, could persuade Dr. Peet that his diagnosis was faulty, that the real trouble had occurred a boat's length from the sports department.

"It was a dastardly thing!" the doctor said through his gums. "It is a felony to hit a man who wears glasses. And from behind!"

"Now, now, Doc!" said Mr. Runyon, as he helped the ex-coach to his feet. "You merely caught a crab. Are you all right?"

"I was cold-cocked!" said Dr. Peet. "Where's my teeth? My glasses?"

Mr. Farnsworth had recovered the glasses. "Why would I hit you, Doc?" he pleaded. "Tell me that! As God is my judge!"

"Here's what I'll tell you!" and Dr. Peet tore up the Farnsworth prescription and threw the pieces into the air. After Marty, the head copy boy, had salvaged the false teeth, the Doc made a shocking promise. "There'll be no more prescriptions for you, or for anybody else in the Hearst service!"

During Dr. Peet's decline and fall, his big-barreled binoculars in their leather case slid across the floor to a place near the desk of Harry Kay, rewrite man. Mr. Kay had risen and then retreated from his desk. He was stuttering and pointing at the spyglass case as if at an infernal machine. He seemed dreadfully upset, and muttered as though to himself, "Tabu! Tabu!"

Mr. Kay was some kind of non-flesh-eating religionist; he would touch nothing that involved butchered animals. The considerate fellow would not even eat sardines; he said they were his "little brothers." Doc Peet's big binoculars were leather-sheathed. Mr. Kay had a close call of it.

Acts of physical violence seldom took place in the editorial rooms of the New York newspapers. So far as I know, nobody ever invaded a journalistic office in Manhattan with a threat to trounce the editor, much less to shoot him, as sometimes happened in the West. I wondered what one of the witnesses to the drubbing of the cab driver would have to say of the fight. The person of whom I speak was our elderly cable editor, Mr. Thomas Jondrie Vivian.

This gentlemanly scholar—an authority on etiquette, protocol, heraldry, medieval parchments, Gregorian chants, and fine foods and wines—was a descendant of Sir Hussy Vivian. Sir Hussy, the commander of Wellington's light horse at Waterloo, had delivered the coup at the great battle—or so Mr. Vivian said—first rallying his shaken horsemen "with a bit of homely language."

Notwithstanding his advanced years, his faultless manners, his social charm, our cable editor was a person of much vitality. In this respect he resembled the late Sir Hussy, whom he described as "more social than noble." His ancestor, according to Mr. Vivian, had displeased his English father by choosing to wed an obscure Irish lass named Hussy. The disapproving sire became so angry and abusive that his son, in revenge, dropped his rightful Christian name—Rodney, I believe it to have been—adopted the name "Hussy," and was so knighted after Waterloo.

Our Mr. Vivian was a small, slender man, as straight as six o'clock in his rough tweeds, and something of a boulevardier. He wore white linen spats and lemon-colored gloves, carried a walking stick, and had a gray military mustache waxed smartly at all times.

Mr. Vivian was a long-time friend of Mr. Hearst's mother, Mrs. Phoebe Hearst. The publisher's mother first met Mr. Vivian when he was a lecturer on languages and English literature at the University of California, an institution frequently endowed by her. Anyone whom Mr. Hearst's mother liked was bound to be favored by the publisher.

Mr. Vivian had flouted the authorities of the school he attended in his youth, the Lycée National at Nantes, Brittany. He had run away from there because he had not wanted to become a priest. Mr. Hearst himself had left school, Harvard, because of a jest played upon faculty members. Perhaps this similarity in their school careers was one reason for his fondness for editor Vivian. Mr. Hearst seemed partial to men who bearded their superiors.

Mr. Vivian also had lectured at Columbia, had served as a newspaper correspondent for James Gordon Bennett, had reported King Jim's downfall in Hawaii and the Battle of Manila Bay, and had written several books. He also composed music, but his work in this field was so complicated that no one else attempted to play any of his scores. Even the composer had to augment his own piano with a bass-playing mechanism, operated with the feet, to interpret his themes.

On the day when Mr. Miles floored the taxicab driver, I inquired of Mr. Vivian if he had ever seen a cleaner blow than the one struck by the copy editor.

"Mr. Miles delivered a superb facer," the cable editor said. "But we must not look with favor on the turning of our editorial room into a fives court. Let us concede, however, that Mr. Miles was somewhat justified in this instance; his honor as well as his vocabulary had been challenged. But fisticuffs, if necessary at all, should be resorted to in the gymnasium of a club. Still, I suppose that would have been out of the question in this case, for the cab driver might not meet the requirements of the membership committee."

Our house physician, Doc Peet, kept his promise not to write prescriptions for us; that is, he kept it for two or three weeks. During this crisis we turned to another quarter, the *World* office, where Dr. Cohen conducted his clinic for parched sufferers. I was particularly fortunate in that two of the finest reporters on the *Morning World* staff, Joseph Jefferson O'Neill and Donald Henderson Clarke, were my close friends. Both men were favorite patients of Dr. Cohen in times of dryness of the throat. The bluff old gentleman did not have writer's cramp whenever I applied for a quick diagnosis and treatment.

Just recently I asked Ross Whytock to fill me in, as the saying is, on the careers of some of our ship-news elders of the 1920s. Two of his favorites of that time were Skipper Walter Scott Meriwether and Captain Edward Simmons.

Skipper Meriwether came of an old Mississippi family. His father was an officer in the Confederate forces. The skipper was well into his sixties when I first met him. I was amazed to see him climb the Jacob's ladder lowered to a bobbing cutter from the port of a liner moored south of the Narrows.

"The beloved skipper died at eighty-four," Whytock said, "after having spent the greater portion of his years on the *Times, Herald,* and *World.* As a young man he enlisted in the U.S. Navy, and served on war vessels powered both by sail and steam. He was the New York *Herald's* newly appointed bureau chief in Havana when the battleship *Maine* exploded. He had served with several officers of the *Maine.*"

When the cable office in Havana was closed to foreign correspondents, the resourceful skipper chartered a boat to take him to Key West. There he sent an exclusive story of the *Maine* affair to the *Herald.* He first handed the office manager a copy of the King James Bible to file to the *Herald,* and instructed that amazed official to accept nothing from anyone desiring wire facilities until Meriwether could complete his detailed story of the *Maine.*

Many old-timers think that this was the first time the ruse was employed by a reporter. In the years that followed, the Holy Writ stratagem occasionally was used in one form or another by first-comers to the scene of a story at some outlying place, or, late at night, when but one operator was on the job.

The telegraph companies sent newspaper copy over their wires at a much lower price than was asked of the ordinary client. However, when they learned that some of the press correspondents had been transmitting the Psalms at press rates, the companies an-

nounced that the newspapers must pay at the regular price level
for matter other than news reports. Bible filing became an expensive practice. Sometimes an important story justified its use.

Reporter Charley Somerville of the *Journal* once put Volume
One of the *Encyclopædia Britannica* on the wire and instructed
the operator to keep on filing it until he could write his story.
No other reporter was able to use the wire until Charley released
it. Meantime the reporter met a lady, got drunk, and forgot all
about the story. Back in New York, editor Brisbane came on duty
to find that his paper had been paying through the nose. A.B.
managed to halt the flood when it reached Aberdeen, Scotland.

One of the picturesque ship-newsmen mentioned by Ross Whytock was salty old Captain Edward Simmons, the last New York
reporter to wear whiskers. That beard was parted in the middle,
and fluttered like the lace curtains of a rectory window. When
the captain climbed the Jacob's ladder he looked like Neptune rising from the sea. On land he was not as nimble, perhaps, as the
younger men; when ashore he seemed to be wearing roller skates
for the first time. Once aboard ship, however, the old boy's sea
legs never gave way. He seemed almost spry after four or five
beakers of uncut liquor supplied—unofficially of course—to reporters who went down to the sea in ships.

I first met the captain at the Press Club, downtown. When off
duty he could be found there; or, some years afterward, at the
Newspaper Club, uptown. He liked to play chess or cards. The
card players sometimes wished that Captain Simmons would stay
at the Barge Office, for, when on the water wagon, he would eat
chocolate ice cream. Not only did his eating delay the deal in a
poker game, but the cards became sticky and smeared. One evening
the captain got so much chocolate ice cream on the Queen of
Hearts as to make her look like the Queen of Sheba.

Whytock recalled a time when Captain Simmons was working
for the old *Morning Sun*. The city editor gave him a clipping from
an evening newspaper, in which it was set forth that a mutiny had
broken out aboard the British bark *Cumberland* anchored off

Stapleton, Staten Island. The Cap took the ferry to Staten Island and there hired a boatman to row him and his whiskers out to the *Cumberland*.

"On board the bark," Whytock said, "Cap Simmons inquired of the first mate if there had been a mutiny. The first officer told him that his lips were sealed and that he would have to see 'the Old Man.' Cap found the master of the *Cumberland* engrossed in a chess problem and a bottle of Scotch.

"After Cap Simmons had introduced himself," Whytock went on to say, "the Old Man inquired if Simmons could play chess. He replied that he could. Whereupon the ship's captain told Simmons that he was working on a problem: white to move and checkmate in three moves. Forgetting the supposed mutiny, Cap Simmons sat down to a liberal pouring of Scotch and soda and began to work out the chess problem. After a considerable time, and a considerable sampling of heather dew, Cap Simmons noticed the swaying of an overhead lamp. He glanced through a port to see nothing but open water.

" 'Lord, captain!' he said. 'Are we under way?'

" 'That we are,' replied the Old Man. 'Before you entered my cabin I gave orders to the mate to hoist anchor and put out to sea.' "

Captain Simmons asked to be put ashore, but his host said they were now well outside Sandy Hook; it would be impossible to oblige. He disclosed that they were bound for Sydney, Australia. He said that he would have Simmons back to New York in seven or eight months. He advised the Cap to make the most of the voyage and enjoy the many games of chess they would have, not to mention an almost unlimited store of Scotch.

For a week or so, Whytock said, the disappearance of the bearded reporter was discussed at the Press Club and at the Barge Office. It was thought that the Cap had gone on a fishing expedition down South.

About seven months afterward the city editor of the *Sun* felt a presence at his elbow. He looked up to see the long absent Simmons, his beard by now as long as Rip Van Winkle's and seeming to glow as with St. Elmo's fire. The captain was exploring a waist-coat pocket with none too steady fingers. He found a crumpled clipping, the one which told about the supposed mutiny aboard the British bark *Cumberland*.

He placed it upon the editor's desk with the remark, "The captain refused to discuss this matter."

I sometimes wonder if those gallant old reporters ever felt "old" as they worked beside us in the busy 1920s. I do not remember that anyone ever spoke of himself as an aged person. The veterans seemed young in heart, and I remember at least three as having been popular among the ladies.

Perhaps the same question might be asked concerning those old reporters as was put by the Abbey Player J. M. Kerrigan to actor Thomas Mitchell. "Tommy," said Mr. Kerrigan at rehearsal one day, "do you suppose the Greeks knew that they were ancient?"

CHAPTER

12

A *new voice hailed me of an
old friend when, first returned
from the Peninsula, I paced
again in that long street of
Damascus which is called
Straight. . . ."* —DOUGHTY,
Travels in Arabia Deserta

On A day of snow and dervish wind two winters ago I returned quite by chance to the first neighborhood in which I had lived in New York. I had been away for almost forty years. Several times when in the East I had meant to revisit that uptown area of my everyday comings and goings as a young man. There I would search out the milestones of yesterday, stand once again among landmarks which had survived the malice of change.

It did not occur to me then—as it would later on—that the belated wayfarer must keep his wits and his emotions in good working order whenever he goes back to an old neighborhood, back to an old love, or back to anything deep in the possessive past. An ambush of ghosts awaits him.

Until that day, some conflicting purpose had intervened each time when I had been of a mind to go on a little excursion to the old neighborhoood.

I had more delays than Lord Howe's redcoats in reaching that same objective when in 1776 they took after General Washington's left wing across the East River from Brooklyn village to Manhattan, then up the island to high ground where the rallying patriots stopped the advance. English historians dismiss this set-to as a skirmish; their American counterparts acclaim it as the Battle of Harlem Heights.

The cathedral church of St. John the Divine now stands on the southern part of the old battlefield. From January of 1919 until September 1921 I lived with my family in a third-floor flat on Amsterdam Avenue just across the way from the cathedral, which was far from completion. It was the second of our homes in this residential quarter. Agnes's parents and her grandmother now had come to live with us. Our daughter Jane was born in this flat. We thought, as did many other inlanders—Ellen Runyon among them—that babies should be born at home.

It was there also that I began seriously to wonder if ever I would come to terms with a matter-of-fact world, and if I should even try to do so. My first rides upon the New York carousel made it appear that a beginner who followed his own rules jeopardized his bread and butter—also his jam. Seldom did a headlong fellow win the brass ring on this swiftest of merry-go-rounds. More likely he would lose a stirrup and fall off his high horse.

I even considered the possibilities of coming to terms with myself, a complex problem indeed. I wisely decided to table that phase of my inquiry until time to keep my unbreakable appointment with six weight-lifters at the crypt.

I did seize upon one persuasive thought, however, while I was making an invoice of the hit-or-miss conjectures which kept bouncing and rolling about like roulette balls inside my skull. This thought grew upon me until it seemed an act of faith. It became my sustaining precept:

Keep the spirit unbroken, win or lose; and never tarry too long in the lotus land of might-have-been.

This became my self-fixed center. I sometimes lost out on material rewards when I refused—wrong-headed or otherwise—to move against that center. Damon Runyon said that I was "a specialist at kicking success."

The continuing wind lashed out from the cold sea lanes and sang wild songs in the minor key. Snow lay everywhere that early morning in December when I went by chance to the old neighborhood. The snow crews had begun to rip ugly seams in the Big Town's new white rug. They advanced like a modern-day Coxey's Army, grotesquely clothed, their breaths rising in puffs of white vapor and trailing in the wind.

I used to think that New York took on a semblance of chastity —short-lived, to be sure—when veiled in snow. This morning, however, the city had the aspect of a wolf in sheep's clothing. Perhaps I was not in a mood to admire its vestments.

I had sat up all night with some durable cronies of old Park Row. These cunning journalists had seen to it that I missed the train to California, where I now lived with Agnes and our cat Frank Moran. My old friends and I had passed the night at the wayside inn of Bernard "Toots" Shor. The massive Mr. Shor, a newspaper buff, as well as a world authority on lentil soup, is known to Broadway cowpokes as the Night-blooming Cereus of the Bar-Nothing Ranch.

My companions at Shor's snug harbor that stormy night were journalists who had been on the various New York newspapers twenty-five or more years ago. They are called Silurians. The Society of Silurians—of which I am a member in more or less good standing—got its name in 1924. Our illustrious though waggish founders used to dine informally at the old Brevoort, the Lafayette, or at chophouses where the ale and the conversation hit the spot. During one of these get-togethers, David G. Baillie—*Tribune* political reporter, scholar, and father of Hugh Baillie, one-time president of the United Press—suggested that the veterans call themselves Silurians. The learned Scotsman explained that the fossils of the Silurian period of geological time represented the first creatures to have emerged from the sea to breathe oxygen and to live on land.

It took but one night at Toots Shor's round bar (alas, he sold that first-aid station in 1959) to make a man feel older than a fossil of *any* prehistoric era. There were no clocks on the premises, not even a calendar. The night of which I write slipped by as we spoke of those Silurians who had gone to God. At the mention of each name a glass was raised—as many as three to the shades of Grantland Rice, Ring Lardner, Don Marquis, Runyon, Ed Hill, and W. O. McGeehan.

During a lull in Mr. Shor's voice someone mentioned that an ex-journalist known to most of us lay dying without the price of a pill at St. Luke's Hospital uptown. I shall refer to him as Dennis Moon, so as not to give offense to his grandnephew, a missionary priest in Madagascar. We made up a purse to pay for a bed for old Dennis to die in, and for his last medical needs. My friends asked that I deliver the gift, look in on the old fellow, and assure him that candles were being lighted for his spiritual welfare in every niche and cranny of St. Malachy's. I was to do anything else to spare him the prospect of joining that seedy exodus which claims so many forgotten journalists of a half-forgotten day.

Toward daybreak Mr. Shor eased me into a taxicab (and gave me some folding money for old Dennis). My host observed that I was behaving like a defective bellows. He suggested that I breathe belly-deep of the outdoor air as a means to regain some of the oxygen I had lost in his pub. Unmindful at the moment that Professor Shor had no medical diploma—other than a Christmas card from Seagram's—I followed his quack advice—but just for one horrifying breath. I sank against the taxicab seat-cushion. I felt as though I had just swallowed the sharpest of the museum's collection of Admiral Peary's ice axes.

I regained part of my senses while the cab was slogging northward on that thoroughfare which the late mayor Fiorello Henry LaGuardia—but few others—called the Avenue of the Americas. I used to know the Little Flower quite well. I thought he had been ill-advised to change Sixth Avenue's name. Someone is always digging up the streets of New York; must they also uproot the signposts?

Before Sixth lost her maiden name and gave up her keepsakes—
the obsolete trestles and iron stays of the "El," and the tramway
rails on which the cars no longer move up and down the right-of-
way below the elevated—in those years before the plastic surgeons
of City Hall lifted the features of the old spinster of avenues—I
used to have many a pleasant visit with her. She was accounted
old and seedy even in my days of forty years ago. She had a
slatternly appearance from, say, 44th to 55th Streets. There one
saw unemployed men standing all day long in front of the hiring
halls. Were they the same men one saw each day? Or did their
common need for bread and shelter make them seem so familiar?

I liked Sixth Avenue next best to Park Row. Somehow I never
felt alone there, or ill at ease. On the day when I rode uptown to
see old Dennis Moon I no longer knew the avenue. For that matter
I no longer knew the city, nor did the city know me. Our love
affair of years ago had gone the way of lilacs kept too long in the
vase.

It occurred to me as I rode along that Ring Lardner also had
liked old Sixth Avenue. I once heard him say that Sixth was "a
street of no pretense." He preferred Sixth to Broadway, where
almost everyone was plainly on the make, but would never admit
that it was so. He thought Sixth even more interesting, more important, than opulent Fifth, where many mansions (not the ones,
he said, which are mentioned in the St. John's Gospel) were still
standing in our day.

I remembered a night when I had sat with Lardner in the grill
room of the Friars Club—the Monastery, as it was called. Ring
had heard that his friend Dorothy Parker had promised to write
lyrics for a Billy Rose musical show. This news distressed my
companion. In fact, he said that he was more upset by this report
than he had been years ago when a Boston newspaper editor fired
him from a twenty-five-dollar-a-week job for "not knowing how to
write." We must visit the talented Miss Parker right off, he decided, and stay her hand.

For some minutes Ring sat in stoical contemplation of a stuffed sea bass mounted on a wooden plaque hung against the wall. This trophy had a mauled appearance. It looked as though it had been clubbed to death, instead of having been landed by a sportsman's hook and line. Cracks were to be seen below the dorsal arch of the banged-up specimen, from which wisps of excelsior protruded. A metal patch, the size of a stove lid, had been set into the midriff of the fish. That piece of armor had been painted to simulate scales.

The belabored bass had quite an interesting case history in a post-mortem sense of the term. A brother Friar (not the fish's brother, but ours) named McNamara hated it. Mac was a most amiable fellow when not too deep in bootleg grog. After six drinks, no more no less, he would beat up on the sad-looking relic of the sea. Fra McNamara would be sitting as quietly as Gentleman Jim Corbett, or Abbott George M. Cohan, or Prior Willie Collier—all decorous members of the club—then, of a sudden, the six drinks inside him, Fra McNamara would whoop, as Chief Red Cloud once did when someone put gunpowder in his calumet. Mac would charge across the floor of the Monastery grill, then pound the sea bass with his fists until the chairman of the house committee arrived. Next day the board of governors would meet to suspend Fra McNamara, then send the fish to the taxidermist's for repairs. No one ever learned why Fra McNamara detested the bass; but his hatred of it was as intense as Captain Ahab's for Moby Dick.

While Mr. Lardner was looking at the punch-drunk fish, George McManus entered the Monastery grill. He stopped beside our table. Mr. McManus was one of the most successful of comic-strip artists, the creator of *Bringing Up Father*. Apparently he was unaware that Mr. Lardner regarded him as being slightly inferior to Frans Hals as an artist, and somewhat less able than Mark Twain as a humorist. Mr. McManus informed us that he was expecting some after-theater guests, all of them comic-strip geniuses. Would we like to join them for some shop talk?

"I will join you," said Mr. Lardner in his solemn manner, "but on one condition. In return, you are to join me, all of you, in a mass-suicide pact. Every last one of you must promise to kill your-

selves. As a mark of sincerity I agree to take my own life. In that
way we shall rid the world of all comic-strip makers, and of their
rolling-pin poverty of wit."

Mr. McManus seemed stunned by this heresy. He stood there
for a few moments, open-mouthed like the stuffed sea bass—or,
better still, like a Tammany boss after a severe set-back at the polls.

He then leaned over to whisper in my ear, "Has our friend been
drinking?"

I nodded. "Drinking *and* thinking."

Mr. Lardner rose. Rather, he loomed from his seat at the table.
"Now," he said, "let us go out and get a breath of stale air."

Although it was quite late, the gracious Miss Parker received us
at her apartment. She listened attentively to Ring's demand that
she forgo the writing of lyrics for Mr. Rose. She promised not to
compose even one iambus for that energetic showman, himself
a lyric writer, co-author of the madrigal "That Old Gang of Mine."

On our way back from wherever it was that Miss Parker resided,
we found ourselves walking along Sixth Avenue. Lardner said that
he had written a song in praise of Sixth, and if we could find a
piano he would sing it. He might even dedicate the song to me.
When I suggested that we return to the Monastery, where there
was a piano, Ring said no. McManus and the assortment of comic
artists might still be there. He decided that we should call upon
Mr. Thomas Smith.

That cherubic scholar was editor in chief for the book-publish-
ing house of Horace Liveright. He was a genuine man about town
and had an impish love of fun, although his mannered ways seemed
a survival of the court of Victoria Regina. Mr. Smith lent us his
key to the Liveright office, in which there was a piano.

Just as we were letting ourselves in at the Liveright headquarters
—a converted brownstone residence in midtown Manhattan—a
police officer on the beat inquired as to our business there.

"I am an editor," said Mr. Lardner, "with the unusual name of
Thomas Smith. And this is one of our lesser authors, a Mr.
Theodore Dreiser. We are going inside to study Mr. Dreiser's latest

manuscript in the hope that we can shorten some of his sentences from ten pages each to a mere six."

We passed muster. Ring sat at the piano. He was a tall man. He had strong hands with which he improvised chords, and he sang in a deep bass voice. I can remember but two lines of his song:

> "Oh, old Sixth Avenue!
> I'll be havin' you. . . ."

Memories of the incomparable Lardner and of other men of our time sprang to mind during my early-morning ride uptown on that day of snow and dervish wind. A montage of piecemeal impressions: the sayings of friends, their faces, the things they had done at one time or another—these odds and ends of remembrance rose as do those unbidden fancies which free themselves from the mist which drifts in upon the crossroads of wakefulness and sleep. Heywood Broun used to call these echoes "the relevant irrelevancies of life."

The taxicab was now leaving Sixth Avenue to go into Central Park. The tire chains flogged the snow of the west drive. It sounded as though the Prisoner of Chillon were making a break from his dungeon.

The cab driver had the complexion of a mushroom picker. His hacking cough made me think of those newspapermen, some of them quite young, who had died of tuberculosis in Denver. Most of them had died with their boots on, as the saying was. I thought, too, of something Arthur Brisbane had said to me one day while discussing reporters and their chances of success.

I came upon his words once again among the notes I found in the old board box—the things he had said in his own thirty-ninth year as a journalist: "The newspaperman must do every day the work by which he lives, and do it all over again. Each day he must create his reputation anew. His greatest asset is enthusiasm, real interest in what he sees and what he tells. And the years are the enemies of enthusiasm. Newspaper work brings disillusion. The reporter is like an electric-light bulb; he sheds light. If he stays too long on the newspapers and is not exceptionally fortunate, time and the current of news running through him burn out his enthusiasm—and burn him out. Then, like the light bulb, he goes onto the scrap heap."

The taxicab driver was coughing like Sarah Bernhardt in the last act of *La Dame aux Camélias*. The cold wind keened. The tire chains clanked. The faulty windshield wiper set up a whooshing flick-flack like that made by the wings of a wounded duck. Thoughts of burned-out men . . .

Whenever I find myself growing too sad for my selfish comfort I reach out for some countering thought, a gay memory if possible. I do not mean to laugh at anyone's misfortune; I laugh to ward off my own fears and sorrows. It is my way of whistling in the dark.

The bronchitic cabbie half turned his head when he heard me laugh. I was thinking of a burned-out journalist, Arthur MacL., and of his wayward teeth. He was one of the editors on the old Denver *Republican* at the time when I was a cub reporter. He had worked side by side with Alfred Damon Runyon on the *Rocky Mountain News*. Both men had been rivals for the affections of sprightly Ellen Egan, society reporter on that newspaper. Arthur was the loser. Long after Ellen became Mrs. Runyon she would twit Alfred about her old beau. The Demon did not like this.

Arthur had been a brilliant editor but something happened to send him down the hill. He became a "wino" in his middle age. After many years of our separate ways I saw Mac again and in California. He was a proud man; this I knew. When I observed that some of his upper teeth were missing, I persuaded him to let my dentist make a bridge for him at my expense.

The next time I saw Arthur he was not wearing the new bridgework. He had pawned it to buy some Napa Valley claret. He then lost the pawn ticket and could not, for the life of him, remember the name or the address of the loan shark. The Shylock had allowed him but five dollars on teeth which had cost me about two hundred. That sum represented only the laboratory expense, since my dentist had asked no fee for his own services.

Mac had a somewhat opaque recollection that the money lender had a red hat, a fez perhaps. My absent-minded friend said that a clue this slight would be of no use as a means of identification, since there was a Shriners' convention in town.

"However," said Arthur, "I feel sure of one thing: this fellow in the red hat is *not* a member of the Sacred College of Cardinals."

My dentist fitted Arthur with a second denture. I suggested that Mac see me the next time he needed a quick five, instead of going in hock. Incredibly enough, the same thing happened as before to Arthur's teeth, and also to his memory. I thought it high time to find a partner in the bridge-building business, or else float a bond issue.

I would have gone to motion-picture producer Joseph Schenck, a generous friend indeed, but hesitated to do so. I had put the bite on him, if you will excuse the expression, for fifteen hundred dollars just a week before this. This sum was applied to a long-overdue payment on the mortgage of actor John Barrymore's yacht *Infanta*.

Creditors were constantly threatening a foreclosure on the *Infanta*. I had acted several times in fund-raising ventures to keep alive Barrymore's vain but poignant dream of once more boarding the beautiful yacht which he had helped design, and in which he had sailed so long ago and had known a brief season of comparative happiness and peace.

Nor did I think it fair to ask my friend Harry Brand to invest in Mac's teeth. It was too soon after he had bought into my firm in connection with another matter: the Tammany Young project. Mr. Brand was the publicity director for Twentieth Century-Fox, and an "easy touch." The late Mr. Young had been an indifferent actor in New York. There he had worked between times as a laundry agent. He would collect the shirts of his fellow actors, who were constantly complaining about the slow service. The reason for this laxity was that Mr. Young would wear a customer's shirt, no matter the collar size, for a day or so before he sent it to be laundered. In Hollywood Mr. Young played bits in motion pictures. He died with a sigh for Broadway. Mr. Brand provided the casket and two railway tickets to send the dead exile home.

My next thought, while looking for a fellow sucker, was of Damon Runyon. Mr. Runyon had come to Hollywood to adapt one of his short stories for the films. He was making more money than the United States Bureau of Engraving. I have a bad memory for anyone's grudges, even my own; I had forgotten that Damon and Arthur were not to be mistaken for Damon and Pythias.

"So this party needs a new china closet, eh?" said Mr. R.

But he gave me the two hundred, and the contract was let. Be skeptical if you will, but Arthur took these newest teeth to Uncle Stoneheart. He once again had amnesia. When I thoughtlessly revealed to him that Runyon had been his benefactor, Arthur blew a fuse. Moreover, while shopping at the liquor store he made snide remarks about Runyon's drinking days in Denver.

Next to Washington, D.C., Hollywood is the world's greatest whispering gallery. Runyon heard that Arthur had been maligning him. When I suggested that he go "halfies" with me on another set of choppers for Mac, he said, "Nix! And also no dice! This man has been lying through *my* teeth!"

It so happened that a newspaper friend of Arthur's and of mine, Ed "Scoop" Gleason, was down from San Francisco on business peculiarly advantageous to our needs. Mr. Gleason was handling the press relations for a picturesque dentist known as Dr. Painless Parker, who advertised flamboyantly and operated a chain-store type of practice at cut rates. When the association of dentists sought to unfrock Dr. Parker, and force him to stop using the word "Painless" in his advertisements, Mr. Gleason saved the day by having the offensive word made a *legal part* of the doctor's name.

I acquainted Scoop with Arthur's dental and financial problems. Scoop prevailed upon Painless Parker to make a pilot set of teeth for a mere sixteen dollars. Duplicates would cost twelve. Artie hocked the pilot set, but got less than a dollar at Uncle's. For a time it seemed that we would have to go into mass production.

Two of these cheaper sets came off the assembly line before Arthur's death.

Not long before that sad event, Mac called on Scoop in San Francisco to ask for four dollars. "Why only four?" inquired Mr. Gleason. "Why not five?"

"Because," Art replied, "I asked Ed Coblentz of the *Examiner* for five a week ago."

"Did he give it to you?"

"Hell, yes! Cobbie came through like a gentleman. But he made me listen to a sermon on the evils of drink. In tapping you for the four, I hoped that you would give it to me but spare me the moral lecture."

We now were leaving Central Park and its snowbound lanes and groves and white-wigged rocks. The cab slewed westward and away from the following wind, which sounded as though all the bad consciences of mankind had met for choir practice.

Old Dennis Moon . . . How long had it been since I last had seen him? And where? I remembered him quite well, though he had never been a person of consequence on Park Row—not one to be placed within hailing distance of such distinguished reporters as, say, James Kilgallen, Joseph Jefferson O'Neill, John Winkler, Alva Johnston, Joe Mulvaney, Joel Sayre, Bruce Rae, Sam Spewack, James Whitaker. . . . The line of great reporters of the 1920s is a long one. Walter Davenport must always be mentioned among those outstanding newsgatherers; and so, too, that all-around champion Herbert Bayard Swope, as well as the pyrotechnical Westbrook Pegler, son of Arthur the Great.

Dennis Moon was to be remembered not for his journalistic feats but for those eerie happenings, the tragi-comical incidents which seemed to bedevil him twice each year, and with time-table regularity. Tall, gaunt, well-mannered, and colorful of speech, Moon was accounted a faithful worker, a staff wheel-horse. He kept sober, too, except for the semiannual lapses when he would take to the bottle, or bottles, and seem possessed by strange frenzies. His periodic nightmares would last a week.

On the first day or so of his drinking, Dennis might be seen in some speakeasy alcove, or else in an out-of-the-way nook at the Newspaper Club. He looked as though he were haunted. In the early stages of stupor he seldom stirred from where he sat, except to go eventually to the lavatory. He would remain there, sometimes for several hours, sitting like Rodin's "Thinker."

One day Moon, sober but wearing his haunted look, went to Bellevue Hospital to call upon his good friend Dr. Menas S. Gregory. Dr. Gregory was a celebrated neurologist, the director of the psychiatric division of Bellevue. He was of Armenian descent. The doctor was a friend to many of us of the newspaper world, ready at all times to help us on stories which concerned the criminal mind or counsel us on our own private problems. Dr. Gregory was an expert in several fields outside that of medical science. I remember a time when he stopped a fellow Armenian from selling me a defective Oriental rug which I had been about to buy for Agnes as a birthday gift.

When Dennis Moon called at Bellevue, it seems that he wanted Dr. Gregory's advice on how to cope with a heartache. A woman whom he had befriended during a trial, in which she had been charged with blackmail, and with whom he had fallen in love, had jilted him.

At the hospital a newly appointed aide told Dennis that the great Armenian had gone to Canada to read a medical paper at McGill University. Dennis called the aide a damned liar. Men in white coats closed in upon Moon to take him to the ward where persons suspected of nuttiness were isolated for observation.

When the poor fellow shouted that he was a bosom friend of Dr. Gregory, the aide at first pretended to agree. "I believe you. Everybody who comes in here is a pal of his." Then he said, "Now pipe down, mister—unless you want to wear a canvas tuxedo with long sleeves tied at the back!"

Dr. Gregory returned some days afterward. He almost doubted his own sanity upon learning what had happened to Dennis, who kept saying, "They threw a net over me!" The doctor set out at once to repair the damage. After some days had passed he sent the patient home in a much better mental and physical condition than when he had walked into the trap. Besides, he now was cured of his heartache.

The last time I had seen Dennis Moon was at the children's party at the Newspaper Club on an exciting day in 1923. Perhaps, in speaking of that year, I might be expected, and with good reason, to stay within the deeper channels of the big news events of 1923. Such minor accents as the memories of Dennis Moon, or of the children's party, or of the Newspaper Club might seem much less worthy of book binding than would the other stories of 1923 with which I had a reportorial intimacy: the death of President Harding; the Dempsey-Firpo fight, and the rise in the popularity of professional sports; the speakeasy episodes, the gang wars; the Teapot Dome investigation by Senator Tom Walsh's committee; and other news.

My present-day editor, Signor Pascal Covici, a man of great patience and good will, has just left town after a visit to my hillside workshed where he read the pages I have written so far. The signor has lived a long time among books and their creators, and has been the father confessor of many authors, John Steinbeck among them. In a friend-to-friend conversation he quietly but earnestly said he hoped to God that I would get around to some of the "important" stories I had "covered" as a reporter in New York. Otherwise, he admonished me, the reader might wonder how I ever had managed to keep pace with the finest reporters on Park Row; and how it was that I became an editor during my early thirties.

Partly to safeguard the sanity of Signor Covici, and partly to justify the claims made in my behalf by Park Row colleagues, who say (not under oath, of course) that I was a first-class journalist, I shall offer this belated promise: From time to time I mean to

deal with, say, fifteen news stories among the hundreds of assignments I went upon during those vintage years of colorful
events between 1919 and 1929.

I should have announced this intention at the beginning of my
tale. But I am one of those unpredictable fellows who, without
meaning to do so, worry their publishers, estrange the critics, and
bewilder almost everyone—except, in my case, Agnes, a few tolerant friends, and my cat—with second guesses and sudden manifestos. The only time I ever spent in consistent, normal preparation for *anything* was the nine-month period just preceding my
birth.

My treatment of the stories I have decided to present will not
be formal. The most perishable of all commodities is the news of
the day. I hold that the half-hidden quirks and the seldom revealed
fancies of the men and women who made the news in my time
were not the least important symptoms of the social, moral, or
economic fevers and contagions which still plague the world. Perhaps my "cross-section" of newsgathering will of itself suggest the
kind of men, and the texture of that time, which prompted Miss
Gertrude Stein to call our generation a "lost" one.

That dismal pronouncement by the high priestess of double-talk
was accepted as gospel by her cry-baby acolytes. Those talented
breast-beaters set the fashion for many other writers, both good
and bad, to place the blame for their generation's woes on shoulders other than their own. Their shrine was the weeping wall.

Miss Stein was not the spokesman for *our* generation of newspapermen. We did not feel lost, nor were we lost, one and all.
Those who did join Mr. Brisbane's "burned-out" regiment seldom
shook their fists at fate, or held anyone but themselves accountable
for their own failures. Miss Stein was a Left-Bank Sappho singing
through an egg-beater.

During my taxicab journey to St. Luke's, when I thought of the
year 1923, it seemed of much more importance to find out how old
Dennis Moon had met life than it was to recall the momentous

headlines of that or of any other year. How was he meeting death?

The snow had stopped falling, but the wind sang on, and the cab driver wheezed, and the tire chains rattled and clanked . . . and my mind returned like a homing pigeon to the children's party at the Newspaper Club, and to the day when Dennis Moon had one of his haunted periods of desperation; and when Blossom the Hippodrome elephant was frightened by Signor Amalfi's trained roosters; and Governor Alfred E. Smith had the belly ache; and United States Senator Royal S. Copeland, dressed as Santa Claus, reverted to his role as a doctor of medicine, and . . .

What a day, indeed!

CHAPTER

13

Each man lays weight on his
neighbor's sin and lightens his
own.   —MONTAIGNE

AFTER a series of factional struggles within the long-established
Press Club, a large part of the membership resigned in the spring
of 1922. The seceding journalists charged that the club no longer
served the best interests of the newspaper profession. The dis-
senters founded the New York Newspaper Club in May of that
year. They bound themselves not to admit to their society anyone
who had not been an accredited staff man of the metropolitan
press.

The more than nine hundred journalists established their headquarters on the third floor of the Bush Building on 42nd Street east
of Times Square. This was a relatively new building, tall enough
to be called a skyscraper. Its owner, Mr. Bush, was well disposed
toward the press. Because of an oversight on our part a neighbor-
ing tenant acquired most of the third-floor plumbing outlets. Our
failure to study the blueprints with a practical eye for soil-pipe
ramifications left us with a lavatory which had the accommodations one might expect to find in a submarine of Admiral Sims'
fleet.

I feel obliged to describe this cubbyhole. It had a single porcelain stall and but one cabinet for the chairing of the bards. It was here that the terror-stricken Dennis Moon played an unrehearsed role during the children's party. A much larger room, adjacent to the lavatory, served as a passageway to and from the skimpy toilet. That unused room was large enough for—well, say an elephant could get into it . . . and, as a matter of fact, an elephant *did* . . .

Something occurred on the morning of the children's party which may illustrate the kind of trouble our restricted toilet facilities caused us. It so happened that sports writer Arthur Robinson got out of the hospital that morning after promising his doctor that he would be back in an hour or two to continue his convalescence. Arthur Robinson traveled with the baseball clubs as staff correspondent for the *American*. He was ghost writer for Babe Ruth, whose main talent for literary composition was the signing of his autograph. Robbie was a war veteran with battle-shattered knees.

He arrived on crutches at the Newspaper Club with one of his great pals, Oliver Herford, artist, author, and foe of stupidity. Mr. Herford's appearance was that of a frustrated gnome. He seemed timid (*at first*), wore nose glasses from which a black ribbon dangled, and was no bigger than a jockey.

Robinson asked Herford to escort him to the club's lavatory before they sat down for a highball and a game of cards. In the jakes, after Robbie and his crutches were properly stowed, Mr. Herford went to the adjoining facility. He had barely assumed his stance there when a fat fellow charged through the doorway. Without any regard for rest-room protocol, the hulking stranger almost knocked Herford off his pins. The artist-author said nothing, but stood to one side. He waited a long time. Nothing was said, nothing accomplished. The unrelieved stranger eventually turned away from the place of his—shall we dare say his Waterloo?—to go to the door.

Mr. Herford touched the fat man's arm. "Pardon me, sir. May I say that you have just demonstrated the truth of an old proverb

—the younger Pliny's, if memory serves me—which, translated freely from the archaic Latin, says, 'The more haste, the less peed.'"

Governor Alfred E. Smith was the official host at the children's party. United States Senator Royal S. Copeland was wearing the robes of Santa Claus and a great white beard; the Honorable Robert Wagner, Sr., at that time a justice of the New York Supreme Court, was on the reception committee. I was in charge of the arrangements—which were soon enough disarranged.

I had had difficulties from the very first day. When, in my enthusiasm, I proposed the party, my city editor (who disliked the club and many of its members) tried to block my participation in the gala event. Even earlier than that he had resented the fact that I had been chosen to edit the club's *Reporter*.

City editor Victor Watson of the New York *American* was a man of brooding suspicions and mysterious shifts of mood. Mr. Hearst's telegraphic code word for Victor Watson was "fatboy." The staff saw in him the qualities of a Don Cossack, hence, as mentioned before, his nickname "the Hetman."

The Hetman's physical aspects were not those of a savage rider of the steppes. Indeed, he looked more like a well-fleshed lay brother of the Hospice of St. Bernard. Nor were his manners barbaric. He had a purring voice and a poker player's immobility of features which somehow conveyed the feeling that he knew where all the bodies were buried. He was the son of a Scottish father and an American Jewish mother, long widowed, with whom he lived in a comfortable home in Flushing. He had worked in the newspaper business since he was nineteen years old, always for the Hearst service. From the very first he regarded himself as Mr. Hearst's disciple, defender, and afterward his prime minister, self-ordained.

It was said that the Hetman plotted to take over the entire Hearst newspaper empire one day by means of various coups: the destruction of editors who tried to halt his course, the unfrocking of publishers whose mistakes of judgment might be magnified in secret reports to Mr. Hearst. Whatever the Hetman's ambitions, his colleagues were kept ill at ease. Among the outstanding members of the Hearst cabinet whom he successfully opposed for a time were the great Arthur Brisbane, Bradford Merrill, S. S. Carvalho, and Colonel Van Hamm. He also disliked Runyon, for no good reason other than the fact that the Demon's talent was so marked as to put him well beyond the Hetman's say-so or his supervision.

Runyon, for his part, had a contemptuous regard for Mr. Watson. "He's a wrong-o," said Runyon, "and I wouldn't trust him as far as I could throw the Statue of Liberty."

Arthur "Bugs" Baer wrote to me just recently, "Vic wanted to die in harness, with his head towards the wagon. He supported his mother and his brother, who afterwards committed suicide. Watson told me that his brother always sent roses to his mother, blossoms bought with Vic's allowance to him. 'And would you believe it,' Vic added, 'she likes him better than she does me. Why?' "

About the only time the Hetman seemed excited was when one of his own pet ideas was born. Then he would get to his feet, as though rising in honor of his own remarkable powers, and say almost invariably, "Gentlemen, this is an amazing story! It's bigger than the Armistice."

Some of the Hetman's "ideas" were dream-ridden, vaguely imparted, and at times preposterous. One day he assigned me to lay bare a "plot" by the Duponts to supply munitions to a wholly fictitious revolution he said was about to occur in Cuba. He said that his information was so secret that he would not be able to confide in me the origin of his pipeline tip.

"I can tell you this much," he said. "It's bigger than the Armistice."

I worked for a day on this plainly ridiculous assignment and consulted several of my own well-informed sources. Then I spent the next two days at the baseball park and at Jack Doyle's pool parlors. When I returned to make my report, the Hetman did not remember having sent me on the secret mission. He was busy, he said, in having someone submit to a monkey-gland operation. And I was to go to work on that odd matter. I shall tell of it later on.

The Hetman had a strong liking for a story, any story which was to be had by means of much sleuthing or by roundabout methods. Most of my stories were obtained by simply seeking out the person who could give me the facts, and not as a rule by playing clever tricks.

One day I tired of following the Hetman's advice of "shadowing" and of the "ring-around-the-rosie" approach to a report that Enrico Caruso had pinched a lady's hip while visiting the Central Park monkey house. I explained my state of mind to artist Winsor McCay and to "Bugs" Baer. Mr. Baer obtained a supply of crepe hair and spirit-gum from an actor at the Friars. We fashioned beards, put them on, and reported to the Hetman at the city desk.

Mr. Baer had an auburn beard, like Longfellow's. Mr. McCay had on a sort of Emperor Maximilian beard and mustache. As for myself, I had on an enormous black "muff." This, together with a derby hat and horn-rim eyeglasses, gave me the appearance of a Russian nihilist.

"We are ready for your next mysterious assignment," said Mr. Baer to the Hetman. "Where to, sir?"

Mr. Watson did not have much humor in his make-up, but he managed a mirthless smile. Just then a reporter telephoned in from the Bronx to give the rewrite desk an account of a murder. The Hetman told me to take the story over the phone and to write it. While I was sitting at one of the rewrite telephones with my derby and my great beard, Arthur Brisbane whizzed in with some editorial copy in his hand. He paused for a moment to look at me, then went on to the city desk to deliver his "Today" column.

I thought it expedient to take off my derby, my glasses, and the beard; and also to change telephones. I managed to do this by the time the great A.B. returned to the place where he last had seen the fierce nihilist. He stood there staring with disbelief at the vacant desk. Then he wrinkled his huge brow and went slowly out of the room. He had a somewhat goggle-eyed expression. He had been "seeing things."

The Hetman's "ideas" for news stories or editorial campaigns were by no means always fruitless or lacking in merit. He campaigned successfully for the riddance of "Death Avenue" and also brought about the ending of pollution of metropolitan beaches by sewage. He exposed the bucket-shop racket with the able assistance of two excellent reporters, Nat Ferber and Carl Helm. In the conduct of these and many other campaigns, the Hetman proved to be a much abler journalist than his critics allowed.

It seems to me now, in a long backward glance, that many of the Hetman's conceits and odd actions—together with his grim posture when brandishing the hatchet in the name of Mr. Hearst—were keyed with the tragedy which was to close over him one day. Alone, rejected on every hand, divorced, and in financial trouble, he leaped from an eleventh-floor window of the Abbey Hotel in 1937.

One finds it difficult to pass censure on the lonely figure who waited for days for a saving word from his zealously served idol, W. R. Hearst. That word was withheld when the need of it seemed the measure of his despair. The unfinished note, written in pencil upon the back of a used envelope, and addressed to the coroner, makes one wonder about many things:

God forgive me for everything. *I cannot . . .*

Much to Damon Runyon's amazement, as well as my own, I got along splendidly with the Hetman; that is, until I became an editor, hence, in his eyes, a rival. Not long after Colonel Van Hamm had foisted me on the Watson staff I received a salary raise and a contract on the Hetman's recommendation. During the next years he gave me the second of the five contracts I would sign with the Hearst Service. It was a somewhat unusual thing for a reporter to have a contract in those days before the epidemic of syndicated columnists. I would like to believe that my ability warranted this advancement. Somehow I think that Watson paid more attention to me than he otherwise might have because his foe, Colonel Van Hamm, wouldn't touch me with a ten-foot blue pencil.

I remember one day when Mr. Hearst (and I never knew why *he* liked me, either) sent the Hetman a telegram: "Please find some more reporters like that young man from Denver." Watson showed this wire to Colonel Van Hamm. The colonel grunted, then made a remark which might be construed in either of two ways. "Don't bother to look any further. We already *have* the only one of its kind."

The Hetman did have friends, but they were mostly outside the newspaper profession. Sergeant Mike Donaldson, Congressional Medal of Honor soldier, was one of them. Dr. Menas S. Gregory was another. I used to go with Watson to call on the eminent neurologist at his apartment, to sit among the doctor's excellent collection of statues, paintings, and books and drink Oriental coffee while Watson seemed to thaw out and become almost affable.

There was one time, however, when his face clouded and he suddenly blurted, "Why did my brother commit suicide?"

I cannot remember Dr. Gregory's reply, if, indeed, he made one. On thinking back to that remark, isolated as it seemed in relation to the otherwise pleasant visit, I am wondering if the Hetman had been seized by some prophetic thought.

No one could foretell just how the Hetman might respond to any challenge to his ego or to his authority. One day he might allow an act of defiance to pass him by, but that same day react to some slight neglect of his orders as though an attempt had been made to assassinate him. As an example of this, he gave me five hundred dollars just before Christmas of 1919 to distribute among twenty needy families on the East side. When I *spent it all on one family*, the first I had come upon—and received their blessings—Watson laughed out loud for the first time I ever had heard him do so. Soon afterward he complained about one of my expense accounts, or rather an item listed in it for the all-day chartering of a taxicab while on a New Jersey murder story. On another day, when there was an explosion of a powder factory in Jersey, he asked night city editor Martin Dunn which reporter had been assigned to the story. Martin said that he had sent me on it. Watson exclaimed, "My God! He'll buy a ferry boat!"

As a rule, however, he was liberal in the matter of expense accounts. I shall have something to say about this elsewhere. I was regarded as a "master" of the expense account, perhaps the best on Park Row. One or two of those accounts have become a part of my legend. Martin Dunn says that long after I had left the *American*, whenever he felt blue he would look in the files for my old expense-account lists, to read them for laughs.

"It was a tragedy of sorts," Martin said just recently, "when the old files were destroyed in a fire."

I was the originator of a theory on how to arrive at a just and equitable sum of one's expenses: "A man who makes a one-dollar profit on his expense account is dishonest. A man who loses five cents on one is a damned fool."

Watson, expense accounts, Park Row, burned-out newsmen . . . a congress of half-forgotten ghosts convening in the winter's sky. As I rode uptown, time did cartwheels. Echoes came from the past, some of them with the sound of muffled drums, others as mere whispers from a hidden world. A lifetime of questions; and now a feeling possessed me that I was coming into a day of answers. I had grown tired of oracles and wall mottos, of slogans, and of prophets who pretended to hold the keys to the kingdom. The weariness that came of an all-night watch with old comrades may have made me vulnerable to impressions of an almost mystic persuasion as I rode uptown on what seemed a small errand: to look in upon a dying reporter who had been of no singular importance on Park Row. He seemed but a guttering candle borne along a dark hallway.

And I thought of the children's party, and of those who had been lively there, and who now were dead. And of old Dennis Moon's strange didos that day long ago.

CHAPTER

14

"There," repeated he, seizing
Sponge by the arm, "that's
what I call shape. You don't
see such an animal as that
every day!" —SURTEES,
  Mr. Sponge's Sporting Tour

EARLY in the summer of 1923 I became editor of the Newspaper
Club's monthly publication the *Club Reporter.* Charles Hambidge,
a much-respected political writer for the New York *Times,* and
president of the club, named me for this post. Victor Watson got
wind of my appointment and did not like it at all. So set was he
against it as to imply that he would not give me a new contract
with a fifty-dollar pay raise.

The Hetman called me to his office the day Hambidge chose me
as the club's editor. It was early evening. The presses had begun to
roll for the first edition of the *American* with a sound like that of
oxen being gored. The floor vibrated, as the pavement of Park
Avenue did whenever the trains of the New York Central passed
beneath its crust. I shut the door behind me. The Hetman motioned to a chair. I had some difficulty in hearing what he was
saying; he always spoke as if through a velvet mask. Besides, my attention was fixed upon the unsigned contract on his desk.

When I refused to comply with his suggestion that I "forget
about the *Club Reporter,*" the Hetman acted as though he had a

piece of ice lodged halfway down his throat. Now, thought I, I really *had* painted myself into a corner.

After a long moment he said, "You remind me of that fellow in Mr. Hearst's favorite story. The fellow winked at his sweetheart in the dark. *He* knew what he was doing—but nobody *else* did."

With that he offered me a pen to sign my name to the contract. Then, to save face, he decreed that I must not write one line for the *Club Reporter* on Mr. Hearst's time, or on Mr. Hearst's premises. Cross my heart.

This meant that I had to go on my days off—and they were few and uncertain—to newspaper offices other than my own to assemble copy for the *Reporter*. I was given desk space and the use of a typewriter at any place of my choice. In any work ever attempted by me I have had the assistance of friends. Among those who stood by me in the publication of the *Reporter* were Walter Davenport of the *Sun*, Edward Klauber of the *Times*, and Christy Bohnsack of the City News Association. Without the aid of these fine comrades it is likely that I would have failed as the club's editor. Klauber read copy and wrote the headlines for our monthly paper.

Ed Klauber afterward became a vice-president of the Columbia Broadcasting System. He did as much as—perhaps more than—any other man to make the broadcasting of news a reputable service. He made the broadcasters feel responsible for their words and for the way in which they presented them. He did much to foster the newscasting careers of such men as Elmer Davis and Edward R. Murrow.

I find it hard to say in which newspaper shop I most enjoyed working when meeting my deadline for the *Reporter*. I had friends in all of them. I must say, however, that I stayed away from the *Sun*, not only in 1923 but also in the years after. Davenport, Don Marquis, Keats Speed, and several others on the *Sun* were my friends, but the atmosphere of the great paper founded by Dana no longer was good, although no cigarette smoking was permitted to foul it.

The owner of the paper was the ice-blooded bachelor Frank A. Munsey. Mr. Munsey was known as the "executioner" of newspaper properties. The one-time grocer-telegrapher from Maine was a specialist in buying newspapers, killing off some of them and merging others, and losing, then recovering, fortunes. Brisbane used to describe Munsey's career as "forty failures, forty millions." A cartoonist for the *Herald* whose name slips my memory (Arthur Robinson says it was Lund) one day drew the picture of a graveyard with the names of Munsey's newspaper casualties on the respective tombstones and the figure of Mr. Munsey as an undertaker smiling in the cemetery. The very next day Mr. Munsey took title to the *Herald*. With that charming spirit of decency and fair play which always distinguished his actions as a newspaper owner Mr. Munsey fired the cartoonist.

After Munsey merged the *Press* in the *Sun* he consolidated the *Sun* in the New York *Herald*. Then in 1923 he renamed the *Evening Sun* as the *Sun* and absorbed it in the *Globe* and *Commercial Advertiser*. These were not the only newspapers he juggled in his game of put-and-take. His *Sun* office reflected his personality.

The *Sun* was published in an old building at Broadway and New Chambers Street. This building once had been the pride of A. T. Stewart, merchant prince, and had been the largest dry-goods store in the world.

It was hard for me to realize that Frank A. Munsey was the same man whose book *The Boy Broker* had seemed to me a literary masterpiece when I was eleven or twelve years old. To say that Mr. Munsey was unpopular with newspaper workers, hundreds of whom he had thrown out of work without warning, would be like saying of a convict who has spent thirty years in solitary confinement that he is not a gossip.

When I became president of the Newspaper Club in 1924, I called a meeting of the membership to see what could be done in behalf of the men fired by Munsey. To my astonishment, while presiding, I received a note which said that Mr. Munsey was at our doors and wished to address the meeting. I read the note to the members, then asked them to give the visitor their polite consideration. A wild cry was heard. An almost nude Zulu, the "wild man" from the Ringling circus, leaped into view. He brandished a spear, jabbered, and was introduced by F. Darius Benham as "Frank A. Munsey."

Mr. Benham was a circus buff and fond of practical jokes. He was a reporter for the *Morning World,* and a very good one, and came of a socially prominent Long Island family. His parents had been none too happy when Freddie decided to be a newspaperman instead of a general or an admiral. Eight Benham ancestors had held one or the other of these high commissions since 1776.

The circus wild man received an ovation. Mr. Munsey afterward held me accountable for the slur on his dignity. He threatened a suit for slander, but instead placed my name on a blacklist. Were I to go near his properties or seek a job on one of his newspapers, I was to be scorned.

One of my favorite ports of call when editing the *Club Reporter* (afterward renamed the *Three-Em Dash*) was the *Morning World.* The forceful Herbert Bayard Swope was in charge there. Swope had distinguished himself as a reporter, then as a war correspondent, and after that as a *World* Washington-bureau star. He returned to Europe to cover the Peace Conference. He worked closely with Bernard Baruch and made more "contacts" in high places than had any other newspaperman I ever knew, or ever heard of. He won the first Pulitzer Prize awarded for journalism. He was also a good poker player.

Swope became managing editor of the *Morning World,* and now, in 1923, was its executive editor. Swope assembled the most colorful group of reporters ever seen on Park Row. He created the "Page Opposite," a symposium of opinion and comment facing the editorial page. He placed no restriction (until Heywood Broun began to write of the Sacco and Vanzetti affair) upon the freedom of expression of its contributors except that of good taste and the libel laws.

In addition to Broun, the writers of the "Page Opposite" included such illustrious men as F.P.A. (Franklin P. Adams), Alexander Woollcott, Deems Taylor, William Bolitho, Samuel Chotzinoff, Dudley Nichols, Charles Michelson, Laurence Stallings, Walter Lippmann, John L. Balderston, Harry Hansen (pioneer of the daily book review in New York, and formerly of Chicago), Arthur Krock, Clare Sheridan, St. John Ervine, Viscount Jeffrey Holmesdale (later on the Earl of Amherst), humorist Frank Sullivan, and occasionally, in the early days of its inception, the great editorial writer Frank Cobb.

All these men could think, Swope once said to me. They were free, he said, from the pettiness and bitterness of personality which began creeping into journalism after the great depression. The time of the so-called depression seemed the twilight of the spirit of good fellowship and mutual trust. Laughter went away. Critics carrying wet blankets set out to smother wholesome sentiment, to stifle at the source any love of life for life's once-sweet sake. It became the fashion among writers of "realistic" renown to condemn the twenties on all sides. Of late a few authors have had some good things to say of the days which cannot come again, but their praises are like the offerings of food placed upon the grave of a Chinaman who has starved to death.

Much as I admired Herbert Bayard Swope, the red-haired comet of Park Row was not the only reason why I liked to drop in at the gold-domed building next to Brooklyn Bridge. Other good friends worked there. I often went with one or more of them downstairs for a glass of the Brown Ruin at Perry's Hole in the Wall, or else to Lipton's, or Hesse's. There we applied silver polish to the linings of all our clouds.

The *World* had three outstanding city editors: "Boss" William Thayer, James W. Barrett of Denver, and Jack Gavin. Gavin took a friendly interest in me, and gave me "the run of the place." Back at my own office in William Street, whenever I was assigned to an out-of-town story—as happened frequently—I would do the unheard-of thing of telephoning Gavin. I would ask that he send Joseph Jefferson O'Neill, Charley Bayer, or Donald Henderson

Clarke—whichever man was available—on the story to which I had just been assigned. I wanted to have a congenial roommate who could get along without sleep.

I think that it was in 1925 when the late Dudley Nichols of the *World* became one of my special friends. We covered several important newspaper stories together—the Ruth Snyder–Judd Gray electrocution at Sing Sing, for one. Dudley didn't like to see these legal killings any more than I did. He had to smile, however, when he learned what happened when I got home to the new house I bought in Kew Gardens, Long Island, in the early 1920s.

Agnes had installed one of the first electric-icebox models there. It had a mechanism separately located below it in the basement. I went downstairs to tend the furnace the night after I came home from seeing Ruth Snyder and her lover die within a few minutes of each other in the electric chair. The icebox motor suddenly started up with a piercing sibilance. It sounded exactly like the Sing Sing death-dealer. I almost fell into the coal bin.

The Ohio-born Nichols had much style as a writer even in the days before he became one of the foremost scenarists in Hollywood. His newspaper stories had both vigor and grace. He also had great spirit as a man, a gallant way about him which gave rise to the rumor that he was the son of Sir Galahad instead of a doctor of medicine in Ohio.

Dudley Nichols became a newspaper reporter—so he told me—because the illustrious Carr V. Van Anda, managing editor of the New York *Times*, was a native of the town in which Dudley was born, and had gone to school with the elder Nichols. Dr. Nichols hoped that his son would become a physician and surgeon. Dudley wanted to be an electrical engineer (a fact which might explain his amusement at my icebox terror). While he was a student at the University of Michigan the United States declared war on Germany. The young man left school to enlist in the Navy. He served in various capacities, first as communications officer for Admiral Sims in London, and then he laid mines in the North Sea. At one time he served under the command of William McFee, the celebrated seagoing engineer, essayist, novelist, and friend (*Casuals of the Sea* is one of his novels).

While in postwar service under Admiral Joseph Strauss, Nichols submitted several articles to Van Anda's *Times*. The editor urged Nichols to take up newspaper work as his profession. Although Nichols had the greatest admiration for his father's schoolmate, as well as for the newspaper he edited, the young man decided to receive his training on some other New York journal. In his judgment he would have "writing room" on a newspaper which permitted a reporter much latitude in terms of individual style while presenting the news.

Nichols worked first on the old *Evening Post*. This property had just recently been sold by Oswald Garrison Villard, a militant pacifist, to Thomas W. Lamont, a Morgan partner and reporter on the *Tribune* in the 1890s. The *Post* was published on Vesey Street. It lay outside the Park Row ferment in other ways. The *Post* was a "literary" newspaper. Its music critic, Henry Finck, had known composer Franz Liszt. Herr Finck had a chronic heart condition. One day he came staggering into the *Post's* city room, waving a newspaper and crying out in anguish that someone had changed the copy in his review of Cantor Rosenblatt's song recital. Because of Herr Finck's heart lesion it was feared that he might join his friend Herr Liszt any moment in the next world. He was crying out, "This will kill me!" and "I am not anti-Semitic!" When the critic was captured inside his office, it was discovered that the paper which he was waving was not the *Post*, but the *Evening Mail*.

Nichols remembered a day when Burton Rascoe and Christopher Morley interviewed Joseph Conrad aboard the *Tuscania* while ship-news men listened in on the literary talk. Our old friend Skipper Williams was present when Chris Morley asked the great novelist which of his works he himself liked best.

"That is hard to say," Mr. Conrad answered. "It depends on the day."

Skipper Williams scooped the literary world by writing of the occasion, "When Captain Conrad was asked which was his favorite novel, he replied, *'It Depends on the Day.'*"

In Nichols' time on the *Post* several of its staff members were as old as, if not older than, Herr Finck. They wrote with pens and ink. The drama editor, J. Ranken Towse, was perhaps the most ancient. One day he came upon Nichols in the reference library of the newspaper (a place known in every shop other than the *Post* as the "morgue") and asked Dudley to get for him a certain book from a dusty high shelf.

"Young man," said Towse, as he fondled the old volume, "when I came to the *Post* at your age, I got down this same book for our editor, the greatest of our American poets, William Cullen Bryant."

Dudley Nichols had become a seasoned reporter when he went from the *Post* to the *World* in the early 1920s. One of his first memorable interviews as a *World* man was with Father Francis Patrick Duffy, one-time chaplain of the 165th Infantry, New York's old "Fighting Sixty-ninth." Father Duffy offered Dudley a glass of prewar Scotch with the toast, "May the Good Lord receive ye— but not too soon."

In these four friends whom I have singled out as reporters for the *World*, city editor Jack Gavin had a backfield as effective and as colorful as Knute Rockne's "Four Horsemen" of Notre Dame. He also had "bench strength and depth," as the football saying goes, in such excellent reporters as Oliver H. P. Garrett and Joseph Van Raalte.

One might suppose that I would become somewhat discouraged when out-reported and outwritten by the very men whom I had asked editor Gavin to send with me on assignments. But their companionship more than made up for any blows to my ego. Moreover, they gave me a post-graduate course in journalism. I earned my degree the hard way, but the best way—in action, and on the field of competition. These and other Park Row gentlemen played hard when off duty, but once they had a story to cover, they re-

vealed themselves as masters of their profession, serious and alert.
They were not chronic drunks, as legend sometimes implies.

One day early in December of 1923 I went to the *World's* city
room to assemble material for the *Club Reporter*. I lacked an editorial. Don Marquis had promised to write one, but had fallen ill
at home in Forest Hills.

While I was casting about for an idea, Joe Van Raalte asked if
I would join him at Perry's. During our visit at the Hole in the
Wall I happened to remark that I seldom had spent a Christmas
Day at home with my family. Some out-of-town assignment was
bound to cancel out the holiday, or else Mr. Hearst would have one
of his third-alarm whims whenever the Yuletide bells began to ring.

I spoke of one Christmas Eve when I had just climbed onto a
stool to put a ten-cent-store Santa Claus doll on our tree, and
Mr. Hearst's secretary Joe Willicombe telephoned. The Chief
wanted me to go at once to Rhode Island. I was to interview
United States Senator Le Baron Bradford Colt at his suburban
home in Bristol County near Providence. Mr. Hearst was looking
for recruits to help him throw spears at the League of Nations. He
hoped that the Republican senator from Rhode Island would announce his enlistment in this crusade.

I told Agnes to finish trimming the tree, then took a train for
Providence. I had no sleep on the slow train. The next morning
I called up the senator from my hotel room in Providence. He
asked did I know what day it was; and did I think it in good taste
on Christmas to annoy him with politics. I rose to a point of order,
as it were. The senator from Rhode Island eventually yielded to the
gentleman from Colorado. At his suburban home he was most
gracious, but said that he wasn't going to say a damned thing about
the League. Furthermore, he had no faith in Mr. Hearst's likes or
dislikes, and indicated that Mr. Hearst changed sides more often
than a ferry boat.

"I do not regard your employer as the Great Manitou," said the
senator. "May I offer you a cup of chocolate?"

And, for the time being, neither did I feel too kindly toward Mr. Hearst or his whims at Yuletide.

At Perry's Hole in the Wall I said to Joe Van Raalte, "There should be no papers published at all on Christmas Day. In the unlikely event that another story were to break, one as big as the event in Bethlehem nineteen hundred and twenty-three years ago, we would provide, of course, for an extra edition. Still, no one would believe the news; for there are not as many as three wise men now living, perhaps not even one."

Mr. Van Raalte was a cynic. He had a habit of talking from one side of his mouth, as did George M. Cohan, who was not a cynic. "Christmas!" he said in a bitter half-snort from the starboard side of his mouth. "Christmas is one hell of a season for the members of three long-established professions: actors, newspapermen, and whores. The actors are oftentimes away on the road at that season, and among strangers. The newspapermen are busy with stories, for the news makers, the murderers, bandits, and frantic lovers, keep no office hours. The whores . . . well, they are perhaps the loneliest of all on Christmas, for that is *one* time when husbands feel obliged to stay home. That is why we have so many suicides among the ladies in red during the holidays: they get to thinking."

"You have given me an idea for my editorial," I said.

I telephoned President Hambidge at the Newspaper Club. I suggested that the Club give a Christmas party for the children of newspapermen and of actors. I wrote an open letter to the children. I became so carried away as to promise them an *elephant* at the party. It was this pledge which disturbed Mr. Bush, the owner of the building in which we were to hold open house. He asked that I call upon him immediately at his office.

Mr. Bush, a handsome man, tall, slender, gray-haired, always dressed in the best conservative taste. He said that he was fond of children. He had no objection to the party, but reminded me that our toilet facilities were limited. He hoped that we were not going to serve lemonade. As to elephants—well, he thought they belonged in a circus, or in India, or Africa. Of course I was only joking when I proposed to bring an *elephant* to the third floor of the skyscraper.

"I cannot break my word," I said. "I promised these children an elephant."

"The promise is yours," said Mr. Bush. "The building is mine. Take the party somewhere else."

Our landlord liked publicity, so I shaped my plea with that thought uppermost. Mr. Bush's eyes began to lose the frost-bitten expression which landlords, loan company executives, and desk sergeants at police stations always seem to have when listening to a petitioner.

"Mr. Bush," I said, "let us disprove the hateful philosophy of Professor Arthur Baer of Philadelphia (I did not tell him that this was my friend "Bugs" Baer), who says, 'Love is the last word in a ten-word telegram.' Show the whole world that you *really* love the children."

Mr. Bush sent for his building-maintenance chief—a Mr. Small I think his name was. "I hope I am not making a big mistake."

Mr. Small did not quite understand the situation. "I can't do a damned thing about the club toilet," he began defensively. "The sewer pipes already are overloaded, and—"

"Not the pipes, Mr. Small," said Mr. Bush. "Mr. Fowler here is going to try, somehow, to get an elephant onto the third floor. Have you any suggestions pro or con?"

Mr. Small's jaw dropped several notches. He had solid-gold lower teeth which may have come from King Solomon's mines. He asked, "Who's kidding who?"

He didn't take his eyes off me as I explained the project. I said, among other things, that we had been elephant hunting for a week or so to find a *very small* tusker; that Dexter Fellows, press agent of the Ringling circus, was unable to bring one down from the winter quarters at Bridgeport, but that his friend and mine, F. Darius Benham, had come upon some spoor during the safari.

Mr. Benham had located just the *right* elephant, a junior member of the herd of Powers Elephants now performing daily at the Hippodrome, only a few squares distant from this very building.

"What are your honest reactions, Mr. Small?" Mr. Bush inquired.

"Do you really want to know?" asked the chief of the maintenance department. "*Do* you, Mr. Bush?" His employer nodded. Mr. Small spoke through his gold teeth. "All right, then. It's nuts! In all the years I am connected with big buildings—first the Flatiron, and then the Singer Building—well, they is some funny kinds of things going on; like the time the Hudson Dusters hang the king of the newsboys to the flagpole at half mast. But *this one* is the most cockeyed malarkey I ever hear! This . . . this elephant . . ."

"She is only a little cow elephant," I said. "Her name is Blossom."

"What in hell difference does *that* make?" rasped Mr. Small. "Cow! Bull! Stud horse! Hell's bells! We got property to pertect, and an insurance policy to look out for, and it's a cinch the insurance policy on the elevator lapses the minute you can even get an elephant onto it. And the city inspector—"

"City Hall has put an okay on all our plans," I said. "Grover Whalen has issued a permit to march Blossom along the streets."

Mr. Bush ruled that we have the elephant. The press agent for the Hippodrome assured us that Blossom would attend the party and be dressed in a clown's costume. Moreover, she was guaranteed to be a gentle animal, not given to tantrums that might frighten the children. Blossom's keeper, however, threatened to block the enterprise. This stubborn mahout informed our white hunter, F. Darius Benham, that his ward had symptoms of a head cold, that any exposure to the December air while on her way to the club would be, as he phrased it, "like asking for double pneumonia in both her two lungs."

I must permit my memory of this gentleman's remarks to enjoy a certain degree of drift, at the risk of having my poet's license revoked. I shall try to put down the things he said in keeping with the way in which he said them. Of all the speech stylists I have ever come upon, Blossom's guardian was far and away the greatest master of the fractured phrase. Even Mr. James Durante might have been left at the post in a match race with this champion.

In his diagnosis of Blossom's sinus condition her keeper said, "A prematurely growned little cow like this here one which is as delicate as a hot-house, mister, can't be shielded with too much care of my attentions. All our bulls is more weaker in their resistance as meets the eye. Why, onct back in Cincy we have a big strong bull conk out and die when he looks like he only has got a touch of the mere sniffles. You can't never be too tedious with these bulls. No, mister, I want that my Blossom stays right here with the herd. Understand?"

We were up against a man in love with an elephant. I was determined not to let his passion defeat our purpose. I made three telephone calls for expert advice. I tried unsuccessfully to locate Frank Buck, the jungle trapper who brought 'em back alive. Then I endeavored to reach Madam Zora of the Sells-Floto Circus, who had been staying at the Algonquin, only to learn that she had checked out yesterday. I had better luck on the third call, a timely one to Grantland Rice.

Poet and sports writer Rice was a naturalist and zoologist, second only to sports writer John Francis Kieran (Fordham *cum laude*) in his knowledge of birds and beasts. One of Granny Rice's best friends was Dr. Raymond Lee Ditmars, curator of mammals at the Bronx Zoo. Dr. Ditmars also had been a court reporter for the New York *Times* back in the 1890s, a good reason why he should come to our aid.

Dr. Ditmars sent a veterinarian posthaste to the club. Mr. Benham and I went with him to the Hippodrome, where we found Blossom eating enough hay to stuff a three-piece set of furniture for the living room. After some clinical procedures the doctor said that Blossom was "slightly resonant on percussion," but otherwise as sound as a Baldwin locomotive.

The keeper became almost hytserical. "How can you stand there and say a thing like *that*, doc!" he cried. "Just lookout! I ask anybody with one grain of sand to see it for yourself: her trunk is running!"

When the mahout quieted down somewhat, I asked that he give me Blossom's measurements and her tonnage. He thumbed his nose at me, said not a word, and I thought that his loved one was following suit. She curled up her trunk in a way which made her resemble a cynical teapot of great size, and regarded me with beady-eyed intolerance.

I had brought with me the dimensions of the entrance to the Bush Building, as well as the width of the elevator-shaft portal on the ground floor and at the third-floor level. I borrowed a tape measure from the wardrobe mistress of the Hippodrome to gauge Blossom's beam. Blossom was only breast-pocket high, but quite buxom. The veterinarian held the other end of the tape, but an accurate measurement was impossible. Blossom swayed and teetered in a hula dance, flogged us with her trunk, and at one point trumpeted.

I appealed to her mahout. "Can't you get her to shut up and stand still?"

He leered. "Gimme one single reason I should ought to!"

"All right," I said, "this is my first experience as a buttocks inspector—with elephants, that is. Be reasonable."

"She thinks you're trying to do something unmodest to her," said the keeper. "Little Blossom don't truss both you two fellas."

I do not now recollect what the figures were as pertained to the Bush Building places of entrance. Nor was I able to get Blossom's measurements other than to make an estimate of her various bulges. I can say, however, that her spread was at least three times the life-size rump of the second Mrs. Peter Paul Rubens, in the nude, as painted by her spouse.

Mr. Benham chose a gay costume for Blossom's debut at the club: a multicolored dunce cap, such as clowns wear, and a white ruff as big as the wheel of a windmill. F. Darius also borrowed for his own use a suit of tattered clothes to wear as a rag-man clown.

Now that our headliner had been fixed upon, I asked Joe Laurie,

Jr., to engage other acts to round out the bill. Joe was a renowned vaudeville actor whom I first met during his legitimate stage debut in *Plain Jane*. At that time I was temporarily serving as a drama critic of the *American*.

Our regular first-string critic, the much-feared Alan Dale, had chosen me to occupy that place while he underwent surgery. I was not quite as able as William Winter as a critic of the drama. Burns Mantle, Bide Dudley, Arthur Chapman (poet, author of *Out Where the West Begins*, and father of today's drama critic John Chapman), all from Denver, coached me in the art of play-viewing and play-appraisal; as did Kelcey Allen of *Women's Wear*, and Broun—and even the gingery Woollcott. It was of no use. Whenever I thought of a poor playwright working his guts out in some Greenwich Village dump, perhaps starving, I simply could not blow a police whistle when he committed that greatest of all crimes—artistic failure.

Among the attractions Joe Laurie procured for the children's party was Professor Enrico Amalfi, newly arrived from Genoa with a troupe of performing roosters. This would be a fine introduction to the press of New York—or so Joe had told the professor during an interview at Ellis Island. Signor Amalfi was having a spot of trouble with the immigration authorities about his visa. Government inspectors, on the lookout for signs of roup and parrots' ailments, had also quarantined the chickens. It enraged the professor, Joe said, that the United States could mistake his educated Leghorn cocks for parrots.

"This Professor Amalfi," Joe added, "is plenty worried about the safety of his roosters, one of which can count up to six by pecking with its beak on a little bell. The kids will go for that routine in a big way. Professor Amalfi once lost his entire troupe during an earthquake in Palermo. He was thrown out of work a whole year while he ransacked all Europe for replacements. He never did get over losing one big capon. He claims it could sing the first two bars of an aria from *Il Trovatore*, and in soprano, no less. The loss of his glands made this possible."

Professor Enrico Amalfi was in a bad cash position, Joe said. We would have to buy some grain for the roosters, take care of the professor's hotel bill for a week, and pay for a truck to bring the cocks from the pier of the Italian Line, where they had been quarantined.

The great day came at last for the children's party. I had wangled some time off by convincing the Hetman that any overt act by him would inspire the club members to burn Mr. Hearst in effigy. Mr. Watson liked children, no matter what his enemies might say of his lack of the milk of human kindness. Moreover, children liked him. So, for this one day, the Hetman buried the hatchet.

I said good-by to Agnes, who was getting two of our three children ready for the party. Our youngest son, Will, was but a year old, and would have to stay home. Ellen Runyon telephoned just as I was going out the door, and said that she was bringing her daughter Mary to the party. Brother (Damon, Junior) was down with some disease or other—the mumps, as I recall it—and could not join in the fun.

I arrived at the club before noon to find everything going splendidly. Jesse, the club steward, had the tree decked out, and had reinforced the makeshift platform which would be the stage for the Duncan Sisters and other visiting artists. Jesse was a capable young man, an athletic Negro, well educated and alert. Ed Klauber once said of him, "I'd like to have enough money one day to afford a Park Avenue apartment, with Jesse to take care of it and of me."

Klauber *did* become wealthy. I visited him in his splendid apartment on Park Avenue one day in the 1940s. He now was married to a woman of much charm. When I mentioned the old days at the club, and spoke of Jesse, my friend smiled. "Jesse was a wonderful man," he said. "But I think he preferred to work for bachelors."

At the club I was asking the two or three survivors of an all-night poker game—all losers, need I say?—if they would not cash in their chips, if any, to enable Jesse to clear away the evidence of gambling and drinking before the children and our visiting statesmen arrived. One of the players was Dennis Moon.

I did not know at the time whether or not he had begun one of his semiannual retreats from the world of reality. He patted me on the back, then went over to the Christmas tree and stood looking at it. He left the club—or so I thought.

Mr. F. Darius Benham, dressed in his rag-man costume, now arrived somewhat out of breath and out of sorts. A rookie police-man, he said, had wanted to arrest him for vagrancy. He would have done so had not Mr. B. displayed his reporter's police card.

"The damned idiot!" F. Darius exclaimed. "I had just come out of Childs Circle restaurant. I was standing near the delivery en-trance with six milk cans beside me when this young cop tells me to get a move on. I explained that I had these cans full of circus lemonade which my friends at Childs had just made, and was try-ing to get a taxi driver to do me the favor of taking the cans and me to the club. Then the silly bastard said, 'That's a good story! We'll get you a taxi, all right—one with a red light on it and a siren, and you can tell it to the desk sergeant. You bum!' No mat-ter, the cans are here now in the kitchen storeroom."

Six huge cans of circus lemonade!

"Jesse," I said to the steward, "our toilet will never stand the strain. Please go upstairs and see if one of the tenants will let us have his wash room for the use of our young ladies and gentlemen and their mothers."

And now there was delivered to us a two-hundred-pound cake which Oscar of the Waldorf had baked and frosted and decorated with his own accomplished hands. Oscar had sent not only the cake, as well as a huge white cloth to disguise our billiard table, but also a punch bowl of bathtub proportions, and much glass-ware. Moreover, he assigned one of his assistant chefs, Monsieur Armand, to prepare something for our honorary hosts, Governor Smith, Senator Copeland, Judge Wagner, and other notables who might stay on for a bite to eat after the party.

Monsier Armand, immaculately garbed in white, with a chef's cap as big as a Boy Scout's tent, could not speak English. Fortu-nately one of our linguists, G. Selmer Fougner, had dropped in to collect his mail. He came to my assistance.

Fougner had been a reporter on several New York newspaper staffs. He also had been a foreign correspondent, as well as a bureau manager in Paris and London for various publications. He occasionally wrote articles under the by-line of "Baron Fougner." The Baron was a graduate of the Sorbonne and the translator of the French novelist René Benjamin's *Gaspard*.

The world-traveled Baron was a gourmet, an authority on vintage wines. Everyone liked him, for he was a person of charm and high spirits. I first met him during the Second Liberty Loan drive. At that time the Baron was in charge of all newspaper publicity in New York for this enterprise. He served in several subsequent campaigns of that nature as an appointee of the United States Treasury Department.

Rare men like Baron Fougner are not tolerated by the solemn bureaucrats of today.

The first time I saw the Baron was at his press headquarters, where I had gone with other reporters to get a statement on the Liberty Loan. The Baron called in one of the several pretty secretaries to take dictation. Without any hesitation, and as if of her own accord, this young woman sat on the Baron's lap to make her stenographic notes.

Next to Ivy Ledbetter Lee—press adviser to the Rockefellers, Bethlehem Steel, the Pennsylvania Railroad, and other large interests—Baron Fougner was perhaps the best-known publicity man of the immediate postwar years. His methods were quite unlike Lee's. The "age of the handout," or the issuance to reporters of carefully concocted statements supposedly written by men of the hour, instead of lively, personal, impromptu interviews, found Lee as its foremost pioneer.

The "handout" has become the grand medium for persons with axes to grind, or facts to conceal, or half-truths to inflate. Fougner's intention always was to get his clients' names into print; Lee's main value to his powerful sponsors seemed to be his ability to keep their names *out*, except on fool-proof occasions which showed his masters as philanthropists and patriots.

Mr. Lee was a man of outstanding ability and unimpeachable personal conduct, but the barrier he did so much to raise between the men who did big things and the public they did big things *to* has increasingly shut out the public's right to know. Politicians also hide behind that wall. They have various solemn names for it, such as "restricted information" or "public security." The people are denied the news they are entitled to; government by secrecy creeps over us. We may expect tomorrow's slogan to read: "Honesty is the best fallacy."

Monsieur Armand saw Baron Fougner and embraced him. When their chattering stopped for just a moment, I asked the Baron what our visitor had been saying, and why was he here.

Baron Fougner smiled urbanely. "Oscar heard that the club is giving Governor Smith and his retinue an intimate supper after the children go home. *N'est-ce pas?* So he has sent Monsieur Armand to inspect our larder, and see if we need some supplies from the Waldorf. I can vouch that Armand is resourceful, a specialist at preparing wildfowl. Perhaps I can suggest something to tickle the palate of Governor Smith, although I am a Republican, and have been offered the publicity work for that great political party next year."

The Baron could not foresee—nor could anyone else know—that Governor Smith would be placed in nomination for the Democratic candidacy the next year, by Franklin D. Roosevelt, as the "Happy Warrior," in a speech at Madison Square Garden.

"Baron," I said, "please thank Armand for us. And thanks to you, also. But Al Smith is a corned-beef-and-cabbage man. So are his Tammany pals. There'll be no wildfowl today."

"I shall not translate what you have just said"—and the Baron looked as though he had been blackballed by the proprietors of the Tour d'Argent. He spoke to Armand, then turned to me. "I have advised Armand to retire to the kitchen, out of earshot, before someone who speaks French inadvertently betrays us as a society of ruffians."

Sirens sounded from the street below us. Governor Smith and other honorary hosts were escorted into the club by Charles S. Hand. Charley was Albany correspondent for the *Morning World*. This personable man and I would have much in common in the days ahead. He was a striking figure, tall, good-looking; Jimmy Walker, whose secretary Hand afterward became, used to refer to him as "Charley Handsome." Al Smith, F.D.R., John Nance Garner, the Robert Wagners, both father and son, admired and liked this man, and at various times appointed him as a confidential adviser.

And now the little guests and their mothers came trooping into the club. I saw two of my children among them: Gene, who had brought along a guest, Herman Depper; and my little Jane. Santa Claus Copeland had on his red costume, a property lent to us by Bernard Gimbel, and a beard as big as a cloud. He welcomed the tots while the orchestra from Earl Carroll's *Vanities* played "Jingle Bells."

Santa Claus was a fine orator today. The Santa Claus filibuster was interrupted when Charley Hand whispered something to him. Governor Smith had the belly ache. Santa excused himself to write a prescription for some paregoric. Jesse took it to the Times Building pharmacy, then came back empty-handed. The pharmacist had charged that the prescription was a rank forgery. Dr. Santa Claus, who until just recently had been Health Commissioner of New York, telephoned somewhat angrily to the drugstore. The camphorated tincture of opium was placed in the hands of a mounted policeman, who is said to have ridden with it like Paul Revere along 42nd Street.

Monsieur Armand had come out of the kitchen to jabber something to me. Baron Fougner had gone. Jesse managed to lure the chef back to the kitchen. And now word came that Blossom had arrived at our very doors downstairs. I hurried down to find maintenance chief Small and his crew removing a revolving door, the first barrier an elephant might expect when visiting a skyscraper. Mr. Small would not even say hello.

There were but a few persons standing on the sidewalk outside the door. Nor did the passing pedestrians seem to be concerned with what was going on. New Yorkers—at least it was so in those days—seldom enjoyed anything that was free. This did not apply to burglars, of course, or to other politicians.

Blossom had on her clown's hat and the big ruff. Her keeper, in a rajah's garments, stood at one side of her, a "jeweled" sjambok in one hand. F. Darius Benham, who had met Blossom at the door, stood at the other side. To my amazement, the keeper spoke to me in a most friendly way. I could not understand his change of mood.

"This way," I said.

Blossom easily cleared the front doorway. I had asked the pilot of one of the elevators to hold his cage at the first-floor level, with the door propped open for Blossom. In my excitement I gave him a five-dollar bill instead of a one. Blossom's mahout tried to back her into the cage. She would not oblige. He wheeled her about, and with a few prods of the sjambok got her to place a forefoot onto the platform. The elevator vibrated. She recoiled.

"Come on now, sweetheart," said Blossom's keeper. "Let's go into the inside and be a good girl. They's nothing to worry you-self with, with fretting. Hup! Hup!"

Blossom wanted no part of that jiggling platform. After a minute or so of pleadings and of jabbings with the hook, the rajah said, "We have got to do something to get her mind off one side. Got any sweet sugar around here? Lumps of it in handy pieces?"

An emergency call brought Jesse downstairs with a pound or so of lump sugar. The rajah used it as bait. Inch by inch he lured Blossom halfway inside the cage. She got stuck in the doorway! My measurements had been inaccurately computed. Blossom could neither get all the way into the cage nor get *out* of it!

"Shall I have Jesse bring some butter, or some lard?" I asked the rajah. He shook his head as he climbed over Blossom from head to tail. The elevator pilot, seen through the metal lattice of the cage, was stiff with fear.

"I'll get her out!" said the rajah in a burst of clarity of speech.

"And in again. It's merely that she's gassy. We got to unflate her."

He finally *did* get her out, with cries of "Back up, Blossom! Back up to the rear! Get your ass out of there, sweetheart! That's it!"

The rajah led Blossom outside the building. He maneuvered her to the edge of the sidewalk. He backed her up to the gutter, then began to give commands: "Mock, Blossom! Mock! Big job, sweetheart! Mock! Mock! Mm-m-m-mmm-mock!"

Thank heaven, Blossom did not make use of the club's facilities for her "unflation"! She was noticeably more slender now. The mahout enticed her into the elevator car with sugar bribes. She was hoisted to the third floor. A new mood possessed her when the rajah asked her to *get out* of the cage. Blossom would not stir.

"A bull," said the keeper, "especially a small little cow, is hard to perdict in advance. Gimme some more pieces of them sugar lumps, if you have got some."

Blossom must have had a sweet tusk.

The children whooped as the elephant walked among them. My daughter Jane became terrified. She toddled behind one of the divans and began to bawl. The other children took turns at riding on Blossom's back, four at a time.

I saw out of the corner of my eye that Charley Hand was admonishing the rajah about something while guiding him away from Governor Smith. Charley then informed me that the mahout had sought this opportunity to ask the governor to parole a lion-tamer friend, serving a term in Auburn Prison for having tried to kill someone—a side-show barker, I think he was. This explained the mahout's air of cordiality toward me earlier in the afternoon. Mr. Hand left off discussing the matter to escort the governor to the washroom. His excellency had a cramp.

And now I learned that Professor Amalfi's chickens had arrived. They had been placed temporarily in the storeroom next to the kitchen. The professor, it was explained, would be here as soon as he could get away from an Immigration inspector, who was annoying him with questions. The orchestra was playing. My daughter was crying and clinging to Agnes. Santa Claus was in top form, and ringmaster Judge Wagner was distributing balloons among the children.

Charley Hand whispered in my ear that someone was holding down the cabinet in our washroom. Whoever it was would not get out of it, or make any reply when Hand had said that the governor would like to know "how soon." "The guy in there may have passed out," Charley said. "You better ask Jesse to see about it. I'll take the governor upstairs."

I was about to go to the washroom but another matter diverted my attention. My son and his guest, Herman, had removed two billiard cues from the rack and were using them as lances in an impromptu jousting tournament. While I was disarming the young knights and telling them that someone's eye might be put out, an ominous disturbance was heard from the direction of the kitchen.

I went there at once to find Jesse standing between two angry gentlemen. They were shouting at each other in alien tongues. One of these men was Monsieur Armand. He held a meat cleaver in one hand. His chef's hat had fallen off; his white apron had been torn. The other man, as I learned soon enough, was Professor Amalfi. He was leaping high and trying to tear his black hair from the roots. Chickens were scampering this way and that, clamoring wildly. One of them escaped into the main room to run amok there.

It seems that Chef Armand had made a terrible mistake. He had assumed that the chickens had been delivered for him to kill, pluck, and prepare for the private post-party meal for our statesmen-guests. Fortunately for the trained roosters—but unfortunately for Armand—the professor arrived just as Armand was holding one of the cocks—the one that could count up to six—and stretching its neck for the meat cleaver.

After the duelists were separated, I went out to where Blossom and her keeper were having a time of it. The escaped rooster—the most highly educated one—had frightened Blossom. It flapped its wings and crowed. Then it fluttered up to Blossom's back, where it crowed again. Blossom showed her resentment of this familiarity by trumpeting and swaying and using her trunk as a flail. I told the mahout to remove Blossom at once. He prodded her toward the room adjoining the lavatory. The musicians played loudly all this time.

The rooster with the mathematical mind was captured, and I was trying to persuade Professor Amalfi to go on with his act when Jesse whispered in my ear, "You better come to the toilet. It's Mr. Moon, and something has happened to him."

I lost no time getting there. I burst past Blossom, who was being given some sugar by the rajah. I went into the small room which was the lavatory. Dennis Moon was standing just outside the cabinet—rather, he was leaning against it, his mouth open. His eyes were trying to part company with their sockets.

"It's happened!" he gasped. "Just as I knew it would sooner or later. My God!"

"Come on, old man," I said. "Let's go outside."

"Outside!" he exclaimed. "Not on your life, after what's happened to me! It staggers the imagination. Fantastic!"

"Suppose you tell me, Dennis. From the beginning. It'll make you feel better. Should I call Doctor Gregory?"

"Don't call anybody—yet. All right, you're the one person I can trust not to think I'm losing my marbles. First, I hear a rooster crowing. No, that is later on. The first thing is when I come to in the can, and think I'll go home. And I look out, and—now don't laugh—I see—and I swear on my mother's tombstone it's true—I see Santa Claus standing right over there at the latrine. I know it sounds nuts. . . ."

"That was Senator Copeland, Dennis. You must have known he was going to be here for the children's party. Haven't you know all along that—"

He interrupted me with "There you go, always trying to cheer somebody up. That's you all over, and I admire you for it. But you haven't heard the worst of my terrible dream."

"What else? It wasn't a dream."

"Then I heard the rooster crow. Three times, like the one Saint Peter hears. And, now hold onto your hat! When I open that door a crack I see an *elephant*, as plain as day. Plainer!"

May heaven forgive me for harboring the imps of mischief which sometimes possess me. "Describe it," I said.

"Not only an elephant," said Dennis in a tone of awesome recollection, "but it has on a hat, a pointed hat. And a big ruff, like Queen Elizabeth's or Sir Walter Raleigh's. It's fantastic!"

"Dennis," I said, "it *was* an elephant. A Powers elephant we brought here for the kids. On the level."

"Good old Gene!" he said. "But why do you treat me like a damned child? I know I'm nuts. You know it. Yes, get Doc Gregory right away."

Charley Hand and Jesse came into the small room to see how things stood. I said to Hand, "Do you think the governor and Doctor Copeland would help us straighten out Denny?"

The two statesmen came to the rescue. They persuaded Moon that an elephant, a real one, was standing just outside the overcrowded doorway. Senator–Doctor–Santa Claus Copeland motioned for us to get out of his way, but permitted Governor Al Smith to go past him to the cabinet in which Dennis Moon had been sitting for many hours.

"Bring me a glass," said Senator Copeland. "A teacup, or anything." When Jesse reappeared with an empty whisky glass, Dr. Copeland put some water into it, then added a dose of Governor Smith's paregoric, stirred it with his forefinger, and offered the cloudy sedative to Dennis.

The harassed fellow downed the potion, then observed that it tasted like absinthe. Governor Smith called out from that place which, in certain respects, makes democrats of us all. He had the voice of three foghorns.

"Better mix *me* another dose of that stuff, Roy," the governor was saying as we helped Dennis out of the chamber of horrors.

Blossom trumpeted.

So many memories came to mind as I rode uptown on that day of snow and dervish wind. Perhaps *too* many.

CHAPTER

15

After the game the king and
the pawn go into the same
box. —Old Italian proverb

SOME hidden influence beyond my reach of mind to identify
or to explain has placed a lien on my wits. This meddling task-
master insists that I review, more fully than I had intended, the
march-past of memories associated with the morning of my return
to the old neighborhood in the winter of the year, and in the winter
of my life. Seldom has the memory of any other day stayed afloat
this long in the tide-race of my recollections.

I had set out that morning on what seemed a matter-of-course
errand. I would call upon old Dennis Moon, pay his hospital bill,
find out if he wished to see the priest, then go on my way. Instead,
I strayed into a labyrinth, every path of which led into the emotional distance.

A feeling of anxiety had seemed to argue against my return to
this place where, once upon a time, the future had lain in my keeping. I had felt that, were I to come upon the half-forgotten evidence of youthful didos I would have to throw myself upon the
mercy of the court.

I had had a premonition that I was to see myself—as though

for the first time—stripped of those flattering brocades with which aging men emboss their reminiscences. A man tells more lies to himself than to anyone else until, toward the last, he looks upon the hoard of pleasing fictions as a treasury of fact. He lives in a sublime hoax. His lost love was the fairest of all. And, of course, she never will forget him or cease to yearn till grass grows at the South Pole.

It is one thing to sit in the sun at some far-off place, and to make long-distance calls to the favorite way stations of one's past. It is quite another matter to walk among the weathered landmarks of a once-familiar neighborhood.

The stones testify against the great hoax. The old stones seem to be saying, "Pilgrim, what have you done with your dreams?"

In other years my memories, for the most part, have come as undertones. They grew briefly resonant, then whispered off and away, like the abbreviated tunes one used to hear while bicycling past the music teacher's window. An occasional recollection, to be sure, stayed on for a much longer time, but left when other guests arrived.

The once-loved faces disappear in the dusk of spent desire. The flower one placed among the pages of Keats' sonnets crumbles at the touch. Its ashes fall without scent or significance of some far-off moment, whether of ecstasy or of heartache. There is left but a trace of this relic, a rust-brown outline on the page, a shadow cast across the young poet's lament:

> The day is gone, and all its sweets
> are gone. . . .

Upon my arrival at St. Luke's hospital that gray morning, I asked the taxicab driver to wait in West 113th Street. I was gone but a minute or so. Hospitals do not receive visitors so early in the day. An attendant with the fattest cheeks this side of the Low Countries set me straight. "Suppose you come back in two or three hours." Mr. Cheeks' jowls stood out like a baseball umpire's coat pockets. "Rules are rules."

The efficient Mr. Cheeks poured himself some coffee from a blue-jacketed Thermos bottle into a paper cup. I went outside to stand in the snow. What to do? Where to spend the next hours? I felt like some road-company King Lear who had forgotten his lines.

I saw across the snow-covered street the massive profile of the cathedral church of St. John the Divine. The greater part of this Gothic temple had been completed since my time of residence in the old neighborhood. There was but one element of the stone fabric which had not changed in appearance, except that it now seemed relatively small and subordinate to the rest of the cruciform design to which it had been groined. This was the apse. There stood upon it, just as in the far-off days, a familiar bronze figure: the Archangel Gabriel.

The first soloist of Heaven's brass section stood upon the apex of the steep choir roof as though perched upon the pommel of God's great sword. His trumpet was upraised to the east in the ageless threat to blow taps for the world. As used to happen whenever I looked too long upon this sculpture, I once again felt a commotion of conscience.

Today a blob of snow sagged from the bell of Gabriel's horn. The pagan wind of last night and early this morning had made off with the herald's mantle of snow, except for a white festoon in the cleft of the bronze wings and the lop-sided snowball in the trumpet's flare. It was not a time for irreverent thoughts, but it did occur to me that the great musician was eating an ice-cream cone wrong-end-to.

The cab driver's voice wheezed in upon my thoughts. "Where to from here?"

It was now that I had that do-or-don't feeling about revisiting the old neighborhood. Want of sleep, as well as the aftermath of too many toasts to the memories of comrades of Park Row, made any decision seem formidable. Well, I just couldn't stand there forever in the cold presence of Sir Gabriel.

The gale had lost force. It still got into the bones, however, as New York's winter winds of any degree will do. The lessening wind had now become a sing-song monotony. In it one seemed to hear a distant company of penitents chanting a litany of woes. Somewhere beneath the slate-gray sounding-board of the overcast the choir of wraiths sang on and on, an endless dirge. This threnody was not one of mourning for the human dead, but for youth itself. For lost youth, for lost dreams, for loves that cannot live again except in wayward moments of retrospection.

The cabbie was waiting for me to get aboard. Finally I said, "Suppose we take a drive into yesterday."

"Come again?" and the obviously bewildered fellow made sniffling sounds. He used a leather-mittened hand to take care of his nose. "Would you mind playing that one back?"

"It's only a little way from here." I was thinking out loud. "I'd like to cruise around for a while in this neighborhood."

"You a tourist?"

"Sort of. I used to live here."

He grunted as he started up the motor. "I ought to pick up some more anti-freeze. How long will it take—this cruise?"

"That depends. Just go around and about, as Damon Runyon used to say."

He brightened upon hearing this name. "I drove Mr. Runyon a number of times," he said. "You knew him?"

"Could be," I replied. "He used to live up here."

We now were crossing Amsterdam Avenue, where the antique streetcars once ran—but no more. Their defective wheels used to sound like a boiler maker's honeymoon.

"You say Mr. Runyon lived up here?"—and the cab driver seemed skeptical. "As I remember it, he lived at the Forest hotel near the Garden. I usedta have a stand outside the Silver Slipper, and I usedta take Mr. Runyon to the Forest just before the sun come up."

"That was later on," I said. "Everything seems later on. Know what I mean?"

"Frankly, no," he said.

My qualms about crossing over to yesterday had yielded to a nostalgic mood. I now had the desire to see the doorways and the windows of my old homes, and of Runyon's home. The once-familiar figures had come and gone, and now were gone forever from those doorways and those windows. But perhaps I could restore to those frames the portraits which time had stolen from the gallery of my youth.

I got out of the car on West 112th Street, about halfway between Amsterdam and upper Broadway. The superintendent of the building in which I first lived in New York had been shoveling the snow from the sidewalk. He was now strewing cinders on the walk to forestall lawsuits charging negligence. I said good morning. He responded like a good New Yorker by not paying the slightest attention.

As I looked at the old flat, all the years since 1918 did a series of backbends and cartwheels in my remembering mind. They flipped on and off stage. Memory is an acrobat.

I remembered a day much like this one. It was toward Christmas of 1918. How clear the recollections of that time! In fancy I see once again the girlish Ellen Runyon as she arrives at our flat. The taxicab in which she has been riding is piled high with gifts. Today she is distributing these presents—not so many of them to her own friends as to Damon's. He is in France, waiting there at some port of troop embarkation—Brest, as I recall it—waiting for his editor to assign him to come home with the American soldiers, or else remain abroad to cover the Peace Conference in Paris. The Demon has written a letter to Ellen, in which he lists the friends he wishes to remember at this Christmas time.

"Alfred has the damnedest assortment of friends," Ellen Runyon said of him and his letter. "He wants I should take presents to each and every one, but doesn't let me know till the very last minute; never a hint of what to get for whom. How can I know what to choose for some bum with tin ears? Or for that waiter at Haan's who used to be a lookout man for Canfield? If Alfred should die—God forbid!—I wouldn't know a soul at his funeral. . . . Well, I can't stay but a minute."

It so happened that she stayed several hours. Nor did it occur to her to dismiss the cab and then call another one when ready to go. The cab meter ticked on the while. I presumed that the driver had excellent kidneys.

Taxicabs were but one of Ellen's extravagances. Later on, Damon bought a Wills Sainte Claire automobile. Neither he nor Ellen could drive, so the Demon hired a succession of chauffeurs. These burly fellows were ex-prize-fighters, or one-time bouncers in Broadway dives, or their like. One of them was the brother of Dot King, a Broadway beauty who had been murdered. I "covered" that story for my newspaper.

The reason Ellen decided to stay on at our flat was that I was behaving like Chief Crazy Horse. Agnes had been pleading with me since early morning not to make a fool of myself. I shall presently tell about this and about other matters, both of a domestic and a professional sort, a mad medley of happenings which beset us.

Ellen Runyon was never happier, in a cockeyed sense of the word, than when she came upon a muddle in the affairs of her friends. She would immediately take full charge, improvise strategies, call the tunes, and issue commands with a field marshal's self-assurance. The tip of her pretty nose would bob up and down as she gave the orders.

I could see her now, in my mind's eye, as I stood, almost forty years afterward, outside the old flat. It is possible, of course, that I am implementing my over-all memories with the random recollections which spring to mind as I write of that day. One remembrance bumps against another, as rolling stones do in a Rocky Mountain landslide. I have asked Agnes to give me her own afterthoughts on matters which ordinarily lie beyond the area of masculine review.

Odd that Agnes had never spoken, until just recently, of the circumstances which foreshadowed the breakup of the Runyon home in 1928. Damon Runyon, Jr., wrote of it in his poignant book, *Father's Footsteps*, in 1954. Hitherto Agnes had said nothing about this, or of certain other sad phases of Ellen's growing unhappiness at home.

But I thought she had been crying over young Damon's book, the opening sentence of which read, "Ours was a house divided by a dark secret."

I had been strangely unaware of this situation at its beginning, possibly because I wore blinkers when with friends. After a day of newsgathering, I would come home tired of having catalogued the tragedies, the sorrows, defeats, scandals, conflicts, the stupid cruelties which negated our boasts as civilized beings. I did not want more of the same when off-duty. Agnes always seemed to sense this.

My wife was Ellen's closest friend and confidante. Even now, she said, she was reluctant to speak of certain things. I pointed out to her that Damon, Jr. had lifted the veil in his book. Anything that happened to mar their happiness, I said, was important to a better understanding of the domestic sadness which so often underlies the surface of worldly success.

As to that morning when I stood in the old neighborhood, I met Ellen Runyon as her taxicab drew up outside our flat. I had been around the corner to pick up the morning newspapers and a supply of envelopes.

Ellen had on a black fur coat (Agnes says it was of sealskin) and a dark red hat worn low on her head, as was then the style. How gracefully she walked from the curbside to the apartment door! She had on a pair of red galoshes, the buckles of which were unfastened on her trim ankles and rang like little bells.

Ellen used to say that she had "the form of a sixteen-year-old girl." She seemed quite proud of her slender feet. She bought all her shoes—a dozen pair at a time—from I. Miller, a firm patronized by Broadway actresses.

Ellen greeted me with a "Hello, there!" and asked that I help carry our Christmas presents inside the flat. Indoors, she kissed Agnes on the cheek, then sensed that something had gone wrong with us. Ellen said nothing for a moment or so, but she changed her mind about leaving on her rounds.

Our visitor peeled off a smart pair of black kid gloves, removed the galoshes, the fur coat. She then walked about the living room, pausing now and then to rearrange this and that. She straightened a framed engraving of the Leaning Tower of Pisa on the bilious plaster of the wall. Next she regrouped bits of bric-a-brac, centered a Grecian urn (made in Japan) on the library table, readjusted the folds of a Paisley piano throw, which had no piano.

Ellen's skirts swished as she moved about the room. Her gown was a dark red gaiety which Agnes says was of hand-twilled silk. "Ellen always wore full skirts," Agnes tells me. "They swished, as you say. Ellen always used the word 'fought' when referring to the sound, which was made because she always wore silk petticoats."

Notwithstanding the fact that I was harassed that morning by problems which now seem ludicrous, something about Ellen's perfume left its fragrance in the alcoves of my memory. Once again I seemed to be smelling that perfume as I stood, almost forty years afterward, in front of the old flat. The fragrance had spread like a cloud as she took off her coat.

With the thought that my senses might be lying, I inquired of Agnes why it was that I remembered but could not identify the perfume. "Wait a moment," I said. "I'm going to turn on the tape-recorder. We'll have an interview. But I hope it will be more fruitful than the only other time I ever interviewed you—the time I asked you to tell me all about Mark Twain as you knew him in Missouri. It was very disappointing."

"But I was only a little girl."

"That's no excuse. And your mother was an even worse reporter. All she could remember was that 'Sam Clemens smelled of whisky and tobacco, but he had nice hair.' It seems unforgivable that you fell asleep during the lecture he gave one evening in Columbia."

"It was past my bedtime," said Agnes. "All children fall asleep during lectures and sermons. I really met Mr. Clemens only twice: once when I fell off the roof of a lean-to shed, and again when I got my frock muddy and my brand-new parasol ruined one rainy day. And he was kind, and he said, 'Little girl, you're always crying when I see you.'"

"The tape-recorder is working," I said.

"Oh, yes. Mr. Clemens and I met a third time. A century plant was in bloom at a neighbor's house, and he was one of the visitors. After he had studied the bloom, he said, 'Look, child. Can you see lots of little soldiers standing there?' A child does not know who is famous and who isn't. . . ."

"Never mind. Now let's get on with Ellen Runyon's perfume. Odd that I seem to remember it, for the nose of man is one of his several accessories inferior to the great apes'."

"Aren't you forgetting that my mother remembered the whisky fumes and tobacco when she knew Mr. Clemens sixty years ago?"

The sound-level indicator, a tiny light on the recording machine, winked. "The perfume?" I said. "Ellen's."

"She probably had on her own extra-special scent that day," Agnes said. "As you know, Ellen was peculiar when it came to the spending as well as the saving of money. On the one hand she would hunt for bargains all over town, waiting, for example, for the post-holiday sales. Like the time she found some earmuffs at Sterns and bought a dozen pairs. Alfred didn't mind her extravagances any more than he did her so-called economies. But he said he wouldn't be found dead in earmuffs, or alive in them either. And she gave you a pair. Remember? They were too small for your ears. And a set to Sid Mercer, as I remember it, and another to Grantland Rice. And I think she gave a pair to Irma Goldberg for Rube."

"But what about that perfume?"

"She would spend a small fortune on perfumes," Agnes said, "mostly flower scents. Her dressing table looked like the toiletry counter at Altman's. She had a cut-glass bottle, pint-size I think it was, that some friend had brought from Europe—an empty bottle to begin with. When she had used up, say, half of the perfume in one of the regular bottles at hand, she would pour the rest into the cut-glass bottle. By the time she had put five or six kinds into it she would have what she called her 'extra-special brand.' "

"I wouldn't mix booze that way."

"Curiously enough," Agnes said, "she had wonderful luck with her mixtures. I think it had something to do with her character, always improvising, changing, mixing, looking for something magical. Going to fortune tellers, and asking me not to tell Alfred. He always hooted at her superstitions. They were both looking for something, I think. I know that she was."

"Are you saying their marriage went sour as early as 1918?"

"Who knows where these things begin?" Agnes said. "She didn't speak to me about it at first. But I sensed it. Her pride was great. Then one day when we were riding the bus . . . we used to take the children and go even in cold weather on top of the bus to see things best . . . Ellen liked to look into the windows of the brownstone houses to see how the Fifth Avenue millionaires lived . . . only there were drapes on most of the windows . . . and those old men with white mustaches and bald heads sitting in chairs at the club windows . . . Ellen could tell who lived where: Carnegie, Frick, and Senator Clark before his house was pulled down . . . Ellen said it had cost six million dollars; had a hundred and twenty-one rooms, four art galleries, and a theater in it. Made of granite, and a monstrosity to look at. Ellen said the old senator had some funny ideas; played Indian with feathers on his head, and rode a bicycle up and down the marble hallways . . . and oh, yes, over on Riverside Drive, the house of Charles M. Schwab, the steel man . . . I think you used to interview him. . . ."

"His private telephone number was Columbus 1324," I said.

"I can't understand," said Agnes, "how you can be so absentminded about most things, but remember a telephone number forty years back. Unless, of course, you are making it up."

"It's listed in one of those little diaries Ellen used to give me every Christmas. The *American*'s number was Beekman 2000. Runyon's home was Cathedral 6158. Only four digits in those days."

"You remember how she would speak of the chorus girls Alfred would sit up with all night?"

"He was looking for characters," I said. "Background, dialogue, atmosphere."

"That's one way to put it. . . . Yes, and we used to see all those other big houses on Riverside from the bus. The home of actress Amelia Bingham, 'The House of Statues,' where Ellen said Joseph Jefferson once lived. It had black curtains, and statues in the window."

"When you get off that bus," I said, "tell me more about Ellen's marriage troubles. I don't remember her as a sad person."

"In summer"—Agnes persisted—"we had a great time on the buses, although the Fifth Avenue mansions were boarded up. Ellen said the wooden shields looked like the doors of privies out West. The rich people escaped the heat by going to Europe or Newport or Long Island. . . . By the way, that perfume bottle, the big one: it had a cut-glass stopper. . . . Yes, she liked to laugh a lot. She said she had been deeply in love with Alfred, but the coolness began about a year or so after Brother (Damon, Junior) was born. He was only a few months old when we went to New York. Not all at once, the coolness, or so I gathered. Nobody was to blame for this, I suppose, at first. . . ."

"Did she ever give you a reason for their 'coolness'?"

"Who knows the reason for anything of this kind? Especially an outsider. I'd say it was the thing that almost always starts things downhill in marriage: loneliness."

"Loneliness," I suggested, "was par for the course in most news-papermen's homes."

"As if I didn't know," she replied. "But Alfred was seldom up and awake when anyone else was stirring. He slept until noon, read the papers, and Ellen cooked breakfast, and didn't interrupt him. Ellen taught me how to prepare bacon. Remember? Draining it on a sheet of absorbent paper to make it crisp. Alfred was very touchy about his bacon and eggs, and about a lot of other things, too. He would spend an hour in the bathroom, and another hour choosing his clothes for the afternoon. Then he'd go out on the town, or to the ball game, or where-have-you? Ellen used to wonder how a man could spend all that time in the bathroom."

"Do you recall the first thing Ellen said on the subject of estrange-ment? And the year? And I trust that you will not leave again on a bus."

"I think it was while Alfred was still in France," Agnes went on to say. "She had received a nice letter from him. I thought it a nice letter, for he asked all about you. And I know he liked you, and always felt hurt when you wouldn't take his advice. She read it to me, and held it out from her, for she was too vain to wear eyeglasses. We were going shopping that day. . . ."

"This was in 1918?" I asked.

"Ellen's maid had just brought in the mail from the downstairs box. Yes, December of 1918. Ellen said, 'He's only being polite. And he's further off than France from me. He might as well be in Siberia, even when he's here in New York.' And now she really let down her hair for a few minutes. But the next minute she was laughing, and spoke of taking baskets of food and Christmas gifts to people I never heard of before. And don't forget what happened that day she called before Christmas of 1918. The letter you made so many copies of, and she tricked you into not doing what you were going to do with that awful letter. And how she used to wonder where you got those God-awful baby sitters for little Gene. I know what you are going to say. We didn't use the term 'baby sitters' in those days. . . . So strange, isn't it? I mean Ellen making Alfred give up drinking before she would marry him. And then, of all things, her taking it up. I think that was one of the saddest things Brother wrote of in his book. You seemed so surprised when you read of it, as though it had happened only yesterday."

"Ellen didn't drink as early as 1918, did she?"

"I'd say it was some time in 1919. Maybe 1920. I knew about it, about her going to the clothes closet and getting a bottle down from the shelf. No, not getting drunk, but nipping . . . Why should I have mentioned it to you?"

"You were right. You shouldn't have."

"You thought so much of her, for one thing. And I always thought it was nice the way newspapermen of that time could have strong affections for the wives, and show it, and with nothing tacky, or involved, or . . . well, it was sort of like a great big family, where everyone loved each other honestly and above-board, and affection did not mean intrigue. How could anyone help loving Ellen, or Julie Pegler, or Kitty Rice? Even though they were all young and pretty, nobody was jealous. . . . If Ellen drank a little at first, and drank more than that when life began to go out of her, I was not going to worry you with it. I have always tried to let you keep your illusions. . . . One thing does puzzle me, and always has. . . ."

"Yes?" I said.

"It is this: You were supposed to be such a good reporter, dealing with facts, seeing all that went on with a story, putting it down, and getting well paid for the job. . . . On the other hand, you could be so hazy about certain matters that seemed plain enough to me. Why was that?"

"I don't know," I said as I turned off the tape-recorder. "I just don't know. Maybe in private life I believe only what I want to believe. Just what do you have in mind?"

"It's about that day which seems to be bothering you, and keeping you from finishing your book the way you wanted to when you set out to do it. And you have overlooked one or two other things."

"Let's have them."

"The things that you seem to *think* happened the one day Ellen called really happened on *several* days. Your facts are right, but you are mixed up in the order of them."

"Well"—and I reacted in the way anyone does when someone near to him comes up with a just criticism—"if I could find that diary Ellen gave me, the one for 1918, I could untangle things."

"There was *no* diary for that year," Agnes said. "The first one she gave you was for 1919 . . . the one you got Mr. Schwab's private telephone number from. For one thing, Mumsie [Mrs. Hubbard, Agnes's mother] was there that day. She had brought Gene from Denver a week or so before this. I can't remember what day. And the things you remember as having bothered us—and they were many—built up to that day, and to the several days afterwards."

Memory is one of the several daughters of experience—a fair-haired lady one day, and a bit of a hag the next. The memory of a memory is, in a sense, the granddaughter of experience, at times undisciplined and headstrong. My memory of the one day was the memory of a memory.

"I may not have been able to recollect much about Mark Twain," Agnes said somewhat mischievously, "but I got to be a much better reporter as I matured." Agnes then said, "Take the day off, why don't you? Go see Tommy Mitchell. He used to live in the old neighborhood when we did. Maybe Tommy can tell you what Coleridge or De Quincy would have done with your kind of story."

"They would have shot themselves," I said. "Or taken over-doses of Chinese mustard."

CHAPTER
16

If a man does not keep pace with his companions, perhaps it is because he hears a different drummer.

—THOREAU, Walden

MY LEARNED friend Thomas Mitchell said that a man looks bigger in the bathtub than he does in the ocean. We were bringing the actor's Siamese cat "Blue" home from the pet doctor's infirmary in Beverly Hills. From inside his wooden crate Blue was sending out protests which could be heard in Pumpkin Buttes, Wyoming.

Mr. Mitchell leaned over to speak into one of the air vents of the crate: "Please, Blue!" I thought for the moment that my gifted crony was about to re-enact his role in *Stagecoach*, a motion picture in which he played the part of a tippling physician with a heart of gold; he had won an "Oscar" for the portrayal. "Please stop that yowling, Blue," he pleaded. "You have been suffering for only three hours. I have suffered all my life."

I had been discussing with Mr. Mitchell the humors, the moods, the compulsions laid upon me and my present work by memories both sad and gay which came of my return to the old neighborhood after almost forty years away from it. Perhaps the presence of the plain board box, in which Blue was causing the air to take on the metaphorical color of his name, prompted the trend of my thoughts. It was very like that old board box which had yielded an assortment of keepsakes—the box of which I spoke some pages ago, and which had smelled of time. In that long-forgotten chest I had found the diary-notebooks Ellen Runyon had given me from year to year. And the old calendar page, and the newspaper clippings which my own cat Frank Moran had sniffed at with an ever-exploring nose.

My old orange and yellow cat had died. Perhaps this loss had contributed to my general state of inability to get on with the book. At any rate I stayed away a long time from my workshed—which Lucius Beebe calls "the Caboose," and Westbrook Pegler "the Wasps' Nest"—and built a rock garden and a fish pool on the hillside where Frank and I had first met. He had come up the hill that day, seemingly from nowhere, gravely wounded and almost starved. He had looked at me with the air of one old man asking of another, "Have you a place where I can stay the night?"

Jack Dempsey had wanted to give me a dog, but I said no. "He's a Boxer," said Jack.

"I wouldn't care if he were a wrestler," I replied. "I am tired of having my friends die. Why invite another heartache?"

Tommy Mitchell thinks that I come to his house to see *him*. Actually it is to see his cat Blue, a great individualist who sleeps on the kitchen stove when it is not *too* hot.

Frank Moran had liked my old board box much better than Blue seemed to be liking the one he was occupying the day we brought him home from the pet hospital. Of course his present situation was not quite the same as Frank's had been. My cat had never been a prisoner in that other box. And now, I thought, I had become a prisoner, in a manner of speaking, a prisoner confined in the seemingly escape-proof dungeon of a single morning—that eerie morning which was the surrogate for a thousand yesterdays.

My friend Mitchell is as good an audience as he is an actor, which is very good indeed. Besides, as Agnes had said, he had lived during our own time, and in our own uptown neighborhood in New York. It seems strange—although it should not—that we had lived so near to each other but did not become close friends until he and Jack Barrymore and I arrived years afterward in California.

It was in November of 1918 that I first met Barrymore (as narrated in *Good Night, Sweet Prince*). And it was then also that I first saw Tommy Mitchell. At that time Jack and Tommy were appearing in the same play at the Plymouth Theatre. Barrymore was the star of Leo Tolstoi's *Redemption* (originally *The Living Corpse*), produced by Arthur Hopkins. Mitchell's part was a slight one. He did not come on-stage until 10:15 each night.

Mr. Hopkins suggested a salary of sixty dollars a week. Mitchell, even in those days, had an eye for bargains. He offered to play three other small parts at five dollars a week each. Fine, said Mr. Hopkins.

The suddenly solvent Michell straightway bought a new suit of clothes, as well as a new coat for his pretty wife Susan. Then, unhappily, the "extra" parts were eliminated, one by one, as rehearsals progressed. The generous Mr. Hopkins afterward pegged Mitchell's pay at seventy dollars a week.

"If Blue will permit me to interrupt him," said Mitchell, "I shall point out that I did not know you then, nor had I seen Jack Barrymore until we met at the Plymouth. At the first rehearsal I thought I needed a cigarette. One of the actors gave me a light. I took this occasion to ask what kind of man Barrymore was. 'I shall sum up his character for you,' said the stranger. 'I personally would have nothing to do with him if I possibly could help myself. Shun him as you would some deplorable disease, the Outer-Mongolian rot, for example. He's the world's number-one bastard!' "

"I must have shown my amazement," Mitchell went on to say, "for this fellow suddenly smiled. He put a hand on my shoulder, then said, 'Look, old man, I mustn't risk embarrassing you. Alas! I am Barrymore.' "

At home, Mitchell released Blue from the box. The pet strode off happily, his tail up like Cape Cod, to find a plate in which

Susan Mitchell had provided enough cold chicken to feed Dizzy Dean.

Mitchell and I sat in his library, where a Whistler nocturne hangs on the paneled wall. The mist-ridden quality of the painting corresponded to my mood. I confided in Mitchell how I had tried to shake off the continuing memories of a certain day.

"I still seem to be standing outside my flat," I said. "If I stay there much longer I'll get pneumonia, and my book will go down the drain. I am the victim of filigree and digression."

"All life is full of digressions," replied the actor-playwright art connoisseur. "Life itself is one large digression. Sir Walter Raleigh said as much three hundred and umpty-umpty years ago." He then went on to say, "I have just finished reading that magazine article by Lucius Beebe in which he says there is a bit of Don Quixote in your blood. As to the morning you mention, it would appear that you were once again tilting at the windmills of your youth."

One of the windmills I was tilting at when Ellen Runyon called upon us in that December of 1918 was the "letter" that Agnes mentioned in the preceding chapter. There were many other conflicting matters, but to set down an orderly account of them is not to be expected of my brown pen. It would be like bringing a sieve to a drinking bout.

A week or so before Ellen called at our home, I had gone downtown an hour earlier than the usual time to ask a favor of Victor Watson. My mother-in-law and Gene, Junior, were to arrive at Grand Central station that same day. I wanted to be excused from work to meet the boy. I also would like to have the next day off to become reacquainted with him. Although the Hetman was operating with a depleted force of reporters, what with the flu epidemic at its worst, he granted my request.

As I was passing Max's Busy Bee en route to the subway, I heard my name called out by someone with a very hoarse voice. I turned in the direction from which the reedy greeting had come, to see two shabby fellows standing beside a battered charcoal oven. As I went over to them my nose sampled the fumes of roast chestnuts. The charred nuts were sending up wispy smoke signals from the ancient grill.

Other noses than mine find this an almost poetic odor, whether in New York or in Paris. My nose reports it as a sickening rancidity, like that of an abandoned floral piece. However mistaken my nose may be, I have a selective ear for voices. When one of the fellows again addressed me in a kind of stage whisper, I seemed to know that voice.

It belonged to the proprietor of the chestnut concession, Dr. DeGarmo. The great healer's appearance had changed a great deal since I last had met him—and not for the better, I must say—the time Damon Runyon introduced us at this same Park Row curbside. By now he had grown a stubble beard. That part of his face which could be seen looked like biscuit dough upon which bits of steel wool had been spilled. The metamorphosed doctor had on a faded blue cap, with fur sideboards lowered to hide his ears. A kind of Abraham Lincoln shawl, moth-eaten and grimy, muffled his neck and draped the shoulders of a much-too-large ulster. The overcoat was held together in front with horse-blanket pins.

"Hello," I said. "Doctor DeGarmo?"

He scotched this Stanley–Dr. Livingstone approach. "My license was issued to 'Anthony Gondolfo,' if you don't mind."

I didn't mind at all, and said so. Dr. DeGarmo, alias Anthony Gondolfo, introduced me to his companion. "Mr. Fowler," he said, "this is Pat Crowe, an old schoolmate. I want that you two good people should know each other."

I shook hands with a thick-set fellow of perhaps fifty years of age. He had blue eyes, somewhat bloodshot, thin white eyebrows, a broad face the color of weathered brick, unwrinkled and masquerading with innocence. I thought that Mr. Crowe smelled of booze, but it might have been that the chestnuts had prejudiced my nostrils.

"At your service," said Mr. Crowe.

It would be just the other way around for the next few years, but of course I could not foresee that inconvenience.

"The name," I said, as we shook hands, "used to appear in headlines."

Mr. Crowe seemed elated by this remark. "The gentlemen of the press," he said, "mentioned me quite often after I kidnaped the Cudahy boy; got a big ransom; spent it. Then I was turned in by a dame." He frowned momentarily. "Just can't trust your sweethearts with a private secret. Oh, well . . ."

In the early part of the century—I forget the year—Pat Crowe had been notorious as the kidnaper of the young son of meat-packer Edward Cudahy. Mr. Crowe served a long term in prison.

"Pat Crowe," his schoolmate volunteered, "has other interests at the moment. Rather, he *had* them until he was fired as night watchman of the Salvation Army hut in Union Square. A false charge of being drunk while on duty. He now wants to give lectures on temperance and on the evil fruits of crime. And I thought that you might lend Mr. Crowe a sawbuck to tide him over. Business is not what it should be with me."

Business was not good with me, either. I was still paying my Denver creditors, and had sent Mrs. Hubbard enough money to bring my child to New York. However, I had a few one-dollar bills in my pocket. I gave Mr. Crowe three of them.

"May God rain down his mercy upon you!" said Mr. Crowe.

Ex-Doctor DeGarmo sought to present me with some chestnuts. I said not to bother about it. He insisted upon telling my fortune. "I do it with nuts," he explained. "I give a customer a reading of their future. Like the auspices the Roman big shots used to get from the Angel of Delphi in Sardinia."

This rogue's "gimmick," not to mention his somewhat garbled reference to ancient practices, enchanted me. "All right," I said. "What do the nuts say?"

The sooty warlock began to flick the hot chestnuts into geometric patterns on the grill. "Well, well, now!" said the soothsayer. He inhaled some of the fumes of the oven. "A great statesman is

going to die soon. You are *not* going to go on that voyage. Damon
Runyon is thinking about you, and hoping that you will be able to
do better by Pat Crowe next time."

"Like hell he is!" I said. "Maybe if you can give Damon the
winners at Belmont when it re-opens, he will pay attention to your
omens."

"What do you hear from our good friend?" The hoarse-voiced
Merlin of the charcoal oven seemed to take no offense at my remarks. "Is Mr. Runyon in touch with you?"

"I just read his articles from day to day," I said. "Why don't
you get in touch with him by reading the chestnuts?"

He turned to Mr. Crowe. "What a sense of humor! Just like Bill
Mizner! Not a care in the world."

That's what *he* thought.

I took a subway train uptown to Grand Central to find Mrs.
Hubbard and the baby waiting near the information booth. The
child had a cold. I held him in my arms all the way home.

"I don't think I'm going to like this hell-hole of a place," said
Mrs. Hubbard as we were riding along in a taxicab. She would like
New York still less in the hours ahead.

At the time when Agnes rented our flat, she had neglected to tell
the landlord that we had an infant son. Babies or dogs—in that
order—were unwelcome in most New York apartments within our
price range.

Our child was cross and colic-plagued. At a late hour, he awakened and would not go to sleep again. He began to cry. I must
admit that this eighteen-month-old boy had the loudest lungs
this side of Texas. The neighbors began to pound upon the steam
pipes. Two or three of them opened their bedroom windows which
faced the court to make suggestions of an impolite sort. One of
these gentlemen implied that Agnes and I had neglected to take
out a marriage license.

Early the next day our landlord, a most amiable man of middle
years, appeared at our doorway. He wore a swallow-tail coat and
starched collar with wings supporting a shallow chin. He suggested

that we had engaged in duplicity by not having told him that we were parents.

"The situation must be remedied," he said. "I shall not ask that you leave at once."

"This man's calling you a liar!" Mrs. Hubbard said to me. She turned upon him with "That's dangerous business where *we* come from."

"My good madam," the landlord said to her, "I am not interested in where *you* came from. It's where you are *going*. And you are going *out* of here not later than January first."

He bowed, then left with the air of an attorney who has just won a case in the court of general sessions.

"Why, the sanctimonious old skinflint!" said Mrs. Hubbard.

The state of siege worsened that night and the next. The cries of the child, the banged steampipes, the bomb bursts of electric-light bulbs dropped among love-frenzied cats in the apartment court, the loud threats to call the police—it was a re-enactment of the Battle of Harlem Heights as fought on this same ground in 1776.

Agnes was worn out from lack of sleep and from trying to find a place for us to move to by January 1. I had to go to work each day, and Mrs. Hubbard was supposed to visit some dying Missourian in Teaneck, New Jersey. Until then I had thought that Missourians never died.

One morning just before sunup I announced to the small garrison of our Alamo that I was getting tired of the loud-mouthed slurs on my family tree. I was going to make a sortie. I would knock upon the enemy's doors and invite the neighbors—come one, come all—to meet me for a series of duels on the staircase.

"Spoken like a man!" said my mother-in-law, who feared no one. And I, who feared no one but my mother-in-law, said, "Glad you are with me on this."

Agnes said no to this plan of mine. She oftentimes annoyed me with her readiness to see the other fellow's side of an argument. "The baby *does* have a loud voice," she said.

Loud? It had a penetrating quality such as I have heard but once since that time. It was in Damascus some years afterward (1935, I think), when my family and I were quartered across the narrow street from a mosque. At daylight of our first morning in the scorpion-infested hotel, I was sleeping under some mosquito netting, as were my two sons. A muezzin in the crow's-nest of a minaret of the mosque sent forth a shrieking summons for the faithful to pray. I leaped out of bed, thinking that someone had caught his scrotum in the lawnmower.

In my bewildered haste I had taken the mosquito netting with me. I stood like a frustrated beekeeper beside the boys' bed. "Listen," I said to the elder one, as the prayer caller continued with his holy yells. "*That* is exactly how *you* used to cry!"

Mrs. Hubbard went to Teaneck. I went to work each afternoon, and did not get home until midnight. Agnes was having a hard time taking care of the fort. Mrs. Runyon, to be sure, would have supplied reinforcements, but it happened that she had gone to Great Neck, Long Island, to manage some friend's affairs.

"It is an epidemic of 'necks,'" I said to Agnes. I pointed upward, not to heaven, but in the general direction of the enraged tenants. "And there are going to be some broken necks if this keeps up."

Hell always seems to do its best for a man when he needs sleep and peace of mind. At the *American* office all that week I seemed to draw the most trivial and tedious assignments. Many of the "leg men" were down with influenza. The copy desk also was short-handed. One day I was pressed into service on "the rim," as the copy desk is called. But I had enough ingenuity to escape after one hour of *that*, and I saw to it that I never would be asked to read copy again. Never.

I was a first-rate copyreader and headline writer, what with my experience on the sports desk in Denver. Also I had been the editor of a weekly newspaper there, the *Great Divide*. But in my day the copy desk was regarded as journalism's Boot Hill. Some of the most scholarly gentlemen I have known were copy editors, but seemed unable as a rule to gain promotion. Ill health sometimes kept a gifted newspaperman on this job. It allowed him regular hours for a sedentary occupation. Then, too, a very able man might have had a drinking problem and been demoted to the "rim."

On the day I was asked to "fill in" at the copy desk, the man in the "slot," the head copyreader, was Captain Marryat. Offhand I forget his first name. I should not forget it, in view of the hilarious episode which occurred at a later time, when I became the captain's managing editor.

Captain Marryat was a dignified English scholar of middle years. He never smiled, so far as I know, and spoke with quiet irony of the "illiteracy existing not only among readers of Hearst newspapers, but also among Hearst reporters." He rode a bicycle to the office, all the way from his home in the Bronx, until age, diabetes, and the increase in motor vehicles combined to thwart that exercise. He was said to have worsted the great Brisbane in an all-night session of stud poker years ago on the *World*. This was an unforgivable act of insubordination. For A.B. regarded himself as a great poker player, and lost money to prove it.

During my first half-hour on the desk I made every mistake known to the trade, and even improvised a few. I had trouble with the copy pencils. I broke the leads again and again. I almost stabbed myself with the long-billed scissors—or so it would appear. I upset my pastepot. As to the pieces of copy dealt me by Captain Marryat, I allowed mistakes in punctuation, misspellings, and possibly libelous statements to pass. I saw the captain watching me as I bungled, faltered, and messed up the Associated Press "flimsy." At length the captain could stand no more of this. I had written a headline which was supposed to fit a two-column space on the page. It was so "fat" that it could not have been ramrodded into the mouth of a Civil War cannon.

The captain took me to one side. "You may safely confide in me. Have you ever, until today, held a pencil and a sheet of paper in your hand? Can you even read?"

I left the copy desk forever behind me that day. I was immediately given a series of piddling assignments. One of them was to investigate the mystery of a man's death in a Staten Island boarding house. It was no mystery. He left a suicide note which contained the best reason for one's self-destruction I have ever come upon, in or out of literature. "I can't stand to live any longer," the note said, "because Laura [presumably his beloved] wants me to shave every day."

One of my assignments, however, during this week of drab drudgery caught my fancy. The Hetman asked me to interview a woman who had been bothering him with telephone calls for three days. She had kept insisting that Mr. Hearst save her from the evil deeds of a witch whose cat had stolen her soul.

She lived alone in a converted brownstone mansion near West End Avenue. I was admitted there after much unbolting of locks, and I went inside to see a wispy woman of perhaps sixty years. She was quite refined in manner and neat in appearance, and her face had been spared many of the cross-hatch wrinkles that age employs in its caricatures of yesterday's belles. She invited me to tea.

Over the teacups she explained that a cat now owned her soul. The animal had been prompted to commit this vile theft by a witch who lived next door. Mr. Hearst, she went on to say, was known far and wide as a great humanitarian. How could she get in touch with him?

I was unfamiliar with the laws of catanthropy, but I wanted very much to help this lovely person. I asked to be excused for a while. I then went to a United Cigar store to telephone the ever-obliging Dr. Menas Gregory of Bellevue. Luckily he was in. He told me what I should do. For one thing, I was to get some fresh liver, then lure the cat to the premises of the afflicted woman.

When I returned with the liver and the secret instructions of the great psychiatrist, the old lady grew suspicious. I managed at length to persuade her to leave the door ajar and to sit very quietly as far away from the plate of liver as the dimensions of the room permitted. I said nothing about Dr. Gregory or his instructions.

It was a long wait. The troubled woman sat like Whistler's mother in a very old chair, and I near her. And now we had a visitor. A carefully inquisitive cat, with a gray head the size of a sofa pillow, came halfway inside the doorway. This cat was in no hurry at all. It drew back when the woman's chair squeaked. After several feints, the animal showed all its gray body in a slow progress toward the plate of liver.

Very gently I addressed it in a speech composed by Dr. Gregory, but embellished a bit. The cat at first seemed uneasy, but did not wish to forego a free meal.

"I do not know your name, sir," I said in substance, "but I shall call you Grimalkin. You have committed a most terrible crime, the stealing of this lady's soul. I must remind you that she is the widow of one of General Robert E. Lee's lieutenants."

Grimalkin was looking at me in a most skeptical way, and then at the liver. "I demand of you"—and I was using an even milder tone than before—"that you surrender up this good woman's soul." I did not like to startle such a fine gray cat, but I suddenly raised my voice, and got up from my chair. "If you don't do as I say, I'll send you to the public pound!"

The cat scurried off like an interrupted safe-cracker. My hostess slumped in her chair. I closed the door, then applied a napkin dipped in lukewarm tea to the lady's temples. She regained her composure in a few moments, and told me that her soul was restored. She said that only a young man of the purest heart and of spotless character could have been Heaven's intermediary.

I thought that she overstated things—not much, but a little bit. I thanked her for seeing virtues in me that the rest of the world had somehow overlooked.

"There is only one thing," she said as she showed me to the door.

"Yes?" I asked.

She wagged a forefinger. "You shouldn't have told the cat a lie. I am *not* a widow." And her fine eyes took on a sad expression as she said, "My fiancé died the day before we were to be married."

At the newspaper office one afternoon Victor Watson said that he had an assignment that was "bigger than the Armistice."

"I am going to invade Europe," he announced. "The Twenty-seventh is waiting for ships to bring them home. We must let these brave fellows know that Mr. Hearst and New York are grateful."

About this time the Hetman, acting for Mr. Hearst—or so he claimed—had asked the governor-elect, Alfred E. Smith, to name Mr. Hearst as chairman of the welcoming committee to greet the home-coming soldiers and sailors of New York. Mr. Smith had replied (Charles Hand, at that time a member of the *World* political staff, told me of this) that he would not appoint Mr. Hearst to the committee, "or even as an assistant to the assistant dog-catcher."

Mr. Hearst had been lukewarm toward Al Smith's gubernatorial candidacy in the campaign of 1918. The governor-elect may well have had that in mind when asked to promise the publisher a place on the welcoming committee. Several commentators have sought the underlying reason for Hearst's seemingly unprovoked attacks on Governor Smith which began as early as 1919.

Some years after the 1919 diatribes appeared (1927) Norman Hapgood and Henry Moskowitz wrote a biography of Al Smith (*Up from the City Streets*). Mr. Smith then was aspiring to the White House. In this book the authors gave the soldiers' committee snub as a reason for Hearst's first attacks on Al Smith. Some months after the book appeared I asked Norman Hapgood to "fill me in" on this circumstance.

At that time (1928) I was managing editor of the New York

Morning Telegraph (not a Hearst newspaper). The *Telegraph* was supporting Mr. Smith's bid for the Presidency. Hapgood was one of our contributing editors.

Norman Hapgood was then about sixty years old. He had had a distinguished career as a writer and editor for several national magazines, the last one having been *Hearst's International*. He had courage, insight, and integrity.

Mr. Hapgood was a somewhat frail man physically, and a food faddist. On the day I have in mind we were having lunch at the Century Club. Vegetarian Hapgood ordered a baked potato and stewed tomatoes, which he "blended" in a fierce-looking mixture on a large plate. He invited me to try this concoction, which I did. Not too bad. Not too good, either.

"Mr. Hearst," Hapgood said, "has one of the world's most retentive memories for insults to his pride. I would not be surprised to learn that his violent attitude towards England had its inception in some mere social slight by the Court of St. James's. When Al Smith refused to name him as a member of the welcome-home committee, it rankled Mr. Hearst. Then, as we all know, the attacks continued. Finally the Hearst newspapers implied that Governor Smith was in league with gangster elements to take over New York's milk supply. Al Smith's ill and aging mother saw one of these articles in the Hearst press. It was made to appear that Smith was responsible for keeping milk from undernourished babies of the poor. It was then that Smith unlimbered his own heavy artillery against Hearst."

I always seem to remember just what a man ate, and how he did it, at times when I should have been paying more attention to matters of professional concern. If I were a gourmet I might be able to understand this quirk in my character. My friend Lucius Beebe, himself a recognized authority on food and wines, winces whenever I order a hamburger or ham and eggs in preference to something magnificent prepared by some great chef. On one occasion (at Chambord, I think it was) Mr. Beebe seemed on the point of calling the police when I happened to say that nothing is as delicious as a bowl of fresh, cool milk and sugared soda crackers at one o'clock in the morning.

My gift of memory for foods and the eaters of it, brings me back to the day Victor Watson called me to his office just before Christmas of 1918. The Hetman, as I have said, was a heavy eater. He particularly liked rice pudding for breakfast. He was having *two* dishes of rice pudding in his office that day. Marty, the office boy, had brought these puddings from a nearby Childs restaurant.

The Hetman frequently had his meals served in his office, was barbered there, and on occasion had a cot set up for catnaps whenever one of his stories grew "bigger than the Armistice." These gestures patently were made to show Mr. Hearst that the captain was always on the bridge when the seas got rough.

On one occasion the Hetman had an infected leg. It became swollen to the proportions of a fire hydrant. He would not leave the office, however, all week long. (I think it was during his bucket-shop campaign.) Mr. Watson slept in his clothes during that entire week. He slit a trouser leg to permit easy access by the doctor to the bandaging of the infected limb.

He was limping one day, and leaning on a cane, when Ed Klauber of the *Times* visited me at the office. The Hetman's flapping trouser leg reminded Klauber of the way a victim is prepared for the electric chair at Sing Sing.

"Is your editor on his way to the death house?" Klauber asked me.

The Hetman overheard the remark. "Leave here at once!" he said to my friend. "I think you are spying for the *Times*."

Mr. Watson was suspicious of callers from other newspapers— unjustly so. It was part of our code never to divulge anything seen or overheard in an opposition editorial room—that is, until the ball of fire Walter Howey became a New York editor in 1924. For some years before that time Mr. Howey had turned Chicago upside down, and a bit sideways, too, with slam-bang methods of newsgathering. I shall write of this presently, and of the time when

I was his sports editor on the *Mirror* in an age of great champions.

On the day of the Hetman's rice puddings in 1918, he spoke of Mr. Hearst's devotion to the fighting men of the Twenty-seventh. He said that the Chief's love of country was even deeper than that of Cincinnatus, Cicero, or Barbara Frietchie. He studied me through his thick lenses, as though trying to ascertain a sign of my mental reservations.

Then he announced, "I am sending you and Jack Winkler to France to interview the gallant lads of the Twenty-seventh and accompany them on the first troop ships to sail home."

"What about Runyon?" I asked. "Isn't he taking care of that?"

"When I need your advice," he said, "I shall apply for it immediately. I am having certain troubles at the moment, but assigning my men to stories is not one of them."

"About a military permit?" I asked. "And expense money?"

"All in due time," he said. "As for expenses, Mr. Hearst is most generous. But he doesn't aim to outfit you for an Arctic expedition. That's Runyon's trouble. Spends Mr. Hearst's money like Death Valley Scotty. Takes a big trunk with him even on the baseball trips. There's a limit. Now get your house in order. I'll keep you advised."

The *American* reporters used to go to Childs restaurant after their assignments at one o'clock each afternoon. This branch of Childs stood at the corner of Park Row and Chambers in the shadow of the old Third Avenue "El." Later on in the day we had meetings in one of the saloons, often at Mike Iorio's, where the free-lunch items were listed on a blackboard. Staff artists frequently drew cartoons on that board. Two of them, Winsor McCay and Joe McGurk of Philadelphia, would collaborate on these bawdy pictures, mostly of Hearst executives. I was sometimes asked to write captions in verse.

I was about to quote from one of these captions; but perhaps I should not. I almost lost my job because of it. The cartoon showed one of our great editors collapsing when about to receive an honorary degree from a certain university. I shall merely set down one line of the slanderous ode:

He suffered paresis while writing his thesis. . . .

I dropped in at Childs on my way home from having been assigned to France. I thought that Pat Crowe was following me, but could not be sure. I went inside the restaurant to see at one of the porcelain-topped tables two of Park Row's best reporters: Jack Winkler and Joseph Mulvaney. I was anxious to ask Winkler's advice as to our overseas assignment, and also hear what my good friend Mulvaney might have to say of it.

Joe Mulvaney was a lean and quiet Irishman of immense wisdom and reportorial insight. A most temperate man, both in his personal habits and in his criticism of the other fellow, he still liked to hear all the office gossip. Joe resided happily in Brooklyn with his pretty wife Florence and one son. Mulvaney, I believe, originally came from someplace near Pittsfield, Massachusetts, but had taken on the speech habits of Brooklyn. He carried a blackthorn stick, wore pince-nez on a short nose, and in winter appeared in a somewhat large overcoat with a fur collar.

The Park Row achievements of John Kennedy Winkler (who died only last year) are still well remembered by the Silurians. Some of his contemporaries say that he was "the greatest reporter" of us all.

The term "greatest" gets more abuse than an icebox door. Brisbane used the word when writing of Runyon. Stanley Walker applied it to Alva Johnston. Editor Frank Pope said it of Walter Davenport. Editor Chester Hope has referred to the excellent James L. Kilgallen (Dorothy's father) in the superlative. And I am tempted to say it of this one today, and of that one tomorrow, from Saint Matthew down to Bob Considine and Jim Bishop.

I believe that *any* notable reporter was "greatest" on a day when he was at his best, and when the story was "up his alley" and the news broke in his direction. Suppose we settle for the term "great" in respect to Winkler, or to Herbert Bayard Swope—or even to *me*.

Winkler was a jovial, athletic young man. He had the complexion of an old English saddle because of his open-air pursuits of golf, swimming, and the rest. His tan lasted well into the winter months, a time when most New Yorkers have a prison pallor.

Winkler never *seemed* to take his work seriously—a most deceptive façade, as when, later on, he beat the town with the news of the Stillman divorce scandal.

Winkler was about a year younger than I. Born in Camden, South Carolina, he had come to New York ten years before I arrived there to go to work on the *American*. He retired from the newspaper field in 1925 to begin a career as a biographer of William Randolph Hearst, John D. Rockefeller, Sr., and J. P. Morgan.

Reporters Winkler and Mulvaney were having oyster stews ("erster," as Mr. Mulvaney pronounced it in Brooklynese) when I came upon them at Childs. When I spoke to Jack about our assignment to France, I was unprepared for his loud laughter.

"You don't mean to say that you take the Hetman seriously!" And Winkler turned to Mulvaney. "Joe, get out your notebook. Take a letter to Runyon. Tell him his Denver boy has a wild gleam in his eye."

Runyon once said that I arrived in New York "with a wild gleam in one eye, and a still wilder gleam in the other."

"I am proceeding on the assumption that we are going to France," I said to Winkler. "Why not?"

"Forget it," he replied. "As for me, I shall enjoy two or three days off, or until the Hetman recovers his poise, then return quite refreshed to my galley oar." He went on to say, "Our Mr. Watson is having some big emotional storms, an affair of the heart. A one-sided matter, I must say. The lady wants no part of him."

To refresh my memory, I wrote to Jack in 1956. In a letter of September 9 of that year he replied in part:

"Re Vic Watson: I knew the guy first when some of us reporters still packed those big, heavy box cameras, doubling in brass as it were. And as the years progressed it was hard but not impossible to find some grains of gold amid the blubber and the bluff. But oh, my! He would snore and snort and writhe like a mountain in heat!"

As to the one-sided "romance" which Winkler had mentioned long ago, he said in his letter to me: "Watson pulled a silly stunt on Norma Talmadge, one of the several women for whom the Hetman (at periodic intervals) professed undying adoration. On this occasion, Vic drove N.T. from his mother's home in the Broadway section of Flushing, wooing madly. When the car approached the Bridge driveway, Watson's mood changed. He guided the car down the sharp declivity leading to the East River and suddenly demanded that Norma pledge marriage then and there or he would plunge the machine into the drink and to certain death, and take the lady with him. Gawd! Norma talked him out of this. . . . I thought later on that Vic might have carried out the dire threat, for a suicidal strain ran in his bloodstream or his brain."

I left Winkler and Mulvaney at Childs. When I arrived home, Agnes asked me to take care of the baby while she looked for an apartment. Mrs. Von Der Heyde, wife of the owner of a grocery store on Amsterdam Avenue, had told Agnes of a forthcoming vacancy across the street from St. John's.

"I have our dinner in the icebox," said Agnes. "Cold roast beef, potato salad, apple pie, and, of course, the baby's bottle."

She had been gone but a few minutes when the door buzzer sounded. It was Pat Crowe. He said somewhat sheepishly that he had "tailed" me home from Childs. He had found a subway ticket and made use of it, but had no money at all.

"Food has not passed my lips since the day before yesterday," said the ex-kidnaper. His false teeth made a sound like the cocking of a shotgun. "May I impose upon your good will?"

I invited Mr. Crowe to help himself at the icebox, explaining that I had not more than sixty cents at the moment. My guest made three or four trips to the kitchen.

Agnes returned an hour or so later. Mr. Crowe was holding the child on his lap. The boy seemed very happy. Mr. Crowe was saying that the "very intelligent child soon will be playing patty-cake."

Soon after I had introduced Mr. Crowe to my wife, she beckoned to me from the doorway of the kitchen. "Your friend," she said, "has eaten the whole roast, most of the bread, and two-thirds of the potato salad."

"The poor guy is starved," I said.

"He doesn't *look* starved," Agnes said. "What are *we* going to do for dinner?"

"Get something from the delicatessen."

"I haven't any money. Have you?"

"Sixty cents, I think."

"Well," Agnes said, "Mr. Crowe seems to be a kindly man. And the baby seems fond of him. Who *is* he? Someone you knew in Denver?"

"He is just an old fellow down on his luck," I replied. "Hasn't had a break since he kidnaped the Cudahy boy."

Agnes seemed stunned. "And you let him play with our baby?"

"He's reformed," I said. "Besides, he loves children."

"Do me a favor," Agnes said. "Get rid of him."

I did not "get rid" of good old Pat for years. He called on me frequently at the newspaper office. Sometimes he would come there when I was writing a story. I used to go right ahead with my work, first having asked Pat to tell me the story of the Cudahy kidnaping. I paid no attention whenever he went into his long recital. As a matter of fact, I never remembered any of the story other than the beginning of it:

"It was a very stormy day when I waited in a buggy. . . ."

One evening, just before the first edition went to press, Pat came in roaring drunk. I was writing the story of a New Jersey explosion (the state was always being blown up, it seemed) and editor Martin Dunn was concerned with my meeting the deadline. Marty, the head office boy, was taking my story, page by page, and then paragraph by paragraph, to Mr. Dunn's desk.

The always courteous Mr. Dunn saw Pat Crowe sitting beside me, gabbing away as I was writing. The editor almost lost his grip

on himself. He came over to us, to say to Mr. Crowe, "You'll have
to stop bothering Mr. Fowler. Can't you see that he has work to
do?"

I rose up from my chair with the manner of an affronted social
leader. "If you please, Mr. Dunn! Mr. Crowe is my guest. I demand
that you apologize!"

Two of our strongest reporters, Robert Watson, a political writer
and one-time worker in the steel mills, and Jack Winkler, seized
Mr. Crowe by the elbows and propelled him outside the room.

The night Mr. Crowe was at our house, Mrs. Hubbard returned
from Teaneck. Mrs. Runyon, home again from Great Neck, said
she would be over to see us the next morning.

We had no sleep at all that night. Early in the morning I
answered a loud knock upon our door. I went outside to find the
hallway empty. I chanced to see an envelope protruding part way
from the slot of our mailbox, one of sixteen metal boxes arranged
against one wall of the foyer.

I brought this unstamped envelope into the living room. As I
read the unsigned note, I contemplated the slaying of the anon-
ymous writer. The note said, "Why don't you take that screaming
brat out and drown him?"

"Don't do anything you'll be sorry for," Agnes said.

"I'm going to smoke out this bastard," I said.

I sat down at my typewriter to write a letter. I made copies of it.
I do not remember the wording. I wrote, among other things, that
my correspondent was a lineal descendant of King Herod—illegit-
imate, of course. I also recommended that the writer of the note
make an immediate appointment with his dentist. For I promised
to bash in his teeth. I signed my name to each copy.

I could find but two envelopes. I placed a copy of the letter in
each one. "I am going out to get some more envelopes," I said to
Agnes, "and pick up the morning papers."

It was on my way back from the newsstand and stationery store
that I met Ellen Runyon. Agnes told her of the letters I had
composed. She then asked Ellen to "talk me out of it."

"I think Gene is entirely within his rights," Ellen said. I was elated by this. I did not know that Ellen's flattery was a part of her strategy to block my purpose.

The telephone rang. It was the Hetman. He asked that I report to him at once, hours earlier than the usual time for assignments. I was to come to his home in Flushing, and waste no time in doing so.

"I'm going to address these letters first," I said to the ladies of my garrison.

Agnes almost caught me off base with a question. "Suppose," she said, "that a *woman* sent you that note?"

My mother-in-law saved me from a put-out by saying, "*I'll* take care of the hussy!" And I am sure that she could have done so. She was of the pioneer tradition.

"Let us do this," said Field Marshal Ellen Runyon, "and it will simplify everything." She turned to me. "You get right along to Flushing, and let *me* handle the distribution of the notes. One in every box. Right?"

"Good enough," I said. I picked up the two envelopes I already had prepared. "I'll drop these in boxes seven and eleven—good dice numbers. And thanks a lot, Ellen."

The Hetman was having some cheesecake and a pack of Piedmont cigarettes when I reported to him in Flushing, Long Island. It was my first but by no means my last visit to this well-appointed home. Notwithstanding his reputation as a hatchet man, Watson was a gracious host. Members of his staff frequently had breakfast with him at his suburban place. Today he had as his guest Nat J. Ferber, an *American* reporter whom I liked very much. Ferber had the mind of a rabbi and looked like comedian Ed Wynn.

Ferber afterward became a writer of novels. He had been an athlete, a long-distance swimmer, but quit the water when defeated by a one-legged man in a race from Coney Island to the Battery. He said that it had been a most humiliating experience. Nat also had been a public accountant, a matter which made it easier for him to find fictions in the ledgers kept by crooked auditors. In 1923, with Carl Helm, a fellow reporter, Ferber uncovered the piratical actions of the Wall Street firm of Fuller & McGee, as well as those of other bucketshop firms. Fuller & McGee was represented by attorney William J. Fallon (*The Great Mouthpiece*), one of the most brilliant but misguided criminal lawyers of the 1920s.

The bucketshop scandal was an impressive newsbeat. It also had strange, unforeseen effects upon the careers of persons other than the stock riggers. The conviction of Fuller and McGee was a costly victory for Victor Watson. In destroying the career of lawyer Fallon, a years-long enemy of Watson, the Hetman was unknowingly preparing his own downfall. I shall have something to say about this at a later time: how he lost face with Mr. Hearst, and took another long downward step toward his personal tragedy.

As Runyon used to say, "Mr. Hearst giveth, and Mr. Hearst taketh away."

On the morning when I called at Flushing in the winter of 1918, the Hetman was six years this side of his frustration. He was dressed like a mandarin that day. As I remember it, he had on a gold-brocade blue dressing gown, pajamas of an awesome hue, and a pair of soft leather boots of Russian design. He seemed to be lacking only a fan and an opium pipe.

I watched the Hetman and Mr. Ferber eat cheesecake. I spoke of the letter, and the copies of it, which I had written to the tenants of my apartment house.

"Never put anything in writing," said the Hetman. "But maybe we can still work out something to bring your landlord to terms: get City Hall to slap a health violation on the place, or order him to install an extra fire escape, or build a new roof, or perhaps give him a fat increase in taxes."

"It's not the landlord," I said. I suddenly remembered something. "May I call up my home?" I wanted to tell Ellen Runyon not to put a letter in the landlord's box.

I was unable to get through to my number. The telephone stayed out of order for the rest of the morning. I did what I usually do when I slip on one of my own banana peelings: sat there like a stunned jackass for several moments, then said the hell with it. I returned to the breakfast table, where the Hetman was having one of his semiannual jokes.

"I was just telling Nat here," the Hetman explained, "that he ought to send his wife over to your flat to take care of those tenants."

Nat smiled. The joke was lost on me. Some months afterward, I met Mrs. Ferber for the first time. I found it hard to believe that anyone so young and pretty and so gay was in reality a ball of fire. I took an immediate liking to her. She was as generous as her husband—which is saying a great deal—and over the years of our friendship I never knew her to lose her temper or say an unkind thing. And *this* was that same young lady who in 1914 invaded the private offices of John D. Rockefeller, Jr., at the Standard Oil building on lower Broadway, threatened to kill him, and was arrested.

Mrs. Ferber's maiden name was Marie Ganz. During the Colorado coal strike (which I reported for my Denver newspaper in 1914) Miss Ganz made speeches against the Rockefellers. She defied the police in Union Square, and continued her orations at the Free Speech Forum. She became known as "Sweet Marie."

Eventually the attempted-murder charge against Mrs. Ferber was changed to one of disorderly conduct, but Sweet Marie spent some time in the workhouse. It was during this episode that Ferber—a reporter on the story—met, fell in love with, then married Sweet Marie. I remember her with great affection.

If I am not mistaken, I was godfather to the Ferbers' daughter, Lenore, a lovely child. At any rate, I used to hold her on my knee. Nowadays I sometimes see the grown women, the children of my newspaper cronies, and think back to the times when I looked upon them as I did my own. There were Jim Kilgallen's baby girl Dorothy, now a celebrated newspaperwoman, and Florence Rice ("Floncey"), the most beautiful child I ever saw, and the daughter of Slim Farnsworth; and Sid Mercer's, and Jack Dempsey's little girls . . . and so many others. . . .

At the Hetman's breakfast table in Flushing, after he had put his sense of humor back in mothballs, he said, "Now, gentlemen, let us turn our minds to Mr. Hearst's enterprises. I have a most amazing idea to build circulation. Our daily circulation is slipping, and only the Sunday paper has leadership in the field—the tail wagging the dog, so to speak. Listen carefully: everyone wants to be young and to stay that way, or else find a way to change back from old age to youth."

"Uh-huh," I said. This was the best reply to the Hetman whenever he was incubating. In fact, it was the only possible reply.

"Let's not leap into this thing unprepared," he went on to say, "but keep it very confidentially in the front of your minds. It has to do with monkey glands. Do I make myself clear?"

"Could you be more explicit?" I asked.

"Nothing is more explicit than a man's glands," he said. "Glands move the world. What would *you* be without glands?"

"Less restless," I said.

"The day will come to you," he said, "and to you, too, Nat, as it does to every man, even to a horse, when he wishes he was once again snorting and pawing the ground." He grew very serious. "A foreign surgeon named Doctor Serge Voronoff has been using monkey glands to do wonderful things for old men. Rejuvenation! I want you to keep an eye out for some fine, deserving old chap who wants to turn back his clock."

I was tempted to make a pun here, but told Satan to stand behind me. "Does this mean I am not going to France with Jack Winkler?" I inquired.

"Nothing of the sort"—and the Hetman tapped a small gong as a signal for the servant to clear the table of its dishes. "David Belasco gave me this antique gong," he said. "Mr. Belasco has many Oriental treasures. You ought to see his collection of jade."

"Then the trip to France is still on?" I persisted. "I have to make a lot of plans. And some expense money."

"What is your idea of expense money?"

"Twelve hundred dollars will just about take care of everything."

I thought that the one-time accountant, Nat Ferber, was about to go into a coma. As for the Hetman, he began a frantic search among the folds of his robe for the lighted end of his Piedmont. It had fallen when I mentioned the twelve hundred.

Mr. Watson put out the live coal just in time to save his robe from damage. "Are you suggesting that Mr. Hearst pay off the national debt?"

It *was* a lot of money for that long-ago time. Just to refresh my recollection of things such as the national debt, I wrote to M. Vilas Hubbard, a Federal Reserve man and president of the Citizens Bank of Pasadena, for some official figures. He replied that the total gross national debt in June of 1919 was $25.5 billion, and in February of 1959, $285.2 billion. My request for that twelve hundred may now look small in comparison, but I do believe that someone in Washington plagiarized my expense-account methods, and thereby made possible the modern-day national policy of spend-it-all-and-more—a splendid philosophy, indeed.

"If I go to France," I said to the Hetman, "it means I shall have to send my son back to Denver, buy equipment, luggage, clothes, and set up a new apartment."

Ferber now did the first of the many favors he was to do for me during our long friendship. "You'll never get the twelve hundred dollars," Ferber said. "Not with Colonel Van Hamm taking personal charge of editorial expenditures."

The Hetman rose to this bait. "What gave you the idea that the colonel has the say-so over *my* staff's expenses?"

"That's the word around the office," Ferber replied.

"It is, is it?"—and the Hetman beat the gong furiously. "Never mind," he said to his worried servant. He then told us "confidentially" that he was asking Mr. Hearst to appoint him as assistant publisher. "When that happens," he said, "we shall *see* who is boss." He smiled mysteriously, then said to me, "I'll see you at the office, and write an order for the twelve hundred."

I got home that night to learn that Ellen Runyon had tricked me; she had not put the letters in the various boxes. I was glad— momentarily so. I now remembered that I had put two of the letters in boxes 7 and 11.

I never heard from box 7. But box 11 responded. A mild-mannered man with a foreign accent called upon me. I saw my letter in his hand. "Have I offended you in some way?" he asked.

This gentlemanly caller was Otto Motzan. He lived with his wife Ethel in apartment 11. Otto was a violinist, a composer, an outstanding musician. When I became well acquainted with him (and we remained close friends until he died in 1937) I learned that his wholesome character and his humility had gained the love of his contemporaries in the American Society of Composers, Authors and Publishers (ASCAP), of which he was a charter member.

Otto was about ten years older than I. He was born in Hungary and had received his musical education in that country. He came to America in 1907, organized his own orchestra for Belle Baker, the vaudeville star, conducted for the Shuberts, then gave up that sort of work to compose music for Broadway productions. Otto Motzan did the scores for the *Passing Show of 1919,* and also for the next year's edition of that musical. He also composed the music for *Very Good, Eddie,* and for various other hit shows. At the time we met he had not reached his full reputation, nor had he as yet written, with M. K. Jerome, the music for the popular song "Bright Eyes," or the instrumental "Elegie."

"Mr. Motzan," I said, "I never make small mistakes. If you wish, I shall put out my jaw and give you a free shot, with or without brass knuckles."

He amazed me by his counter-offer. "Mr. Fowler, my wife and I have no children. If you don't mind, we'd like to take care of your baby whenever you and Mrs. Fowler want to go out for the evening."

Another "baby sitter"! We promptly took advantage of this offer.

We planned to have Christmas where we now lived. Then Mrs. Hubbard would take our child back to Denver, to keep him there while I was in Europe.

Mr. Motzan ran into a spot of trouble while taking care of our baby. My wife, mother-in-law, and I went one evening to see a motion picture at a neighborhood theater. On our return we found out that the tenants had a new complaint. It seems that the child had quit crying whenever Motzan played his violin, but immediately started up again each time the musician paused in his fiddling.

Otto would have said not a word about this, but his wife revealed that *they* had been asked to move. "Those tone-deaf boobs," Ethel said, "object to good music after ten o'clock at night. Genius is completely lost on them."

My friend the taxicab driver must have thought me a burglar "casing" the neighborhood. "If you don't mind," I said to him, "let's go around the corner to Amsterdam, opposite the entrance to the cathedral. That's where the twenties came roaring in."

"The *what?*"—and I fancied that he was now sure that my wheels had left the rails.

"I don't get up this way very often," I said. "About every forty years or so."

"It's your money, mister," he said. "I got all day."

17

I know not if it was a dream.
  I came

Unto a land where something
  seemed the same

That I had known as't were
  but yesterday,

But what it was I could not
  rightly name.

  —AMBROSE BIERCE

To THOSE gray fellows who count nothing good that is new, but burn candles only to the old, this question: Was it a golden age, the one you now extol? Or does it borrow its present luster from the memories of your own prime?

I was standing before the cathedral which had risen high above the old neighborhood since the time when I had lived there. The 1920s had been my golden years. Now I was remembering them in terms of my youth and its aspirations. How big the dream! How little the man!

A sculptured array of preachers, prophets, saints, and martyrs looked down upon me—figures surrounding the five front portals of the Cathedral of St. John the Divine. A cathedral is an illustrated church, a holy narrative in stone. Could anyone feel self-important when in the presence of this grand jury of saints and patriarchs?

The Roaring Twenties must have had a special influence on the world, golden or otherwise. Stories of that time seem of particular interest to the men and women of today. The historians, however, cannot agree among themselves as to the dimensions of that period of gusto and caprice, the ten years of experiment and error, the tumultuous aftermath of the fall of kings, the coming apart of empires at the seams. It was an age of paradox and enigma.

I am not equipped for a journey into the forest of whys and wherefores of the moral, the economic, or the social insurrection of the 1920s. Besides, too many birds have sung in those trees. Perhaps, however, I may be permitted to touch upon one aspect of the time: the change in the complexion of the news. The color of the news for some years had been a battlefield red. Now the public interest in current events began to move across other bands of the journalistic spectrum.

There are vintage years for the news as well as for the wines of quality. The yield of 1919 was of the best. This transitional year brought flash floods of prosperity to some, and financial drought to others. New fortunes meant new names in the headlines. Politics became a floating crap game.

The war correspondents came home to find their city desks no longer concerned with tales of battles lost or won on the fields of France. Instead, they and the other reporters now wrote of economic dislocations; the Ku Klux Klan; Henry Ford's libel suit against the Chicago *Tribune*; the advent of Prohibition; the attempt of the Navy's NC hydroplanes to fly the Atlantic; the arrival in New York of Eamon de Valera of Ireland soon after his escape from the British; the coldest April in forty-five years; Jack Dempsey's winning of the heavyweight championship on a hot July 4 from Jess Willard at Toledo; the visit to America of King Albert and Queen Elizabeth of Belgium; the many strikes, among them that of the New York actors; the deportation of anarchist Emma Goldman; Caruso's silver jubilee at the Met; the ban on smoking by women at all New York hotels except the Ritz. . . .

To be sure, there was a noisy season of welcome for the returning war heroes. It began with a series of parades, the pomp of victorious flags, the ballarag of drums, speeches, promises, anything for our boys . . . and then the veterans went into an eclipse. Few of them could find jobs.

Sergeant York received the Medal of Honor. The City of New York was his for the asking that day. Eventually he would lie paralyzed in his old age, and hounded by the tax collectors of a grateful country.

Woodrow Wilson became the most conspicuous martyr of them all. This was the year of his travail. The gaunt idealist seemed to be acting the part of the *Christus* in the Passion Play. No village of Oberammergau, but the nation and the world, provided the background for this portrayal.

Early in 1919 the liberated people of Europe received Mr. Wilson as the new messiah, and strewed flowers at his feet. They shouted amen, amen, to his gospel of brotherhood and lasting peace. He sat among the pharisees of diplomacy at Paris and at Versailles. At home the sanctity of his mission was impugned. The senate and the press fashioned a cross for him—the treaty of peace he had proclaimed. Of his Fourteen Points they made for him a crown of thorns.

We saw the lines deepen on his face. We saw him start out on his last attempt to perform a miracle, to plead his cause to his countrymen. His Presidential railway car *Mayflower* left Washington in September. The dark blue car was conspicuous among the red cars of the Pennsylvania line. The special train carried the crusader eight thousand miles across the land. Mr. Wilson spoke in seventeen states, delivered forty sermons on the mount. A group of senators who, in his sight, acted as modern Pontius Pilates, said the words of doom over the peace treaty.

Wilson the Just suffered a stroke in the railway yards near Wichita; and there his last great agony began. The long journey home became his *via dolorosa*.

The most hazardous of all occupations is that of the idealist.

Forty years ago the newspaper was the world's information booth, the most immediate agency of public reference. This should be kept in mind when one thinks of the newspaper's place in the scheme of the 1920s. The great change in the character of the news reflected the change in men's thoughts and deeds, and recorded their growing worship of the machine.

The newspaper lost its spark of immediacy when radio and television pre-empted the headlines. Now the spot news comes piecemeal every hour or less over the air. It is like eating between meals; by the time the newspaper arrives at the table your appetite has been spoiled.

Other problems harass the newspaper, some of them self-induced. A newspaper must stay free of obligation to anyone other than the public, but it also must be solvent to survive. With rising costs, as well as the intrusions by other media—the news magazines, for example—the wonder is not that the press sometimes falters in its mission, or that daily papers fail, or merge to keep in business, but that the Fourth Estate still has a voice.

It has become more and more a publisher's voice, however. In other days the editor was in command. Editors, for the most part, were one-purpose men. They tried to reflect the public interest, to defend the public's right to know. The old-time editor had an austere disdain for the complaints of the business office. This independence still obtains in the outstanding newspapers, but the besetting evils of a haywire economy, as well as the reprisals exacted by ferocious minorities against anyone who prints unpleasant truths, has taken much of the do-and-dare spirit out of the makers of newspaper policies. When appeasement supplants editorial enterprise, and silences the outspoken criticism of evil men, the newspaper forfeits its character, loses its influence—and eventually its life. Public servants become public masters. All freedoms are endangered when that of the press is assailed.

Were it not for the small date-book given me by Ellen Runyon for 1919, I could not now so readily place in sequence the things remembered, the things which otherwise would be vaguely recast as in the private idiom of a dream. These guiding notes become the white line of the highway when night comes on and the fog rolls in from the sea.

On New Year's day of 1919, says the tiny log-book, my assignment to Europe was canceled. Our son was in Denver with his grandparents. Agnes and I had moved into the apartment on Amsterdam Avenue. And I had spent $1353 on the European trip that failed.

"Hearst editors," Ellen Runyon said, "never can make up their minds. It is very hard on the wives. Sometimes I wish that Alfred was a plumber. Besides, he could fix the pipes."

I seem always to have had enormous luck in respect to expense accounts. It was the only ability I possessed which was superior to any of Runyon's several talents. He did not do badly, however, in the collection of expense money, but admitted that I was his master in that field. Whenever the Demon could not balance his books, he would set down the amount needed to get him out of the red, and then explain it with the phrase, "Spent while going around and about."

One day Bugs Baer found that he had squandered fifteen dollars more than he could justify in his itemized account. So he wrote, "Fifteen dollars, for going around and about like Damon Runyon." The auditor flatly refused to honor the claim.

When I put in my expense account for $1353, auditor Chester Vaden showed the list to Colonel Van Hamm. The colonel saw that I had bought a complete wardrobe for myself and a coat for Agnes, and luggage, and paid moving-van costs, and had exchanged fifty dollars for French francs to use as pocket money aboard ship. He almost fell out of the Island of Manhattan.

"This man," he was overheard to say, "thinks that Mr. Hearst is the mother lode. Disallowed, in toto!"

It so happened that the colonel and the Hetman had now locked horns in a test for Mr. Hearst's favor. The colonel won the first onset when he countermanded my assignment to France. My expense account now became the issue for the second phase of the contest. The Hetman not only won this flurry of influence but credited me with an even $1500. He also allowed me to keep the fifty dollars' worth of francs.

For no apparent reason the Hetman accompanied his generous action with the words, "I hope you haven't forgotten the monkey-gland project. Find me a worthy old man who wants to get fixed up."

With this thought temporarily in mind I gave Pat Crowe half the French money I had in my pocket. He said that he preferred American currency, and seemed embarrassed when I suggested that he submit to that which he called "monkeying with my glands."

I gave the remainder of the francs to Dr. DeGarmo. "Merci, monsieur," the chestnut vender said. "But as a former man of medicine, I question the success of that surgical procedure. I also doubt the wisdom of any man who would re-equip himself with the very tools with which he dug a pit in other days." The philosopher poked among the chestnuts as though playing with symbols. "The grand passion died for me while I was in college the last time. Too much saltpeter, perhaps. Shall I tell your fortune with the nuts?"

"Not today," I replied.

Dr. DeGarmo reminded me that he had been correct in predicting that I would *not* go on a voyage. His other forecast, he said, would come true soon—the death of a great statesman. It did.

I went that night with Ed Klauber of the *Times* to report a benefit for war orphans at the Hippodrome. Three celebrated composers took turns leading the orchestra: Victor Herbert, John Philip Sousa the March King, and Reginald DeKoven, of "Oh Promise Me" fame.

The next morning Ellen Runyon called at our flat to take Agnes to a post-holiday clearance sale at Arnold Constable's. "Mrs. Abraham Lincoln used to trade there," she said.

I asked if she was going to buy a Lincolnian shawl for Damon. Before she could reply the telephone rang. The city desk wanted me to go at once to Oyster Bay, Long Island. Colonel Theodore Roosevelt had died in his sleep at four o'clock in the morning. A clot of blood had detached itself from a vein and entered his lungs. He was a few months this side of sixty-one years when he died at Sagamore Hill.

"Here's one for you," I said to Ellen. "An old con-man friend of Damon's predicted this."

My mention of the fortune teller made Ellen forget Arnold Constable's sale. She cross-examined me about Dr. DeGarmo. As a pretext for keeping me on the witness stand she took charge of the packing of my overnight bag. I am one of those reporters who travel light, as the saying is, but Ellen would have none of my abbreviated choice of on-the-road necessities.

"Why," she said, "Alfred always takes a trunk, and two suitcases, no matter where he goes." She examined my long nightshirt, a flannel masterpiece created by Agnes. "I haven't seen one of these," she said, "since Papa Egan died. He was a railroad superintendent." She handed the garment to me. "I guess it's all right. Here, fold it yourself."

The memory of that long nightshirt now seems to be the main symbol of my recollections of the burial of the statesman. Before I set out for the Long Island side of Penn Station, I telephoned Jack Gavin of the *World* city desk. I wanted to have a congenial roommate at the Octagon House. That picturesque old inn at Oyster Bay was bound to be overcrowded with reporters and dignitaries.

"John O'Leary is already at Oyster Bay," said the amiable Mr. Gavin. "He was, as you know, one of the colonel's closest newspaper friends."

Mr. O'Leary, the *World*'s labor specialist, was a fine man in all ways, but somewhat strict in respect to the decorum of his fellow journalists. As dean of the New York newspaper delegation he would of course assume charge of press headquarters.

"However," Mr. Gavin said, as though in answer to my silent prayer, "I am sending Joe O'Neill to do the color story."

Joseph Jefferson O'Neill was one of the ablest reporters of that day. He was ten years older than I, a handsome man, and most generous with advice to younger reporters. His closest friend, reporter Sam Fisher, had just died, and Joe seemed to have chosen me as Sam's successor in his affections.

O'Neill had one dangerous fault. He smoked in bed. He did this while relaxing, a few drinks inside him, after having filed his stories. Don Clarke and several other friends had warned me of this, and suggested that all Joe's clothing, even his shoes, should be searched for matches at bedtime.

"After you have had a few narrow escapes with Joe," Don Clarke had said, "you will wish that Prometheus had never stolen the fire of the gods and brought it to mankind."

On the night before the Roosevelt funeral I saw to it that Joe was safely asleep—or so I thought. I had a few additions to make to my story and to his before I went to bed. A sculptor—I think it was James Earle Fraser—was making a death mask of the late colonel. Also, a troop of New York's mounted police officers had been delayed somewhere along the North Shore Drive while on the road to Oyster Bay.

Colonel Roosevelt had at one time been police commissioner of the City of New York. A detachment from Traffic-A had been riding all afternoon from City Hall to act on the morrow as a guard of honor.

"Sign me off," I said to the telegraph operator. So far as I know, none of us ever used the supposedly classic term "thirty" at the end of our stories. That, and several other words and phrases which occur in motion-picture scripts, was not a part of our supposed lingo. For example, I never heard one Park Row man describe another as a "star reporter." And if one of us ever telephoned in with the legendary cry of "Stop the press!" he would have been turned over at once to Dr. Menas Gregory of Bellevue, or else fired.

When I opened the door of our tiny room, I smelled smoke. I snapped on the light to find a patch of the bed quilt slowly widening in a ring of smoldering fire. I managed to put it out by means of water from the night-stand pitcher.

Mr. O'Neill awakened, ignored the mishap, and demanded a drink of Bourbon. I undressed and got into my long nightshirt. I told Mr. O'Neill that the bar had closed. Dean O'Leary had ruled out all dice games, late drinking, or other pastimes which might reflect upon the solemnity of the occasion.

"Find me a drink," Mr. O'Neill threatened, "or I shall rise from my bed to make a public denunciation not only of Mr. O'Leary but of the colonel, too."

I was too tired to get into my clothes again. It was a cold night. My diary says it was "sloppy weather." I had no bedroom slippers —Ellen had neglected to pack them. I looked outside our door, saw no one, and the whole inn seemed to have gone to sleep. I decided to go to the bar on the errand of mercy.

My first thought was to awaken the proprietor. This was not necessary. I happened to come upon him in the closed bar. He was sitting, half asleep, waiting for the mounted police guard to ride in and register for the night. He was not cooperative at first, but let me into the bar reluctantly. He then explained that it was against the law for him to sell me a bottle. He could not let me take even a glass of the creature outside the barroom. His liquor license would be revoked.

"You should worry," I said. "Your license will be no good after July when the whole country goes dry."

He finally permitted me to order a drink, and said he would turn his back if I decided to sneak off with it. As he turned his back, I felt that I needed the drink myself. My bare feet were getting colder. A draft was reaching under my skirts and taking immodest liberties with that which biblical heroes always girded for battle.

I had another helping of the sauce. And another. Then, while working on the third one, I heard a sound of cavalcade, a rattling of bridle bits, footfalls in the corridor. Now several officers of Traffic-A, cowled and slickered against the weather of their forced march, tromped into the bar. Their conversation stopped. They looked at me with a kind of lusty amazement.

One of the officers pointed, then called out, "Lookut! The Nightgown Kid!"

I had a somewhat hard time living down this nickname. But it was not until early in February that I really felt too bad about it. And, as so often happened, my mentor Damon Runyon was the cause of this embarrassment.

Runyon returned from France early in February, or so says my little date-book. He invited me to go to the hotel where Captain Eddie Rickenbacker, America's war ace, was staying. Damon said that he had ghost-written a speech which Rickenbacker was to deliver at a welcome-home dinner. These men had been friends during Rickenbacker's automobile-racing days. Damon also had called at squadron headquarters on the Western Front and written several stories there about the captain's feats as an aviator. He knew that Captain Rickenbacker was my favorite of all living heroes, so he took me to see him in New York.

There is a conflict of dates between the entries in my diary and a letter which my friend Rickenbacker wrote me in October 1955. Eddie's letter says in part:

"Damon helped me work up a speech, and a good one, which was delivered in the Boston Symphony Hall, where I was introduced by the late President, then Governor, Calvin Coolidge. I got home February 19, 1919."

There must have been *two* ghost-written speeches. My book says that Joe O'Neill and I covered the Rickenbacker speech at the Waldorf the evening of the same day I had interviewed Malvina Hoffman, sculptress and pupil of Rodin. That was February 3.

The discrepancy puzzles me, but no matter. The bravest of men was a bit on the nervous side when he thought about his debut as an orator. He seemed to regain some of his strong spirit when the Demon confided that the mere thought of speaking in public gave him what he called "the triangular jim-jams."

"I envy a self-confident man," he said. Then he turned to me with that deadpan manner which I had learned to recognize as a sign of impending irony. "It takes a man with nerves of steel," he went on to say, "to appear in public in a meal sack, and in his bare feet. Like Mr. Fowler does. The Nightgown Kid."

I let this pass. But do not think for a moment that I always spared the Demon when *he* wanted to keep some of his old didos under cover. We used to sit after press hours in the sports department while a gallery of colleagues listened to our tall tales of Colorado. Runyon would speak of his father, and of the days of the gun toters; and I would talk of my Uncle Dewey Wheeler, a powerful and courageous man. Bugs Baer turned these tales into a newspaper series about "Gink Fowler of Rufftown," a place where the citizens played tiddly-winks with manhole covers, and the canary birds sang bass.

One early morning I told the story of how Runyon had played Santa Claus in Denver and kicked at the children. The Demon's face turned as red as a brakeman's flag. He did not relish jokes about himself, unless *he* told them. Indeed, he was very sensitive to adverse criticism, implied or otherwise. When columnist Frank Adams (F.P.A.) one day took him to task for his faulty syntax, Runyon became his lasting foe.

The matter of nightgowns was settled early in May; and a very cold month it was along the Atlantic seaboard. Appropriately enough, my friend Joseph Jefferson O'Neill of the *World* had a fiery connection with the episode. We were roommates once again, this time in a ramshackle "hotel" at Rockaway Beach, Long Island. Rockaway Beach was a seaside summer resort; perhaps it still is. We found most of the inns, boarding houses, or hotels shuttered against the gales of winter when we arrived to cover the United States Navy's attempt to fly the Atlantic.

The Navy had built and commissioned four hydroplanes, called NC-boats, for this pioneering flight. Destroyers were stationed along the Great Circle route to refuel the planes. The double-wing, one-pontoon seaplanes were to fly a three-leg course from Rockaway Point to Trepassey, Newfoundland, then to the Azores, and then set down off Plymouth, England.

The metropolitan reporters found quarters conveniently near the Navy hangars at Rockaway Point, but O'Neill insisted that he and I stay at the Wakeham House in Rockaway Beach. He explained that this hotel had a romantic association with his past, a pre-marital adventure, of course. Mr. O'Neill was not only a man of the World but also of the world. He was said to have found romance even on the Henry Ford Peace Ship, a dedicated ark where moral discipline allowed for no hand-holding in the moonlight.

The Wakeham House was boarded up and deserted. Joe, however, located the manager, a middle-aged lady of the build and height of a first-baseman. She took the padlock off the plank door, assigned us the "best" bedroom on the second floor, then produced some bedclothes which reeked of camphor flakes. The electricity and the telephone had been shut off. The landlady found a kerosene lamp for us and recited some instructions on fire prevention. She may have known of Joe's reputation.

"I suppose you have plenty of matches?" she said.

This was like asking Australia if it had any sheep. "I think so," Mr. O'Neill said.

"Of course you'll have to eat out," she advised us. "Not many places open this time of year." She beamed at Joe. Women always did. He clicked his heels, a habit picked up while riding through Germany with the Ford peace party (although they had been sealed up in private railway cars during the entire journey).

"Toodle-doo," Joe said, and he kissed the tall lady's hand.

The Navy project seemed to have had a curse laid upon it. Bad weather, accidents, fire in the hangars, and other happenings set back the takeoff of the ships. The day before we arrived one of the ships was put out of commission with a damaged wing panel.

Assistant Secretary of the Navy Franklin D. Roosevelt, tall, active, and optimistic, went on one of the trial flights. He left the Point with the comment that history was in the making. While

we were inspecting the ships on May 6 one of the flight engineers
—Howard, I think his name was—lost a hand when spinning the
propeller of the NC-4.

During the NC-boat assignment Joe and I subsisted mostly on
hard-boiled eggs, available as free lunch at a dingy saloon owned
by "Oyster Tongs" McGee. Mr. McGee wore a gold ring in the
lobe of one ear. He kept a huge stoneware bowl piled high with
eggs on the bar. At first he seemed to think that we ate more than
our share of them. He chanced to overhear me recite from one of
my several unpublished poetical works, then decided that I was a
man of letters. He asked that I write down the verses on a paper
sack. He proudly tacked them on the wall next to a framed photograph of pugilist Jim Jeffries, crouched low and clad in fighting
trunks. Fortunately for everyone I can recall but two verses of this
work:

> Ah, come to me, my sex-starved pet:
> I'm hotter than a crêpe suzette. . . .

Since we had no live telephone at the Wakeham House, Oyster
Tongs McGee volunteered to safeguard our interests. He appointed three of his hangers-on as sentinels. They were to apprise
us if the NC-boats took off while we were in residence.

There was a fire one night in the hangar of one of the NC-boats,
I forget which one. Perhaps this mishap stirred Mr. O'Neill's love
of flames. We had gone to bed. I had been painstakingly careful
when blowing out the lamp. I was full of hard-boiled eggs and
very tired.

In the early hours of morning I awakened with the warmest
backside I had experienced since the time I was hazed as a fra-
ternity freshman. The whole room seemed afire. Even Joe was not
indifferent to the danger. "Man overboard!" he shouted.

How we managed to get out, I do not know. And how we happened to save our shoes and trousers and a very few other items
of clothing, I also cannot remember. I do know that I had to beat
out the fire from my nightgown; and that the volunteer fire

department arrived, with Oyster Tongs McGee in command of a chemical tank, his earring glistening beneath a World War helmet.

As we were getting into the clothes we had managed to save, I said to Joe, "How in the devil are we going to square *this?*"

"Oh," replied Mr. O'Neill, "just put it on your expense account."

The hotel did not burn down, but looked barbecued, especially in the region of our upstairs window.

The three NC-boats took off that morning. Joe, as usual, wrote a beautiful story. He likened the airships to the caravels of Columbus. Joe chartered a taxicab to take us to our respective homes, for he was almost as particular as Runyon in the matter of personal appearance. Right now we looked like a pair of chimneysweeps. I had left my singed nightgown at Rockaway Beach. I decided never again to wear that sort of thing.

The NC-boats had hard luck all the way. The NC-1 was forced down and sank, but the crew was saved. The NC-2 went astray in the fog and disappeared in the sea. Its crew spent fifty-two hours in the water. The NC-4 made it to Horta in the Azores, after fifteen hours' flight from Newfoundland. After one delay and then another, the NC-4 was the only one of the Navy craft to reach Europe. It landed off the coast of Portugal, and then off England twelve days after it had left the United States.

It was the first plane to cross the Atlantic. I would report several first flights of airplanes in the 1920s, including that of Lindbergh and of Commander (afterward Rear Admiral) Byrd. But I like best to think back to Smokey Joe O'Neill, and to the time we saw the single-pontoon Navy crates take to the early morning air off Rockaway Point.

Early that year (Arthur Robinson says that it was *before* Christmas of 1918, the day he came home on the *Paris*) the Hetman spoke to me in his office.

"How are you coming along with that monkey-gland assignment? Surely some nice old man is waiting around to get back his youth, also to glom onto a thousand-dollar bonus."

"I'd volunteer for the operation myself," I said, "especially at *that* price, but I don't exactly need it just yet."

"Fowler," he said, "you'd have a great future if you didn't make jokes about serious things. Think it over."

"I *have* thought it over," I replied.

"What conclusion did you reach?"

"None. I laughed so hard I couldn't make up my mind."

"All right," he said. "Here's something for you to do, and it's dead serious. It concerns Mr. Hearst's reputation as a patriot. Mayor Hylan is forming a committee to welcome the soldiers and sailors. Rodman Wanamaker is to be chairman, and Grover Whalen his assistant. Mrs. Hearst is to be chairman of the Mayor's Committee of Women. But Mr. Hearst, modest as he is, must be in the picture for his own deserved good. Are you following me?"

"Kind of," I said.

"As our first move," he went on to say, "Mr. Hearst is going to finance a patriotic gesture. The *Paris* is arriving tomorrow morning with a number of wounded soldiers. You are to charter a ship, provision it with sandwiches and coffee, and see that these boys are given a *real* welcome by meeting them off Ambrose Lightship."

"How many people? Isn't this short notice?"

"At least a hundred," the Hetman replied. "And don't worry about short notice. Life itself is full of short notices; and death is a short notice, as a rule. Just get that ship ready to sail at seven o'clock tomorrow morning."

It now was five o'clock in the afternoon. I knew nothing about ships, other than prairie schooners. I called Don Clarke at the *World* office. He advised me to go to the Whitehall district and gave me the name of a friend who managed an excursion-boat line.

"Better hurry, though," said Don, "the offices are closing. I'll put in a call to Mr. Balderston to wait for you."

This *must* have been before Christmas, for I have no entries in

my 1919 diary pertaining to the episode. My old newspaper friend
Ross Whytock was control officer of the Port of New York for
Military Intelligence at the time. Just recently he helped me piece
together some of the details of my assignment.

I found Mr. Balderston in an aged two-story building on the
north side of Battery Park, a short walk from the Bowling Green
subway station. Mr. B. was a thick-set man of perhaps fifty years
of age; he had on a derby hat which seemed a half size too small
for his head. When he shook my hand it felt as if the door of a
bank vault had closed upon it.

The Balderston firm operated a fleet of coal-burning one-stackers
—small steamers which plied between the Battery seawall at Pier 1
on the North River and various Hudson River ports of call. When
I said that I wished to charter a ship for Mr. Hearst, Mr. Balderston did not seem too enthusiastic.

"The only vessel available," he said, "is tied up at Pier One, just
around the bend of the Battery from the Aquarium. And the crew
has been dismissed."

I told him I wanted the ship tomorrow morning, early, explained
the mission, then asked the cost of it.

"Oh, let's see," he replied. "Well, two thousand dollars would
just about cover everything."

I had not the least idea of a fair price for the chartering of a ship
of *any* tonnage. "That seems mighty steep," I said from the depths
of my seafaring ignorance. "This is for Mr. Hearst, you know!"

Mr. Balderston's tone was that of a district attorney. "You don't
know a damned thing about this business," he said. "Do you?"

"Mr. Balderston," I admitted, "my only contact with the sea
has been the reading of Lord Byron's apostrophe to the ocean.
May I recite from it?"

"No," he replied. "Much as I don't give a damn for Mr. Hearst,
I'm going to let you have a ship for tomorrow morning, three to
eight bells, for fifteen hundred dollars. The *White Swan*, Captain
Hughes commanding."

I had a difficult time that evening in getting provisions for the

White Swan. I finally persuaded the manager of the Childs restaurant nearest our office to make four hundred ham sandwiches for Mr. Hearst and the other patriots. Circulation Manager Joe Bannon of the *Journal* assigned one of his trucks to deliver these rations at the Battery seawall at dawn.

The *American* staff was not on duty early next morning. I checked with the "lobster trick" man of the *Journal* as to the whereabouts of the *Paris.* She was said to be encountering heavy seas off Sandy Hook, but hoped to dock "sometime today."

It was a cold, blowy morning when Mr. Hearst and perhaps a hundred assorted dignitaries boarded the *White Swan.* White? Perhaps so, at some ancient day. She had the complexion of rust and coal smut. To my inexperienced eye she didn't seem worth fifteen dollars at an auction sale, let alone the fifteen hundred I had pledged for the charter.

Everyone was bundled against the wind that drove in from the gray sea lanes. The *White Swan* strained at her mooring lines and made rheumatic complaints. Mr. Hearst was dressed as an Arctic explorer in a fur cap and shaggy fur coat, similar in its haystack contour to that of the racoon coats then popular among college men.

I went ashore from time to time to get word of the *Paris.* The press-service bulletins were contradictory. I reported each message to Mr. Hearst. After the guests had exhausted their flatteries of their host and begun to wander about the deck, Mr. Hearst asked that I join him at the starboard rail.

"What is your favorite city?" he asked. "New York? San Francisco?"

"Athens," I replied.

Mr. Hearst had an amazing faculty of expressing himself obliquely, and in a voice described by Ambrose Bierce "like the fragrance of violets made audible."

"Athens?" he said. "Somehow I thought that *Chicago* was your favorite city."

He was, of course, referring to my bad time at the 1918 World

Series. He smiled. His was a curious smile, somewhat mirthless, noncommittal; not quite an upside-down sneer, but midway between the conventional smile of an Etruscan tomb effigy and the crescent smirk of a Halloween pumpkin. His pale blue eyes never blinked as he looked at and *through* you.

At eleven o'clock I received word that the *Paris* was delayed by the gale at sea. By now about half the patriots had left the ship to go to their offices or their homes.

I said to Mr. Hearst, "These people are getting restless."

"Well," he said, "that's a habit people have."

"Do you think we should take a little sail?"

"Yes," he said, "let's take a little sail."

Captain Hughes said that his orders were to dismiss his men at noon. However, he permitted us to cruise past the Statue of Liberty, then back to the Battery.

After we had made fast I went ashore to learn that the *Paris* would not dock today. Mr. Hearst and the surviving patriots departed. I visited a saloon near West Street and had enough beer to float the *White Swan*. Toward five o'clock I called my office to be told that the *Paris* was going to dock, after all, at nine o'clock that evening. I was to get the ship ready once again. Mr. Hearst would be down when the *Paris* was reported off the Quarantine Station.

Mr. Balderston was just closing his office when I arrived there. "Impossible!" he said. "The fires are banked, and the crew dismissed."

I prevailed upon him to notify Captain Hughes. When a second fee of fifteen hundred dollars was suggested, I managed to have it lowered to a thousand for the repeat performance. I then decided to hire an orchestra for dancing aboard the *White Swan*. My friend Otto Motzan recruited five of his musician friends, one of whom had the largest bull fiddle I ever saw.

From now until ten o'clock that night the bulletins were confusing and contradictory. The *Paris* was behaving like the *Flying*

Dutchman. Besides, we now had no guests at all, other than the musicians.

I had set up my press headquarters at the West Street saloon. At a little past ten o'clock, Martin Dunn informed me that the *Paris* was on the horizon; that Mr. Hearst could not come down, but had said to put to sea anyway to greet the wounded soldiers in his name. I was to drum up some patriots, no matter who they were, or how I did it.

In my desperation, I enlisted several stalwart customers of the saloon to play patriotic roles aboard the *White Swan.* Then I went to Battery Park and to Bowling Green to find a few romantic couples keeping one another warm on the benches. I promised them an evening of free dancing while riding the waves.

At eleven-thirty the *White Swan* had steam up, the orchestra was playing "The Blue Danube," and I was at a pay telephone in the saloon to receive last-minute instructions.

"Call everything off," said Martin Dunn. "The *Paris* is not coming in until tomorrow night."

I scribbled a note to the master of the *White Swan* to abandon ship. I gave a dollar to one of the bar flies to carry it to him. I then took up a position at a subway kiosk, to see from a distance what might happen.

The message was delivered. The music stopped during a sweet passage of one of composer Strauss's works. Next there was a fight, the details of which I could not see clearly, except that the big bull fiddle went overboard like a badly launched lifeboat. And now my friends from the saloon, as well as the lads and lassies who had been dancing, were being expelled from the ship. I went down the subway steps. After getting onto and then off several wrong trains, I found myself at the Woolworth turkish baths.

Mr. Hearst neglected to order a patriotic voyage next day. I turned in my expense account for the rental of the *White Swan,* and for the sandwiches, the orchestra (including a new instrument for the bass violinist), and for something which I listed as "sundry emoluments for reluctant recruits." The bill was in excess of $3000.

The Hetman validated the expense, but said, "It's a good thing Mr. Hearst has a big income from the Homestead mine; otherwise he might die in the poorhouse. . . . By the way, let's get that monkey-gland project going."

I was at my desk in the city room one early afternoon, and at the mercy (temporarily) of a sweet-mannered but somewhat odd gentleman named George Tuttle. Whenever Martin Dunn or little Pete Campbell or Royal Daniel left their respective posts on the city desk for an hour or so, Mr. Tuttle would sit in for them.

Mr. Tuttle was our exchange editor. His regular job was to analyze the daily newspapers—the local ones as well as those on our mailing list. He would compare our stories with those in the other papers, then send a marked copy of the *American* to Mr. Hearst.

Tuttle had an amazing memory as to when, where, and how any and all stories had been handled. He could tell you the exact dimensions and context of newspaper articles printed as long ago as four or five years. His was a freak memory, and so were some of his gestures. He was called "Bugs" Tuttle. This was not meant to reflect upon his mental caliber, but to denote his ability to ferret out the least fault or "bug" in one of our printed efforts.

On the day of which I am speaking, Mr. Tuttle was not exactly himself; personally I thought this an improvement. He had just had the narrowest of escapes. Among the stories which he had criticized and marked for Mr. Hearst's scrutiny was one which had to do with a Louis XIV desk. This antique had been presented by the estate of John Pierpont Morgan to the Metropolitan Museum of Art as a memorial.

Mr. Tuttle had gone to town, as the saying is, when evaluating our account of the Morgan gift with that of the *Times*. Among other adverse criticisms, Mr. Tuttle wrote that our story was deficient in its general context, badly written, ambiguous, and insulting to a reader's intelligence.

Martin Dunn rescued this marked paper just as a special messenger was about to take it to the Clarendon. Mr. Dunn informed Bugs Tuttle that the article had been written by Mr. Hearst himself, with instructions not to alter a word.

Bugs Tuttle was one of several editors who dreaded to have Mr. Hearst send word to them, particularly a telegram. An office anecdote (apocryphal, but revealing) had it that Mr. Tuttle one day received a telegram but delayed opening it. Finally he asked one of his aides to open it and read it to him. The telegram was from a cousin, who said that the editor's mother had just died.

"Oh, thank God!" Mr. Tuttle is supposed to have exclaimed. "I thought it was a wire from Mr. Hearst!"

On the afternoon of Mr. Tuttle's narrow escape in respect to the Louis XIV escritoire, he was understandably dazed. He gave me a sheaf of copy left over from yesterday's report by the City News telegraphic printer. Somehow it had not been properly discarded.

Instead of rewriting this stale material, I decided to catch up with my personal correspondence. And now I heard voices. I looked over to the city desk to see a thin gentleman with snow-white hair. He was trying to interest Mr. Tuttle in a series of articles on the reformation of the calendar. He had introduced himself as Irving Bacon, and said that he wanted to put thirteen months into the calendar, the thirteenth month to be called "Sol," and each month to last for a cycle of the moon.

"We are not interested in the calendar or its defects," said Mr. Tuttle. "Mr. Hearst does not like the thought of time passing, because it suggests death, and Mr. Hearst is definitely opposed to death."

The Hetman now arrived after a rice-pudding session at Childs. When he glanced my way, I began a pantomime which, in my opinion, portrayed a monkey scratching its torso for fleas.

Mr. Watson came over to where I sat. "Something wrong?" he asked. "A skin disease?"

I directed his attention to the scholarly old fellow at the desk. "There, if I am not mistaken, is the man who needs a thousand dollars, and some new glands."

"You are *not* mistaken," said the Hetman. "Bring him to my office."

Mr. Bacon was about to leave the premises when I intercepted him. "Would you like to make a thousand dollars?" Apparently he thought that I was jesting, but followed me to Mr. Watson's lair.

The Hetman patiently explained the situation, then led Mr. Bacon into a question-and-answer report on his love life, or lack of it. Mr. Bacon said that he now was working for a low wage at a monastery up the Hudson. He was a Latin expert, and translated communications from Rome for the Catholic brothers.

"As for women"—and he seemed reluctant to speak of them—"well, I . . ."

"Please continue," the Hetman urged. "Anything you say to us is sacred."

"Well, then"—and Mr. Bacon thought things over—"I never was what you might call a full-blooded man. But I do have an occasional carnal thought. And I am ashamed to admit it."

"How often does this occur?" asked the Hetman. "Once? Twice a month?"

"Oh, no! No! About once a year, or at the most not more than twice."

"Same thing here," I said, and the Hetman glared at me. "Once a year. But usually twice."

Mr. Bacon left the office with a signed agreement. He also took with him a hundred dollars as a down payment.

The Hetman now said, "Please, after this, keep your great wit in reserve for bar-room display. Now, let us clear the decks for action."

I was to find a surgeon, a monkey, and an operating room. "We shall earmark five hundred dollars for the doctor," said the Hetman. "We'll need a surgical nurse, of course. As to the monkey, get a good, vital animal, but don't go spending a fortune for one, or buy the Bronx zoo."

Dr. Gregory of Bellevue warned Mr. Watson that any member of the County Medical Association who even so much as spoke in favor of the operation risked expulsion. I managed to find a young surgeon who said he could use the five hundred. I shall call him Dr. Masters, and his nurse Miss Frohm. The doctor was an energetic and personable man, and our first story of the project described him as a disciple of Dr. Serge Voronoff, and an outstanding expert in the field of glandular transplantation. Our story also described the "special" monkey we acquired for the operation.

I had come upon the monkey—a nasty-tempered fugitive from an organ grinder's beat—in the window of a pet shop which did business at the head of the escalator leading down to the Long Island side of Penn Station. I delivered the monkey (whom I called "Ponce de Leon" in print, but referred to privately as "Fireball") to Dr. Masters' office. Ponce promptly bit the doctor in the hand, but took a liking to Nurse Frohm.

No hospital would allow us to operate on its premises. I then made the round of hotels that I thought needed publicity. To the Hetman's pleased amazement a Mr. Townsend, owner of a hotel off Central Park West, agreed to let us use the bridal suite of his somewhat old place—this in spite of the fact that he had religious scruples about the practice of medicine or surgery. Columnist O. O. McIntyre persuaded Mr. Townsend to lend us the suite free of charge. O.O. was doing publicity for the hotel as a sideline.

Dr. Gregory said he would not be present as a spectator at the gland operation. However, three other doctor-friends of Mr. Watson—including a doctor who was medical adviser to Florenz Ziegfeld and to the *Follies* chorus—reluctantly agreed to look on, but asked the Hetman to keep their names out of the newspaper. He promised.

The heart chart, or cardiogram, was a relatively unpublicized device at this time. An eminent Dr. Smith of Philadelphia was said to be a pioneer in this kind of work. The Hetman himself took Mr. Bacon to Philadelphia and, without revealing the true identity of the patient, or the underlying purpose of the call, got from Dr. Smith a chart of Mr. Bacon's heart action.

Back at the *American* the Hetman assigned one of the staff artists to do a bit of "editing" of this chart. The artist put in some India-ink strokes here and there and did a few splurges with an air brush charged with Chinese white to create blank spaces in the chart.

"In this way," Mr. Watson explained, "we can print a 'before-and-after' diagram."

The amended chart looked like a profile of the Canadian Rockies. The gaps in it suggested that the patient had died several times. There was hell to pay when the great Dr. Smith learned what had been done to his cardiogram. The matter was quashed, however, when it appeared that the doctor might possibly be embroiled in (dare I say it?) an off-beat situation.

In recalling the day of the operation I forget some of the details. I remember, however, that the donor was in one room of the bridal suite, and the host in a second room. The monkey got loose again, and again bit the doctor. The nurse captured him and lashed him by means of strips of surgical gauze to a rack shaped like a miniature sawbuck. The monkey was chattering with rage, possibly sensing the loss of his keepsakes.

In the next room, Mr. Bacon had been placed on an examination table from Dr. Masters' office. The Hetman stood at his head, offering words of encouragement. The three doctor friends of the editor sat in chairs ten feet away. They almost went out of their minds when a staff photographer took their picture.

At this time I was in the room where the doctor was putting an ether cone over the monkey's face. The little fellow suddenly passed out, not only for the time being, but for all time. He was as dead as Charles Darwin. Dr. Masters quickly removed the monkey's glands. He popped them into a bichloride of mercury solution, then went to the next room to prepare Mr. Bacon's area of reception.

Mr. Bacon had been given a local anesthetic. But he paled and began to perspire. Mr. Watson applied a cold compress to the scholar's brow. I was taking round-by-round notes, as if at the ringside of a prize fight. Dr. Masters decided that one gland was enough to suture to the *vas deferens* of the host. Mr. Bacon fainted. He was removed from the table and put in a bed above which there hung a picture of Catherine the Great reviewing her troops.

The Hetman ordered an eight-column, first-page headline for this story. To the consternation of the three doctor-spectators Mr. Watson had their pictures printed on an inside page, as well as a statement by each. All three were subsequently suspended by the County Medical Association.

For a week I was assigned to stay at the hotel to record the expected miracle of rejuvenation. For my companions I had Medal of Honor Sergeant Mike Donaldson and Little Billy. Billy was a vaudevillian of tiny size. He referred to himself as a Lilliputian. If anyone spoke of him as a "midget" he became outraged. Sergeant Mike, Little Billy, and I lived very well indeed, that week in the bridal suite. The room-service tab was enormous. We had many callers, among them Bugs Baer, and a large part of the membership of the Friars Club.

Mr. Bacon suffered an infection. The other newspapers got wind of this mishap. We moved out of the hotel one evening, and went to Long Beach to hide there until the patient recovered.

It was a wooden hotel, huge and old. The taking of pictures (it was the day of flash-pan-and-powder photography) was expressly forbidden. A society dance was going on when our staff photographer took a picture of Bacon to show that he was "in the pink," and enjoying a vacation at a "seashore place somewhere in Maine." The camera man had overloaded the flash pan. The explosion startled the ballroom guests. The hotel management ruled that we leave. I pointed out that legally they could not evict an invalid guest. We stayed the week while Mr. Bacon got rid of the infection.

After his "rejuvenation," Mr. Bacon looked ten years older than when he had first come to the *American* with his idea of calendar

reform. I saw him a year or so afterward. One result of the operation was the complete riddance of his carnal thoughts. He had
retired to a monastery, did a great deal of translation for the
brothers, and finally died there while reading a Latin version of
The Temptations of St. Anthony.

"It seems that all you newspaper alumni are writing memoirs,"
said my friend Thomas Mitchell. "It must be some kind of com-
municable disease. Even our friend Jack Dempsey is writing an
autobiography. The year while you have been standing in our old
neighborhood—it *seems* you have been there at *least* a year—was
the one when Jack won from big Jess Willard."

"Yes," I replied, "and when he came back to town an army of
hangers-on gathered about him." He now lived at the Alamac. A
clever sports paragrapher, George E. Phair, wrote a jingle which
applies to most men who come suddenly into prominence:

> Hail, the conquering hero comes,
> Surrounded by a bunch of bums.

Mr. Mitchell's cat, Blue (a literary cat if I ever saw one), came
into the actor's library. "Both Blue and I," said Tommy, "would
like to know why you have not written about any murders so far.
Most reporters' books tell about murders and hangings and deaths
in the electric chair. Have you no grisly scenes to give us?"

"Well, now," I said. "I covered many murders, and attended
my share of electric-chair and gallows events. I saw Ruth Snyder
and Judd Gray die at Sing Sing. And I saw Gerald Chapman
hanged in Connecticut. I remember the slaying of a mighty queer
chap named Jacques Lebaudy, who called himself 'the Emperor of
the Sahara.'"

"How about the Ford libel suit against the Chicago *Tribune?*
And that bigamy case involving the vice-chancellor of my home
state of New Jersey?"

"Be patient," I said, "as you used to be with your spinster aunt back in Elizabeth Port—the old belle who enjoyed attic privacy among her mildewed dance programs and musty valentines."

"Well," said my friend, "at least tell me one thing now: Did you see old Dennis Moon, and pay that hospital tab? And quit listening to those ghostly flutes and violins?"

"I paid the bill," I replied, "and the nurse on the ward let me look in upon Dennis. I saw a wasted old man, of skeletal weight. Stretched out and dying of cancer of the blood cells. His eyes open, and staring, the pupils like decimal points, from the sedation, I suppose. Fingers stiff, like sticks of bamboo. Called me Doctor, and said he hated bedpans. A week or so afterwards I got word that he was dead. Nobody remembered his last words; nobody ever quotes a burned-out newspaperman."

"Many deaths there were that year," I went on to say. "Mr. Hearst's mother died, and it obviously was a great loss to him. Henry C. Frick, actor Nat Goodwin, Sidney Drew, Adelina Patti, all died. And finally Colonel Van Hamm, tired of the slings and arrows of his rivals, died in December during a visit to Florida. After the colonel's death there began a parade of new managing editors. They arrived and vanished. The list reads like a martyrology. Damon Runyon once said of this:

"A new managing editor walking in sometimes met himself walking out, which gave rise to a rumor that there was a mirror in the entrance. We always suspected there was a mysterious ogre living on the premises who fancied managing editors as a diet, and ate 'em alive. We could account for their sudden disappearance no other way."

"What did Runyon say when *you* were made a managing editor?"

"He said that I was climbing thirteen steps to stand on the Jim Julian."

"Meaning?"

"The Jim Julian was the name of the gallows back in Colorado and Wyoming. It worked by means of one of those toilet-tank floats. When the victim stood upon the platform it released a catch. This in turn let the water drip out of the tank. When the hollow ball-float sank to low tide, boom! Technically a man hanged himself, a way society has of passing its guilt onto someone else."

"Runyon kept close watch on you."

"Yes. And I think I was a disappointment to him, at least in those early years. I remember that he was raking me over the coals for something—I believe it was the time I interviewed Cardinal Gibbons at the Irish Race Convention in Philadelphia [1919] and had filed a story in which I mistakenly quoted His Eminence Cardinal Farley. You know how I am on names. But that great gentleman Martin Dunn knew my weakness for names. He corrected the copy and passed it along to the headline writer. Cardinal Farley had been dead for a month or more.

"While the Demon was reprimanding me," I continued, "I showed him a letter from my Aunt Etta. She said that my grand-father Norman Wheeler had died. The old prospector, who never had hit it rich, but always thought he was about to do so, had died sitting in a chair at the front window, and looking out at the mountains he had hammered at so vainly for so many, many years.

"Damon was deeply touched," I went on to say. "He said it was not the time to criticize me. And I replied, 'It never is. My grandfather was a failure as the world sees such things. And so am I. He was always looking to tomorrow, and saying it would bring the big strike. And I am that way, too. And I wouldn't change my way of thinking if I could.' I remember Damon's reply as clearly as though it were made yesterday. 'My old man was that way,' he said. 'For him there was always a tomorrow. But me? There ain't no tomorrow, never. Just today. But I suppose it's kind of nice to play kissing games with the future.' "

18

Nimrod the mighty hunter.

— Genesis

WHEN the game-birds were in season down South, Alfred Damon Runyon would quit his studies of Broadway wild life to deal instead with that of the tidelands of Georgia. The Demon and a party of New York sportswriters and baseball men regularly went hunting there each winter as guests of Colonel Tillinghast L'Hommedieu Huston. The stout and merry colonel was part owner, with brewer Jacob Ruppert, Jr.—himself a colonel, as was almost everyone else with a million dollars on tap—of the New York Yankees baseball club.

Colonel Huston looked like Friar Tuck, especially when he took off his iron hat, got into an old brown bathrobe, and latched onto a stein of his partner's best brew. He had leased an island near Darien, Georgia, on which he raised hell and dairy stock, in that order of emphasis. There he built a hunting lodge for his friends. And there sports reporters Runyon, Grantland Rice, W. O. McGeehan, Bozeman Bulger, and other nature lovers *pro tem* gathered in happy season to bag quail and wild ducks or, when the tide was right, to scatter-blast the marsh hens.

The favorite of everyone at Dover Hall was Wilbert Robinson, catcher for the Orioles in his and John McGraw's early days with the Baltimore club. He now managed the Brooklyn team. Your Uncle Wilbert, as Runyon always referred to him in print, was a man of girth and gusto; even the umpires liked him. Editor Ralph McGill of the Atlanta *Constitution* recalls that Your Uncle Wilbert used to send an elderly colored man at daybreak each morning to wake up the guests at Dover Hall with hot toddies well laced with corn whisky.

"This will start the blood," Your Uncle Wilbert would say.

The hot tonic sometimes made a guest trigger-happy. Editor McGill remembers a morning when Babe Ruth had several helpings of the alien corn. The great fence-buster thereupon charged outdoors, broadjumped the veranda, and fired two rounds of birdshot into the brisket of Colonel Huston's prize-winning bull, Kenesaw the Third, having mistaken it for a bison.

Runyon, of course, never had one of Uncle Wilbert's eye-openers. No doubt he thought it a dangerous way to set out for the duck blinds, the man and the gun both loaded. He was too polite to condemn this practice, but did touch upon it indirectly one early morning when he pointed out to Bill McGeehan that the left hip-boot was not meant to go on the right leg.

"Only a dude would have noticed," said Mr. McGeehan, a grizzled essayist, known on Park Row as "the Sheriff."

Runyon was indeed the dude at Dover Hall, or anywhere else, for that matter. When Beau Damon waded among the cattails and the watercress it was as though some meticulous squire had stepped out of the frontispiece of *Field & Stream*. His weapons were of the finest; his bird dogs were aristocrats of the bench shows; even Pabst beer had fewer blue ribbons. Well-trained in the field, these retrievers seldom barked out of turn, and the pointers seemed to be saying, "Excuse me," whenever they pointed quail.

My friend knew much about dogs. Over the years he owned a variety of them. The first one, he told me, was a mutt back in Pueblo, when Damon was a boy and his old man a printer. Now, years later, a more prosperous Runyon paid attention only to purebred animals. He would have liked to keep them as household pets, but his landlords seldom permitted him to do so. Damon, Junior, says that his dad occasionally had a dog in their home, but not for long at a time. Damon boarded his various dogs at kennels remote from Manhattan, but always referred to them as though they lived within whistling distance.

"My dogs know all about telepathy," he once said of them.

Runyon stayed well informed about the canine imports from Europe. He acquired a Doberman pinscher in 1919. Until then I never had heard of that breed. I would have thought it some kind of tool. Jack Dempsey one time planned to give Damon a dog called a Bismarck, an enormous beast lacking the social graces. The heavyweight champion of the world had bought this monster while on a delayed honeymoon in Europe with Estelle Taylor. Runyon refused the gift, for reasons touched with pure horse sense.

Dempsey and the Bismarck had several misadventures when abroad, as well as some troubles afterward in America. First off, a German citizen sued Jack in the Berlin courts to determine the ownership of the animal. Dempsey won the lawsuit, but at much inconvenience and expense. The Manassa Mauler had not wanted to buy this immense creature in the first place. But, in Jack's words, Estelle had gone nuts about the dog.

When Estelle Taylor Dempsey made up her mind about anything, the heavyweight champion was in for a harder time of it than when he won the title from big Jess Willard in Toledo. It was early in 1926 in Berlin when Estelle first saw the Bismarck. The big dog's name was Castor—appropriately so, as Dempsey soon enough found out. Castor weighed almost three hundred pounds, ate four times a day, and looked like the Abominable Snowman. Estelle wanted to take her new dog everywhere she went—when out shopping, or while viewing the monuments. Castor was much too large to ride in a motor car with his owners. Dempsey hired two cars each time they toured the countryside: one for Castor, the other for himself and the bride.

Castor did not like to travel alone. Besides, he mistrusted chauffeurs, growled at them, and finally bit a driver who tried to pet him during a visit to Sans Souci. Dempsey paid out several hundred marks because of the man's injuries. Estelle now decided that Castor should have an escort. Jack persuaded an ex-lightweight pugilist, Lee Moore, to accompany Castor on the daily tours, as well as to exercise him each morning Unter den Linden. Moore served but one week as Castor's keeper.

One morning at the Hotel Adlon, lightweight Moore was about to set out with Castor for a so-called stroll. He and the dog were at the head of the grand staircase, the double-strength leash looped to Moore's wrist. Estelle and Jack were standing in the lobby when Mrs. Dempsey saw her dog.

"Here, Castor!" Estelle called out. "Here, Castor, sweetheart!"

Castor understood this much of the English language. He lunged down the staircase. Moore, his wrist ensnared at the other end of the leash, now performed a series of involuntary head stands, high dives, and pratfalls. His cries for help were lost among Castor's barks of happiness. It was the most violent plunge ever seen, except at the ghastly accident in 1899 on the ski course of Chamonix. Mr. Moore sustained a broken arm and an assortment of contusions.

Estelle demanded that Jack reprimand him. "What for?" asked Dempsey. "He almost got himself killed!"

"Because," said Estelle, "he called Castor a 'son of a bitch.'"

Had Estelle been familiar with the German language, she would have been shocked beyond measure at the way the various cab drivers and hotel managers spoke of her darling Castor. Among its many faults, the big dog was not housebroken. And Estelle insisted that Castor have a room of his own, and the use of the sitting room of the Dempsey suite.

His master had to pay again and again for the damage done to rugs and upholstery, as well as for the big dog's habits while a passenger in taxicabs. In Paris, Dempsey was threatened with a lawsuit when Castor ruined an Aubusson rug, then did terrible things to the wallpaper and the window drapes. The dog disliked French cab drivers more intensely than he had those of his native Germany, perhaps because of the terms of the peace treaty of Versailles.

"Castor cost me well over five thousand dollars in all," Dempsey told me. "He was seasick all the way home. The ship's doctor refused to take him as a patient. Estelle spent most of the voyage in the ship's kennel."

When Dempsey offered Castor to Runyon as a present (the dog had just torn the pants off a bell captain at the Astor), the Demon said, "I thought you were a friend of mine. The answer is no, in spades!"

Arthur Robinson says that Dempsey gave Runyon a Belgian griffin. The dog was forty times smaller than Castor, and well behaved. I never met Castor or the griffin. The only Runyon dogs I ever saw were a pair of whippets. He showed me these skinny hounds during my visit to his estate in Florida in the early 1930s. At that time Damon owned a place on Hibiscus Island, Dade County, Florida.

The whippets, Runyon explained, had been a going-away present from one of his neighbors, a Mr. Alphonse Brown. Mr. Brown was a retired Chicago businessman of sorts. Just recently, under the more familiar name of Al Capone, he had been invited by his Uncle Whiskers to take a long holiday on another island, Alcatraz. The sport of dog racing was impractical there, because of the rocks.

One evening (I forget what year it was, but Damon and Ellen were living apart, and had been for some time) I called upon Runyon by appointment in New York. He had just moved from the Forest Hotel—a hop, skip, and jump from the Garden—into a suite in the Park Avenue sector. We were to have dinner that night at Dinty Moore's, then go to the St. Nicholas Rink to see the fights.

My friend was being dressed by his new valet as I arrived. This gentleman's gentleman was built along the lines of Grant's tomb. He had more scars than those of a chronic loser of Heidelberg duels. Perhaps he was an ex-mountain climber who had tripped over one of the Pyrenees in the dark. While the valet (who also served as Runyon's chauffeur) was laying out my friend's attire, I inspected the arsenal of hunting weapons just outside the dressing room. We talked through the open doorway.

Runyon spoke of Dover Hall, and of the pleasures of the chase. He had often wondered, he said, why I had little interest, if any at all, in the killing of wild animals. I had just returned from a fishing trip with Bill McGeehan in Canada. I said that I had enjoyed the scenery up there, and had liked paddling the canoe much more than I had cared about hooking salmon. I told Damon that I had turned down McGeehan's invitation to go moose hunting.

"Not only am I a bad shot," I went on to say, "but I certainly would not like to kill a moose."

"I'd say you *are* a hunter," he replied. "You're a hunter, but don't seem to know it. Want to know what you're hunting?"

"Sure. Unless you expect a fee."

He was almost dressed now. He asked his valet to select a cravat, a blue one from Sulka's. "Fella," he said, "I wouldn't know whether to call it hunting or groping. But the thing you are hunting is *yourself*. Quite a chore."

I was somewhat disturbed by this remark, as are most men when an unwanted word of truth streaks in like a put-out throw from the outfield to home plate. Before I could reply, Damon raised a hand, Indian fashion. "Big Chief Bellybutton has spoken."

The valet now was showing the Demon perhaps six neckties, handling them like a snake charmer. "That one," said Runyon, indicating his choice. Then he said to me, "We are all hunting most of the time. We hunt for all sorts of things, a bit here and a bit there, to get what passes for happiness, which doesn't come in one big piece and by the bale. Me? I hunt for ducks and quail and such."

"You also hunt men," I said.

"Yeah?" and his tone was one of challenge. "Let's see your hole card."

"Those heavyweights you're always touting," I said. "Do you really think you'll ever find a champion among those blokes?"

"Lack of faith!" he said. "That's Broadway. That's you. That's me, too, except when I get a yen for something, and believe in it, and go for it." Then he said, "Maybe you'll change your tune when you see my boy in the semi-finals tonight."

We were going to the St. Nicholas arena to watch Runyon's latest protégé in action. His name, as well as that of his opponent, escapes me. Runyon's long-time search for a heavyweight of the championship potential became a joke among the sports writers. He did not like this. Bill McGeehan said that one of the Runyon hopefuls, Napoleon Dorval, had been christened not for the emperor but in honor of a French pastry. Damon advised his sensitive fighter to "keep a stiff lower lip."

Once in a black-and-blue moon, a Runyon pugilist was able to get into and then out of the ring under his own power. But for the most part the Demon's athletes ate like lions and fought like lambs. For example, Monsieur Napoleon Dorval's greatest ability was to down several large helpings—at one sitting—of broiled chicken livers, a favorite breakfast dish of his patron. Arthur Robinson says that it cost Damon more to feed his heavyweights than it did, later on, to sustain his string of racehorses.

McGeehan once said that the frequent high dives of Runyon's pugs frequently put the Fordham seismograph out of order. He went on to say that Runyon one time kept a heavyweight prospect in a suite at the Gotham Hotel. "This canvas inspector finished several breakfasts one Sunday morning, and was trying to read the comic pages of the *American*. He had just about mastered the spelling of the hard word 'Wow!' in a Barney Google episode when the bells of nearby Saint Patrick's began to ring. Down went this fighter to the rug. He roared out, 'Foul!' The house dick burst in upon him to see the splendid athlete holding his groin, moaning like a busted pipe-organ, and refusing to come out for another round."

When Runyon's newspaper work took him to various cities or towns, he always found the time to visit the local gymnasiums, with a long-shot hope of coming upon *the* heavyweight. In New York he enlisted scouts to advise him whenever a lineal descendant of the Cro-Magnon man was to go on exhibition at Lou Stillman's gymnasium. So dedicated to this quest was Mr. Runyon as to call off his other plans—even an afternoon at the track—to watch a newcomer work out at the second-floor gym in Eighth Avenue.

Professor Stillman's classroom for students of the more-or-less manly art seldom was mistaken for the recreation hall of Mrs. Spence's finishing school for girls. Sometimes it was difficult to see just what, if anything, was going on in the two practice rings. The unwashed panes of the seldom-opened windows, the haze of rosin dust and tobacco smoke, contributed to eye-strain. The old place had the charm of a Hogarth engraving of debtor's prison, and smelled like a bat cave.

Professor Stillman took a dim view (how could he have taken a clear one?) of the modern conveniences. Complaints that the plumbing was out of kilter—the hot-water faucets and shower taps having been connected with the Bering Sea—got less than nowhere with the professor. When some upstart suggested that the gym traps be brought up to date (or at least up to the time of John Sholto Douglas, the Eighth Marquis of Queensberry) Professor Stillman was quoted as having said, "Great fighters come from the gutter. Bad air, no sunlight, lousy food, and all the other blessings of the slums make a candidate want to fight his best."

As Jimmy Durante once said, "You gotta take some things for granite."

Notwithstanding the shortcomings of this ancient academy— the lack of oxygen, the miasmic mists, and the hazards of acquiring athlete's foot—many great fighters had trained here. Spruce and fussy though Damon Runyon was about his own personal habits, he was never heard to say that an hour at Stillman's qualified a spectator to play on even terms with the goats of the Bronx

Park zoo. His man-hunt for a champion seemed to overpower his finical viewpoint while at Stillman's.

Writers other than Runyon have had strong likings for prize-fighters and their profession. George Bernard Shaw saw himself as an expert in this field. But his judgment, when trying to pick winners, was almost as bad as that of James J. Corbett. Ex-champion Corbett, the foremost stylist of the modern prize ring, named but one winner among all his attempts to call the turn. That successful forecast happened by mere chance, a fluke. I should know, because I was responsible for Gentleman Jim's lone triumph as an oracle.

I was Corbett's ghost writer at the time when he was retained by Hearst's Universal Service to submit daily articles during the training period and then cover the first fight between Jack Dempsey and Gene Tunney at Philadelphia in September 1926. Mindful that Corbett had *never* picked the winner of a championship match, I thought it but fair to keep his record above reproach. Like many other newspapermen, who *might* have known better, I felt sure that Dempsey would keep his title in the Tunney fight. Gentleman Jim had been telling his friends at the Friars Club and the Lambs that Dempsey would knock out the challenger in about the sixth round of the scheduled ten rounds.

As a means to counteract Corbett's foolhardy impulse to destroy his unblemished reputation as a false prophet, I sent a ghost-written article from the Dempsey camp at Atlantic City on the eve of the match. In it I had Corbett say that Tunney would win the decision after ten rounds of left jabs and superb footwork to off-set the champion's renowned hooks and crosses. I did not, of course, believe a word of this. I showed the dispatch to my old mentor, Otto Floto, who had come on from Denver to cover the fight.

Otto did not join in my laughter. "Son," he said, "I am picking Dempsey to win, but am doing it against my better judgment and experience. Your joke on Corbett may very well be the way the fight comes out."

And the fight came out that way almost to the letter. Corbett had known nothing in advance about this story. Nor did he learn of his triumph of judgment until his telephone began to ring at his Philadelphia hotel next day. The messages of congratulation confused him. He thought that the sarcastic sportsmen were trying to tease him. After he read his story in the newspapers, Mr. Corbett began to puff up and want to show himself in the lobby. By the time he got back to New York, Gentleman Jim believed that he really *had* chosen Tunney to win. At the Lambs and at the Friars, however, he had some explaining to do. Why had he said one thing to his friends, and then written another?

Some famous writers, from Lord Byron to Hemingway, have been not only students of the fight game but also quite handy with their fists. Among our present-day book men, Budd Schulberg and Paul Gallico know how to use the mittens. Indeed, Mr. Gallico once faced Jack Dempsey at the training camp, then wrote a story for the *Daily News* on how it felt to be knocked out. That was early in Mr. Gallico's writing career. He was a husky young man, a one-time gunner seaman in the Navy, and before that an oarsman at Columbia. He arranged with Manager Jack Kearns to appear, unannounced, as one of Dempsey's sparring partners. The champion did not as yet know Gallico. When he saw the earnest fellow charging in on him, Mr. Dempsey mistook him for a "ringer"—someone thirsting for a reputation of potting the champion. Jack flattened Gallico. It was the beginning of a lasting friendship.

None of these writers, old or new, tried, as Runyon had, to find, develop, and manage a heavyweight champion. It was a curious obsession—or so it seemed to his colleagues on Park Row. Runyon was a comparatively frail person. His only physical participation in a sport had been a brief attempt long ago out West to become a jockey.

Arthur Robinson thinks that Damon's urge to come upon a champion had its deep-down roots in a provincial type of vanity. "He had several coats of sophistication, self-applied," Robinson said just recently. "But the varnish wore thin at times; the grain showed through. And then Damon seemed the small-town boy, standing in front of the village poolroom to watch the boys and girls go past."

Robbie was one of Runyon's earlier protégés. They spent much time together both in the Big Town and on the sports trail away from Broadway. They had many pre-dawn discussions about this and that, such as the essays of Montaigne or the delicate drinking manners of the horse. I remember that Ellen gave a four-volume translation of Montaigne to Runyon on Christmas Day of 1920. It became his Bible.

Robbie maintains that Damon's quest for a heavyweight boxer was a revealing symptom of the man's provincial naïveté. If so— and I am inclined to accept the theory in part—it might help explain the Demon's urge to manage a champion. Although he had not as yet come into his full fame as a Broadway fabulist, his newspaper work had won the praise of critics even as far away as London. Nonetheless, he seemed to think it important that he find a champion to become a *real* Mr. Somebody among the dese-and-dose sharpies of the Rue Regret.

It is beyond my reach of discernment to sift the whimsical in-and-outs of the men of mark whom I have known. Isn't *anyone* satisfied with his share of the laurel leaves? Many of the celebrated persons of my acquaintance did unpredictable things when out of sight of the crowd. During their private moments they were not quite the same kind of persons that the newspaper headlines implied. They came down from Mount Olympus when not on public display.

Jack Dempsey told me of his having seen a great man in an odd situation. The ex-champion had happened to go to a drugstore at Princeton, New Jersey, some years ago. He had refereed a wrestling bout the night before, and had got something in his eye. While the druggist was selecting a clinker remedy, Dempsey observed an elderly gentleman at play with a yo-yo at the far side of the shop. This gentleman was happily studying the way the toy bounced.

"I recognized him from newspaper photographs," Jack told me. "Professor Einstein playing with a yo-yo! Who am I to think *he* was nuts?"

Mr. Dempsey himself has two or three hobbies not ordinarily expected of a tiger of the ring. On the day when he told me about Dr. Einstein and the yo-yo, the mighty ex-champion was making fudge in the kitchen of his Santa Monica apartment. My children seemed to think this a strange contradiction of the Dempsey nature, but I didn't. He likes candy and so do I. Moreover, Mr. Dempsey is an expert at making it. He is also skilled at cooking fruit for preservation in Mason jars. It is his habit to prepare several crates of strawberries each season in the old-fashioned way taught him by his thrifty Mormon mother. The moral of this, I might say, is: Never risk a trip to the hospital by accusing a heavyweight cook of being a softie.

Damon Runyon hunted still another kind of men than heavyweight prize-fighters. He was as successful in finding them as he was unlucky in turning up pugilists of the first class. He liked to come upon ambitious young reporters. Hither and yon he looked for newspaper hopefuls, discovered several excellent prospects, then helped them make good on Park Row. Nor did his watchfulness over them relax even when they had come to feel that they were able to think and do for themselves.

Talent scout Runyon's protégés seldom got beyond his critical influence, no matter how old they became or where they may have wandered. Some of them left Park Row to write magazine pieces, others to do motion-picture scenarios, books, or plays. Their hair turned gray—or else was missing at the summit. This made no difference to Runyon—or so it seemed, for he kept on clucking like a mother hen to these chicks, unmindful that they had become old roosters with coops of their own.

Runyon also wanted things done *his* way. This was a very fine way, indeed, for him that got a dollar a word, instead of a penny, for his published thoughts. For example, Broadway's Balzac liked to face a bare wall when writing a story of Guys and Dolls. He recommended that his pupils do likewise.

Professor Runyon could be three thousand miles away from a graduate of the class of 1920, yet somehow find out what that fellow was doing, and just how he was doing it. If there were pictures or other decorations on the wall of the place in which you wrote, he would find out about that, too. Or windows, or anything else which might cause the eye and the mind to go off course. Then he would send one of his "cease and desist" letters, as when Arthur Robinson was at work on the libretto of the opera *Gettysburg*.

Robbie now was several years past his newspaper days of ghostwriting sports-page dillies for Babe Ruth and for other literary stalwarts of the bullpens and the locker rooms. Now he was living at Pacific Palisades. He had as his neighbors the eminent novelists Thomas Mann and Lion Feuchtwanger. He also lived near the motion-picture actor Tony Quinn, who didn't care who wrote what or when, unless there was a fat part in it for him.

To Runyon's dismay, he learned from some gabby visitor to Florida that his friend Robbie liked to work while seated on his front porch. The porch looked out upon the Pacific Ocean. In the Demon's opinion this was an even worse hardship on the muse than a wall covered with pictures of naked women.

One morning Robbie was writing about the Great Emancipator. He chanced to see the postman deliver Mr. Quinn's fan mail, a bale or so of it. Soon afterward the fellow put but one or two letters into novelist Mann's box. Mr. Robinson was properly impressed by this evidence of the public's good taste in not pestering a Nobel Prize winner with too much correspondence. Robbie could not see author Feuchtwanger's mailbox. He wondered, however, if the public was as fair to him as it was to Dr. Mann.

"Does Mr. Feuchtwanger get much mail?" he asked the letter carrier.

"Only on the first of each month," was the reply. "It's people like Mr. Quinn whose mail gives us public servants lumbago; like carrying the hod did to my old man, who was a bricklayer's helper, till he bogged down and also ruptured hisself. Here's a letter for you. Hope it's good news, or something."

The letter was from headmaster Runyon. Get off that front porch instantly, it read in effect, and pull down all the blinds. This business of gaping at the sea, the letter went on to say, is okey-dokey for whale hunters, for lovers, or for beachcombers, but not for a man who hopes to write. Do as I do, the professor commanded: get yourself a bare wall. And if your wife Beth tries to hang so much as a smidgin of something nice and cosy on that wall, slap her down. Apologize afterward.

The Runyon gospel of workroom privacy and the bare wall might seem inconsistent with his fondness for Broadway excitements, the roar of the town. Back in the 1920s he usually wrote his column "The Mornin's Mornin'" at home. However, many other assignments found him and his typewriter at public places. There, like other reporters of that age of hurrah and tumult, he had to forego the benefits of monastic peace. Hermits seldom appeared to advantage on Park Row.

More often than not, the working press was harassed from all sides, jostled, given scanty space in which to sit or write. In certain emergencies, a reporter had to fight both mankind and nature itself while trying to win a place beyond that door upon which some misinformed signpainter had put the legend: "Gentlemen."

I cannot recall, however, that occupational hardships, the sardine conditions of the press box, the hullabaloo of the crowd, or anything else bothered Runyon. He seemed well insulated at all times. He would find a place for his typewriter, a feat comparable to pouring a quart into a pint bottle. After a quick look-around and some grunted hellos he would sit down, unhinge the lid of his typewriter, then feed a sheet of pulp paper into the machine. He would glare at the blank copy paper as though it had just told him an off-color story, and puff the while at his cigarette. Now he would draw his hatbrim low over his spectacles, readjust his necktie, then . . . bingo!

Damon wrote with the forefingers, as did most other newspapermen. He typed rapidly, steadily, with the tempo of a woodpecker in search of breakfast. He seemed aloof and alone in the crowd. In some respects he seemed alone always, everywhere.

There were no bare walls during the Fifth Avenue parades of soldiers home from the war. Of all the military parades, I best remember that of General John Joseph Pershing and his army. Damon Runyon and I covered that celebration for the New York *American* early in 1919. The ablest reporters of Park Row marched with that parade down Fifth Avenue: Martin Green of the *Evening World*, Don Clarke of the *Morning World*, Ed Klauber of the *Times*, Boyden Sparkes of the *Tribune*, Ed Hill of the *Sun*, and many others.

Arthur Brisbane, I've already mentioned, once said that Damon Runyon was the grest reporter of his time. Many of Brisbane's statements, like Powder River, were a mile wide and an inch deep. This, I think, was one of them. A.B. made his pronouncement for promotional reasons, to advertise the wares of the Hearst syndicate. Had he said that Damon was the greatest reporter-writer, then we might free the man's real celebrity from the needless overtones of eulogy.

Many times, however, Runyon's stories *were* the best to appear on the newsstands. His account of the Pershing parade was one of the finest examples of his genius for style. The grace of the writing, the atmosphere, the sense of movement, the rightness of phrase—well, his story made mine look like something taken from the wastebasket of poetess Ella Wheeler Wilcox.

The next day, after I had finished reading the several newspaper accounts of the Pershing parade, I asked editor Martin Dunn to do me a big favor. "From now on," I said, "please don't send me on any story where Runyon is assigned."

"I know just how you feel," the wise editor replied. "You see, I used to work alongside Al Runyon back in Denver. Pretty good, wouldn't you say?"

An extraordinary thing about Runyon's performance was that

he had stayed but a few minutes at the line of march. His own experience, of course (as the "Colorado Kid" in the Spanish-American War), had given him an eye for military concerns. Moreover, he had just spent several months as a correspondent at the battlefront with Pershing's army. His intimate pattern of writing about the American foot soldier had been shaped as early as 1916, during the campaign against Villa. In the Second World War, the renowned Ernie Pyle followed—and, in some respects, enlarged upon—Runyon's appealing style when reporting army life.

The "Colorado Kid" of the Spanish-American War seemed never really to have been mustered out of military service. His son says that Damon Runyon often demonstrated the *Manual of Arms* in the privacy of his home, barking orders to himself and using one of his elegant fowling pieces for the ritual.

A brief, owlish appraisal of the Pershing march-past gave Runyon the over-all dimensions of his story. Much of his reporter-writer ability lay in his gift of quick perception, his response to a first impression. As in many passages of life itself, the emphasis tends to shift or subside when a reporter, or almost any other quester, overstays that effervescent moment of strongest address to the senses. A second piece of pie is not always as tasty as the first.

While other reporters were marching behind General Pershing, the Runyon was on his way to Jack Doyle's billiard and pool establishment in the Broadway sector. There he played a few games of snooker with the proprietor. Toward evening he appeared at the newspaper office in William Street to write his memorable story. Night city editor Dunn had placed a fat envelope of City News copy in the "R" pigeonhole of the staff mailbox. This was an old wooden honeycomb screwed to the wall next to the bulletin board just outside Colonel Caleb Van Hamm's cubicle. Runyon merely glanced at the City News report, then put it in *my box*.

The New York City News Association report carried the details of the parade—statistics, sidelights, factual matters submitted by a staff of competent, underpaid, and unsung leg men. City News was a cooperative news agency, the first of its kind. Its daily reports were sent by means of the teletype to all member clients in the Greater City. The City News often saved a reporter the trouble of explaining why he had missed some important development while covering a story. It sometimes happened that a City News bulletin arrived just in time to protect the fellow who had muffed his assignment entirely.

Had Runyon marched behind Black Jack Pershing on the day of the great parade, he might have observed a somewhat revealing "slant." It had to do with the things the general said to and of his horse—the first of the two mounts which, one after the other, the hero rode along Fifth Avenue. The general wore a set smile for the crowd, but between his teeth came words which belied that smile. It appeared there were two sides to a general on parade.

John Joseph Pershing was a native of Missouri, a circumstance which may have explained his strong opinions of horses, or of anything else. A handsome figure, tall, straight, and with nothing brittle about him except his temper, he now was approaching his sixtieth year, but with no concession to that age. He had an air of courtesy, but of a most formal kind—an arm's-length manner.

Interference by the civilian high brass left him cold, as the expression is. When the War Department decided to do away with the Sam Browne belt, General Pershing continued to wear it. The broad leather waistband, with the supporting shoulder strap extending diagonally from right to left, had been designed by Colonel Samuel James Browne of the old British Indian Army.

As a one-time cavalry officer, Black Jack's horsemanship was superb. It was said that the riding hall at West Point had not seen his like since the days when Ulysses S. Grant was a cadet at the Academy. Cavalryman Pershing had ridden against Geronimo in 1886, against the Sioux in 1890–1891, and afterward against the Moros in the Philippines, as well as in Mexico during the vain pursuit of Pancho Villa. Francisco Villa, too, was an expert horseman, but not a faultless dresser. Indeed, he looked like the Heywood Broun of equestrians.

Today on Fifth Avenue both the Pershing horsemanship and his temper went on trial. The assembled thousands saw his half-smile, but could not hear his epithets. Nor, in the brief glimpse of the passing hero, could the spectators sense, as did the reporters who marched within earshot of Black Jack, that he and his mount were fighting a duel.

The Commonwealth of Virginia had given this horse to the general with the request that he ride it during the welcome-home celebration. This came as something of a surprise to Black Jack. When the parade formed at the northeast corner of Central Park, he didn't have time to look the gift horse in the mouth, or to inquire into its lack of experience in a big city.

The stallion had ancestral papers almost as detailed as those of the First Families of the Old Dominion. I cannot remember the steed's name. I think it was Shenandoah, but am not sure. It was a magnificent animal, all of sixteen hands, splendid in conformation. It had a deep chest and a sleek coat which, in the sunlight, seemed touched with bronze. The mane and tail billowed out like a hair-tonic advertisement.

Shenandoah (if that was its name) had never been in a parade before this day. Nor had the horse hitherto seen waving flags, other than a small Confederate ensign on the roof of a Virginia barn. The handsome beast also was unfamiliar with the flatulence of police motorcycles and the roar of the spectators. Its ears were unaccustomed to the brassy gales of bands playing "Over There," and that tune about the accommodating lass from Armentières.

No sooner had Black Jack straddled Shenandoah than the stallion tried to charge across town, as if bent upon taking the ferry to Tenafly, New Jersey. The general managed to rein in the steed, then headed it southward. It was plain to the reporters that Black Jack was mad as hell at not only Shenandoah but at Virginia as well.

From then on, for the fifty-one blocks of park-side pavement, the general had a counterfeit smile for the crowd. He occasionally risked taking his right hand from the reins to salute. Meantime,

Shenandoah was foaming, slobbering, breaking wind, and veering this way and that under the restraint imposed by the angry horseman. Behind the mask of his synthetic smile the general was using four-letter eloquence such as we now come upon between the covers of modern novels.

At St. Patrick's Cathedral steps, the high dignitaries of City, State, and the Church awaited the coming of the hero. Governor Al Smith was there. So also were Mayor Hyland and Archbishop (afterward Cardinal) Hayes. The saluting, half-smiling, *sotto voce* cursing general finally rode up on the lathered demon from Virginia. A military aide dismounted, then took the bridle bits of the Pershing steed.

The general now too dismounted. He was still beyond the hearing range of the archbishop.

"What shall I do with the horse, sir?" the aide asked him.

The smile vanished for just a moment. "Take the G.D. son of a bitch out and shoot it!" said Black Jack. Again smiling, the general walked up the steps, accepted the hand of the archbishop, and said, "Your Excellency."

After a minute or so of hearing how great he was, the general went down the cathedral steps. A mounted traffic policeman now offered him his own horse. This horse had no noble bloodlines; it had never romped over a grassy estate. But one thing was obvious: it was quite at home amid the roar and bluster of Runyon's town.

"This is more like it!" said the general.

He now heard someone say that Caruso was taking a snapshot picture of him. For the first time that day General Pershing seemed *really* interested in somebody among the spectators. "Where's Caruso?" he called out. "Where is he?"

He saw the great tenor leaning out from a second-story window of the Mark Cross building. Caruso was holding a small camera at the ready. The general waved at him—the only time I saw him wave at anyone that day. Caruso waved back.

Although Runyon spent but a few minutes at this parade, a dozen other reporters, myself among them, marched for hours along Fifth Avenue. Some of us grew weary, or thirsty, or both. Reporter Boyden Sparkes went all the way to Madison Square. The stout Mr. Sparkes had just recently been mustered out of service. He was in splendid physical condition. He paused but once to bawl out some uniformed spectators who had called him a slacker. Reporter Ed Klauber also lasted out the long march. Ed was not an athlete. In fact he liked sedentary assignments, such as a night at the opera or at the horse show. But he was a *Times* man. As such he dared not reveal signs of weakness, moral or otherwise, while on duty. Don Clarke and I were of less admirable mold. We were foes of getting old too soon. Life was for us, and we for it.

Mr. Clarke had been an athlete at Harvard (briefly, for he had been invited in his sophomore year to leave that institution). Don Clarke was a brilliant, brave man. He never backed down in a fight, even when he lost his eyeglasses, without which he could see but dimly. In later years he underwent the agonies of cancer without complaint or signs of self-pity. Instead he read Horace and other Roman poets in the Latin text, and managed somehow to hold fast to his ability to laugh at his own predicament. Whenever I saw Don Clarke I felt as though I was looking upon some great gay truth.

I was no weakling myself, except in matters of character and moral restraint. Mr. Clarke and I treated ourselves to two or three saloon breaks during the big parade. Then, having refreshed our bodies and our minds, we deployed each time in a taxicab along a street parallel to Fifth. With our police cards displayed in our hatbands, we would work our way through the crowd and once again take our proper places behind the general.

When the parade was over, Mr. Clarke and I went to the Woolworth turkish baths in Park Place to steam out our kinks and have a dip in the pool. I dang near drownded (as old Scout Wiggins used to say) in the pool of the skyscraper. Somehow, every stroke kept me at the bottom of the pool. Upon saving my own life—accidentally—when I had recovered the use of my left lung I denounced Mr. Clarke.

"What in hell kept you from coming in?" I demanded. "Did you think I was getting baptized?"

Mr. Clarke was not now wearing his thick eyeglasses. Nonetheless, I believed that he should have sensed my peril. "Good Lord!" said my alleged friend. "I thought you were giving an under-water exhibition. A most magnificent one, I would say, for an amateur."

Both Mr. Clarke and myself were glad to refer to the City News reports when we reached our respective offices. Were I a younger man, with a somewhat brighter glow than the present candle power my skull affords, I would write a book about the New York City News Association. If nothing else, this would be a token of gratitude for its nick-of-time assistance during my own moments of gathering wool instead of news. It would also be a memorial to the men who worked, anonymously and the clock round, in Manhattan and in the Bronx—men who did the shoe-leather labors so seldom acknowledged in terms of pay or praise.

Notwithstanding their drudgery, their anonymity—the take-it-for-granted contributions of these men—several alumni of City News became famous. Novelist Louis Bromfield once pounded the night news beat at Bellevue Hospital and police headquarters. Jack Alexander, *Saturday Evening Post* writer and editor, was in the boot camp of City News. So also was Louis Stark, afterward the outstanding labor editor of the New York *Times;* and Edwin Lanham, novelist and member of the *Tribune's* great rewrite battery. There were several other notable men who had worked in the old newsroom at No. 2 Lafayette Street.

The New York City News Association was born in 1894. Its foster parent was the Associated Press. That sponsoring agency had just recently (1893) been reorganized—in both a functional and an ethical sense—by Melville E. Stone, its new general manager. From the beginning of Mr. Stone's long term, and on through the administration of his able successor, Kent Cooper, the Associated Press held fast to the doctrine of accuracy, impartiality, and integrity in the gathering and the distribution of world news. This code rubbed off on the AP's foster child, City News. During the forty-eight years of its service to the New York newspapers, the metropolitan agency abided by that article of faith.

City News had twenty-two member clients in New York at the time of World War I. Its leg men kept twenty-four-hour watches at police stations, jails, courts, hospitals, morgues, and administrative offices. On occasions of disaster—the burning and sinking of the *General Slocum* in 1904, the Triangle Waist Company fire in 1911, the arrival in New York of survivors of the *Titanic*, the Wall Street explosion—City News men went on the job in force. At election time the news service was at its peak of efficiency and accuracy. It never elected the wrong candidate.

The mergers of metropolitan dailies, the increased costs of operation, and the resignations of member newspapers caused the demise of this venerable agency. It folded at seven p.m. February 11, 1942. The Associated Press thereupon took over the functions of City News. The members of the staff placed a wreath on the switchboard. The beloved Anna Daly Sullivan, cashier for more than thirty years, sat looking at a placard upon which was the legend, "Profanity is vulgar and offensive. Why not quit it?" Miss Sullivan got up, closed her desk, then announced, "I'm going to swear!"

In the year when City News began its career, Grover Cleveland was in his second non-consecutive term as President of the United States. The Vice President was Adlai Stevenson, grandfather-to-be of the man whom many of us now admire. Governor Roswell Pettibone Flower was rounding out a somewhat undistinguished term as chief executive of New York State. He had been a securities broker, and had run successfully against capitalist William Waldorf Astor in 1881 for a seat in the United States House of Representatives. During that campaign (the "golden canvass"), as well as in the gubernatorial election, it was charged that Tammany Hall rigged the polls in Flower's behalf. Tammany Hall

could do more things to and with a ballot box than merely admire
its frail lock. Even today some of our ablest politicians take off
their masks and stand with bowed heads when the names of
Tweed or Croker are mentioned.

Richard Croker was boss of Tammany Hall at the time when
City News was founded. His mayor was Thomas F. Gilroy, a
Grand Sachem of the Tammany wigwam. The chief of police was
William S. Devery, perennial winner of the golden blackjack. The
chief grew a bit round-shouldered—a deformity brought on by the
lifting of black bags, tribute exacted for his guardianship of the
city against virtue.

City News came into being midway in the Gay Nineties. How
gay were they in point of fact? Legends come down to us in fragments, as do pieces of heirloom chinaware. By means of some quirk
of survival, a few names persist in the public mind. They become
symbols, accepted all too readily as trademarks of a time past. A
plump Miss Leonard of Clinton, Iowa, a lass who smoked cigars,
became Lillian Russell of the stage. Diamond Jim Brady, a gross-
grained show-off, who lived for his belly's sake and for a puff in
the press, in reality was so tight-fisted as seldom to have given his
women a reward other than a dinner at Delmonico's, or the tem-
porary *use* of a bracelet, a ring, or a glittering pin. The frequent
mention of these names in a modern story or in a present-day song
would have us believe that Miss Russell was more comely than
Helen of Troy, and that trencherman Jim was generous, gay, devil-
may-care, and the age itself a Strauss waltz.

Not everyone was prosperous and gay at that time. Nor did that
newer legend-ridden era, the 1920s, find everyone roaring and carefree. Nostalgic minstrels who sing of Broadway's merriment seem
never to have met the hungry men of Brooklyn, or heard of the
Gold Star mothers of the Bronx.

How gay was the year when the City News began its chores? It
was 1894, the year after the great panic. Nation-wide strikes had
tied up the railroads and the coal mines. President Cleveland sent
government troops to Chicago, ostensibly to watch over the United

States mails, during the bloody strike against the Pullman Company. Eugene V. Debs led his American Railway Union in a sympathetic boycott of servicing Pullman cars, then called a general railway walkout. The government indicted Debs for conspiracy. Clarence Seward Darrow kept him out of jail.

This was the first celebrated case of Darrow's long career as a defense advocate. He was now thirty-seven years old, and looked like a young lion. He had already established a reputation as a corporation counsel; the Great Northern Railway was one of his clients. Now he turned his energies and his eloquence to the practice of criminal law.

That was the year when Hawaii became a republic. It also was the year when Captain Dreyfus was degraded in France. The Chinese-Japanese war began. Congress passed a graduated income tax. It was nullified the next year by a decree of the United States Supreme Court as an unconstitutional method of making a citizen unhappy. The ladies were reading Anthony Hope's *The Prisoner of Zenda* and George du Maurier's *Trilby*. A buck-and-wing dancer, Charles B. Lawlor, sold his song "The Sidewalks of New York" for a few dollars (so the late Gene Buck told me in speaking of those pre-ASCAP days) and afterward went blind.

That also was the year when the jockey-size "General" Jacob S. Coxey led his "army" of the unemployed in a march upon Washington, D.C. The peppery little general was a social reformer. The purpose of his march was to persuade President Cleveland and the Congress to issue fiat money to finance public works and thereby create jobs. The general was somewhat ahead of his time.

"All I got for my pains," General Coxey told me years afterward, "was to get arrested for walking on the grass of the Capitol grounds."

The general was about sixty-six years old when I chanced to meet him in April 1920. He was still lively and full of juice. He attributed his vitality to the fact that he had never wasted his energies by resisting temptation. When I last heard of him the general was in his eighties, as spry as an elf and ready to march at the drop of a helmet upon Washington or on any other citadel.

When I came upon the general in 1920 I had just wrapped up a newsbeat concerning a plot to assassinate Venustiano Carranza, the graybeard provisional President of Mexico. (His murder occurred the next month.) It was now Prohibition time. I learned that the safest beverage of the District of Columbia was native corn whisky, and that the best place to get it was the Ebbitt Hotel. The National Press Club now stands on the site of that old hotel where several Presidents-elect had stayed just before their respective days of inauguration.

The man to see, I was advised by Henry H. Stansbury, Washington bureau manager for Hearst's Universal Service, was the hotel porter. Until now I never had tasted corn liquor in its primitive stage. Mr. Stansbury said that the flavor of it would grow on me. He was a Southern gentleman, having been born near Etowah Shoals, Rome, Georgia, at the confluence of the Coosa and the Oostanaula rivers. The best corn liquor, he said, was made with those waters. He added that he had been weaned on the stuff.

"Ask for the porter," said Stansbury. "He does business in the baggage room of the Ebbitt."

The baggage room was dimly lit; and so was the porter, or so it seemed from his thickness of speech. He smelled of cloves, and one of his eyes was shut in a sort of perpetual wink. Before I could introduce myself, he asked how many jars did I want. I thought a quart might be enough—if he could spare it.

Spare it! He opened a huge trunk. I saw inside it a cargo of old-style Mason jars with metal screw-caps. Well, perhaps I should take two, just to be on the safe side.

While the porter was putting the merchandise in a paper bag, a brisk little fellow came in to ask "Why the hell that medicine I ordered has not been delivered." This was General Coxey. He was then in residence at the Ebbitt. When the porter mentioned the gentleman's name and rank, I introduced myself. He thereupon invited me to his quarters for a discussion of social conditions.

The corn liquor had the complexion of highly diluted milk, and tasted as though it had been keeping company with old 'tater sacks. Although the general did not approve of Mr. Hearst or his foreign policies, he offered to drink to his health. He believed that my Mexican story was somehow linked to the fact that Mr. Hearst had extensive land holdings south of the border. It seemed to interest General Coxey that just recently I had seen Senator Albert B. Fall. I forget whether the senator had just returned from the Southwest, or was about to go there in connection with trying to buy a newspaper. At any rate, he was chairman of the Senate Committee Investigating Mexican Affairs, and had supplied me with much information.

"I know Fall quite well," the general said. "Perhaps too well. He can't buy a paper or much of anything else. He's stony broke." And then the general made a prediction: "Certain oil people are setting out to run, not only the country, but the world. Watch the Republican convention [1920]. Out of it will come—I don't know who, but I do know what—somebody easy on the oil boys. And then we'll see fellows like Senator Fall making it still easier on them. Well, let's drink to somebody's health. What have you been reading lately?"

"A bit of Dante. This year is the six-hundredth anniversary of his death."

The general refilled his tumbler from one of the Mason jars. "To Dante!" he said. "Right now Mexico is an inferno. Did the junta give you any trouble?"

"Quite a bit. I was followed, threatened, both in New York and here. Somebody ransacked my hotel room. Only yesterday a wild-eyed blonde, built like a first baseman, barged in and began to yell that I not only had taken a biological advantage of her but also had appropriated her earrings as a stud fee."

The general nodded as one who had been through the mill. "The badger game. Then her 'husband' showed up?"

"Yes. But he didn't have time to make his pitch," I replied. "You see, I had taken in a friend the night before: Sergeant Mike

Donaldson. He's a Medal of Honor soldier and, since he is a hero, is of course broke. Mike happens to suffer from frequent calls of nature. He was in the bathroom at the time the big broad threatened my amateur standing. Mike is chesty and tough. He used to train middleweight champion Stanley Ketchel. When Mike came out of the jakes, and with his pants at half-staff, the nice married couple ran a dead heat for the door."

"Let's drink to the health of Sergeant Donaldson," said my host. "I wish someone would accuse *me* of those things. Oh, well! It was different years ago. Why, in this very same hotel—maybe in this room—I was talking politics with a lady, a very heavy-set lady. And never mind her name. We were discussing this and that, while making ourselves more comfortable in the folding bed. And the damned thing closed up suddenly on us, like a bear trap. What a panic! Worse than the one of 1893. The house dick saved us from smothering to death. Luckily he was a friend of mine."

The general raised his glass. "To Edna!" he said.

After we had drunk to Edna's memory I proposed that the general seek new fame. "Suppose you change your rank from general to admiral, and form Coxey's Navy?"

I said this in jest, but the general seemed to be hearing bugle calls and bosun's whistles. He refilled his glass, raised it. "To Coxey's Navy! Please announce in your newspaper that Admiral Coxey is about to move on Washington with a fleet of rowboats, punts, and rafts, from the Potomac."

I wrote a story about Admiral Coxey's navy. It was printed the next morning on the front page of the New York *American*. I think a better story would have been the tale of the folding bed. Without using Edna's name, of course.

If Damon Runyon was the great newspaperman so many persons say he was, you may ask: Then why did he never win a Pulitzer Prize? Many outstanding reporters of Damon's time won no prizes, other than the greatest of all: the recognition of their abilities by fellow workers. As to Runyon's place in journalism, perhaps I should quote someone outside the Hearst fold, since the evidence presented by Runyon's devotees, Walter Winchell for one, or by Brisbane, might appear prejudiced. I shall cite Herbert Bayard Swope in this respect. Swope was the first newspaperman to win the Pulitzer Prize (1917) for his superb report of the Battle of the Somme.

Swope, in the opinion of many journalists, was one of the greatest newspapermen of this century. He and I were close friends over the years. We corresponded frequently until just before his death in June 1958. In November 1954 he wrote to me in reply to my request that he name ten outstanding editors and ten of the foremost reporters of the 1920s.

I think it of interest that he named Runyon as his number-one choice. It also interested me but did not surprise me, in the light of Swope's ability to be just to the talents of his adversaries, that he included Westbrook Pegler high up in this list. He did so, however, with the parenthetical remark, "(Damn him!)." Swope's honor roll of reporters reached not ten but sixteen; his editorial choices numbered twenty-three. It *did* surprise me when he named Mr. Hearst as number one and Joseph Pulitzer as number two among the editors.

In passing, I have to smile at Swope's way of sometimes addressing me as "Young Gene" in his letters. One facet of his enormous charm was his whimsical manner of regarding old, old friends in terms of the days of the green bay tree. To his mind, the young knights of Park Row still rode out with pomp and circumstance to the tournaments of world news. He refused to admit that the old crusades were forgotten, or that the once stout lances now lay broken in the dust and rubble of the long ago.

For some years the omission of Hearst men among Pulitzer winners was attributed, by certain observers, to the Hearst-Pulitzer feud of an earlier time. I. Kaufman, widely known veteran of the old Brooklyn *Eagle*, recalls that his newspaper's cartoonist, Nelson Harding, twice won the Pulitzer Prize. Mr. Hearst lured Harding to the New York *American*. There the cartoonist became the first

Hearst man to receive honorable mention from the committee on awards. The resourceful Arthur Brisbane celebrated that event with a headline which, when quickly read, suggests a great victory: HEARST MAN WINS PULITZER PRAISE.

As far as I know, the only Runyon newspaper story ever rejected by an editor was the one he wrote in Boston the night before anarchists Nicola Sacco and Bartolomeo Vanzetti died in the electric chair. They had been indicted, tried, then convicted on circumstantial evidence linking them to the robbing and killing of a shoe-company paymaster and his guard in South Braintree in April 1920. During the following seven years of appeals, postponements of execution of sentence, and furors of opinion both in America and abroad, Sacco and Vanzetti were looked upon as martyrs. Many writers, including columnist Heywood Broun, poetess Edna St. Vincent Millay, Upton Sinclair, and playwright Maxwell Anderson spoke out against the killing of the two men.

Runyon went to Massachusetts in August 1927 to cover the electrocution. Edmond D. Coblentz, the gentlemanly San Franciscan with an excellent editorial mind, was then in charge of the New York *American*. When Runyon's story came over the teletype machine, Mr. Coblentz read the opening line, then turned the color of old beeswax. The opening sentence read, "They're frying Sacco and Vanzetti in the morning." Mr. Coblentz paid a hasty trip to the water cooler. He did not bother to fashion one of those drinking cups which staff members made by folding a piece of copy paper into a sort of miniature dunce cap. He picked up one already made, which had been used and then flung aside. When the groggy editor regained his poise, he ordered his subeditor to use the Associated Press story instead of Runyon's.

There were no bare walls at the political conventions. There were none at all at the World Series games, or at the outdoor prizefights. Nor could one expect privacy at the murder trials, or at the City Hall steps whenever Mayor Jimmy Walker and New

York's official greeter, the Hon. Grover A. Whalen, welcomed Channel swimmers or transatlantic aviators, or awarded fancy scrolls to crowned or uncrowned members of royalty. These publicized darlings were soon forgotten after their hours of noisy exposure to the Big Town. It was a time of synthetic wonder-workers and ersatz miracles, a carnival spin of mass make-believe—the world's last brief holiday from fear.

CHAPTER

19

<hr>

I remember the man or the tree, but where I saw them I mostly forget. —COLERIDGE

Iᴛ ɪs much too early this March morning to expect a crack in the stillness of our sleeping neighborhood. Across the quiet mile of glen, along that ridge called Tiger Tail, the homes are dark but for the occasional wink of a bathroom window. Bandmaster Lawrence Welk last night forgot to switch off the tinted lamps in his terrace-garden. I can see a blue-gold mist over there, a halo for a shrine in the patio of the music man.

Both sides of the valley floor rise up in silhouette and serenity, to all appearance exempt from the mischiefs of the world. Perhaps I, too, am but a silhouette profiled against my own horizon of foreclosed intentions. It is an hour or so before sunup of my seventieth birthday.

How am I to celebrate this debut among the ancients? I cannot, of course, be as gracious about it as Grandma Moses or Pope John. I would like, however, to stay reasonably buoyant of spirit; skeptical in some respects, but free of peevishness. And I would hope to die a long time off without too many false starts. As for that last grand slam in spades, I shall rely upon the stratagem which so far has kept me out of the boneyard: I make it my business to go to everybody's funeral but my own.

I did not grow old on purpose. Men seldom do—women, never. Old, that is to say, in the sense of the Psalmist's threescore years and ten; and with that dread of an aftermath of labor and of sorrow. I am as reluctant as anyone else to throw a farewell kiss to youth; to say good-by to its escapades, its gay sorceries, the dreams wrapped in cellophane. I shall not, however, take myself to the wailing wall. Nor do I mean to engage in that folly which causes the wrinkled sloganists to maintain that old age is just fine and dandy, a real boon. Let them quote Robert Browning's invitation to grow old with him. Let them pipe-dream on his assurance that "the best is yet to be." When the poet shammed that dilly, he had his head caught in an inkhorn.

How quiet this early morning! The dogs leave off their barking; the frogs, their wooings at the fishpond. Even the cats declare a moratorium on whatever it is they like to do these nights at winter's end. Other than the bongo beats of my coffee percolator, and the muted flurry of clock-bells in houses nearby, my small world has nothing much to say out loud on this, my seventieth birthday.

A clock somewhere to the right of me strikes four; booms slowly, with senatorial assurance. Another clock, a fast-counting referee to my left, disputes the testimony. It rings eight times with tinkling impudence. I am not to be misled, however, by this contradiction of the clocks, left or right. Our democracy allows the clocks freedom of speech.

It so happens that *both* clocks are correct. A reporter who has been around for as long a time as I learns—if he learns at all—that well-made clocks and well-made men tend to obey their respective rules of action. The clock to my right obviously is a grandfather's clock. As such it must toll a traditional and patriotic four when it *is* four. The other, that more sprightly timepiece, has the lilt of a toy piano. It strikes eight when it is four; for it is a ship's clock now on shore duty. When it beats eight bells at four of the dial, it does so in the idiom of the quarterdeck and of the chart-room.

Let clocks and freedom ring. As for me, my own clock has no chimes. Its hands point, not to four, but to seventy. Not hours, nor days, but years . . . so many birthday cakes ago . . . so many candles burned . . . and the merry guests have ridden out and far away. . . .

The stillness of this new day belies the reputation of a month known for its ill-tempered winds and the knifing of Julius Caesar. No winds blow this March morning; no winds at all, other than the gales of time. These echoes, too, die down; soon they become as faint in memory as the whispers of conspirators.

When a patriarch-elect rises too early on his birthday, he is apt to make second guesses about his past. This is a disturbing exercise, indeed; one which could bring on a siege of senile delinquency. Should I go back to bed? Stay there until the carrier boy porches the morning paper? And the hillside trees come alive with the daybreak fugues of birds?

Of late years in Southern California I have been rising early each day—not this early, to be sure—awakening at those hours which used to be my curfew time on Park Row. This change of habit need not imply a gain in character. I find, however, that my point of view has changed in some respects since the 1920s. The shifts of time and circumstance play tricks upon the perspective scheme.

When I think of the several revisions of view which age brings, I wonder if I am not now quite another person than the Mr. Myself of the headlong years. Why did I ever lose sleep over those huge trifles of times past? Why did I squander those mornings of fickle spring chasing thistles in the wind? Or try to win a laughing contest with the gods?

The arteries may have something to do with change of view. Or, more likely still, the glands, now that one has survived the sweet swindles of passion.

This morning, the silence of it, the darkness outside, becomes a time of flashbacks. In a manner of speaking, this birthday morning brings with it a revival of half-forgotten nouns; that is to say, a resurgence of persons, places, things from the long ago. These inflections and reflections come without any order of their importance or in their proper sequence. Then, too, the five senses keep intruding upon these recollections, as though resentful of anything less real than the here-and-now.

The past and the present ride a seesaw. My own sensibilities go up, then down on this teeter-totter of alternating moods. At one moment I see with the mind's eye the rag doll of a woman: Ruth Snyder in the electric chair at Sing Sing Prison. Then the smell of coffee abruptly brings me out of that particular yesterday. Next I am looking on with thirty-six-year-old eyes at a scene in the prairie near Minot, North Dakota. Queen Marie is preparing to review a rodeo. She is to ride sidesaddle as queens must do when on equestrian display. Again I can see a hurriedly built outhouse in the background. It is plainly labeled "Ladies" and "Gentlemen" at its respective doors. But the queen's official host, Old Colonel Carroll, cannot see too well. He has but one eye, and it is not trustworthy. The colonel is sturdy, gruff, purposeful. I see him as he stoops to allow his high silk hat proper clearance as he goes through the *wrong doorway* of the privy.

I then seem to hear his long-ago howl of: "I'll be a sonofabitch! . . . Your Majesty!" And then he backs out unsteadily from the makeshift throneroom, and from the memory of that day.

I become seventy years old once more when I hear a dry branch fall on the roof of the kitchen in which I now am sitting. But soon again I return to the Park Row days.

The actors' strike of 1919. Of its several phases I recapture one moment of pathos. An actress who has chosen not to join the ranks of Equity, Bessie McCoy, is in tears. The musical-comedy beauty, the widow of Richard Harding Davis, bends over the make-up table in her dressingroom in a theater. Not only have her fellows called her a strike-breaker, but someone has written, in soap, on the mirror above the make-up table the word "Scab!"

I come back to present thoughts when a misplaced seam in my pajama pants causes me to squirm on the kitchen chair. I wonder how the devil gets his pants on over his tail. Now once again the seesaw tilts and the past rises. Memories of stories and of their makers spring to mind. The Ku Klux Klan, and the time I played a trick upon an ex-Klansman whose confessions I was ghost-writing for the Hetman.

The reformed Klansman has brought with him his robes and hood for the purpose of photographs. He also wears a pearl-handle pistol, by virtue of a permit the Hetman got for him. He is very much on edge, and keeps on saying that death is headed his way. I dress myself in the Klan robes in the photographer's room. Then I suddenly appear in the Hetman's office. And I call out the password I have learned from our nervous news source:

"Klexter, what of the night?"

The young fellow is very quick on the draw. His pistol looks as big to me as a Civil War mortar. Bravely, I wheel. As the saying is, I take a powder before I get a literal dose of it in the guts. Fortunately, indeed, a rewrite man, Steve Dunleavy, disarms the ex-Klansman. This makes it possible for me now to be sitting here this early morning of my seventieth birthday.

Mr. Dunleavy was an Irishman of middle age. He had blue-black hair, the kind Jackie Gleason has these days, and a mustache to match. He smoked a huge, curve-stem pipe, and had a brogue that sounded like a cavalry charge. Bugs Baer said that Steve couldn't get his consonants past his teeth.

I seem to be at Mt. Clemens, Michigan, a health resort thirty miles out of Detroit. The air is charged with sulphur; the fumes turn one's silver coins black overnight. Here I am to have a grand reunion with old friends: Joe O'Neill and Charles MacArthur. Henry Ford is suing the Chicago *Tribune* for a million dollars; not that the automobile magnate needs the money, but his honor and reputation have been thrown up for grabs. Two or three years before this the *Tribune* in an editorial had described Mr. Ford as an ignorant idealist and an anarchist.

Joe O'Neill would leave the *World* to become a public relations man for Mr. Ford. They had met on the Ford Peace Ship at the time Sir Henry was going to get the boys out of the trenches by Christmas at the beginning of World War I. On the other side of the libel suit, Charles MacArthur, still in uniform, would be handling press relations for the *Tribune*. There would be plenty of whisky on hand, all of it bad, supplied by these press agents.

I was covering this trial for Hearst's Universal Service, the morning news wire. The fact that Mr. Hearst and Brisbane were admirers of Mr. Ford, together with Joe O'Neill's guarantees that I was pure in heart, noble of purpose, and a moral giant, would mean that I would have easy access to Mr. Ford, take long walks with him and his courtiers, and study King Midas in his incarnation of a wiry, sharp-featured farmer in a black derby.

The trouble with this short-lived intimacy was that almost everything said by this phenomenal gentleman was not to be published. He permitted an occasional quote, as when he told me that his first ambition had been to make a dollar watch, but that Ingersoll had beaten him to the draw.

Under no circumstance was I to reveal that he had modeled his empire upon the two organizations which he said were the greatest business concerns in history: Standard Oil and the Roman Catholic Church. And only when I convinced Mr. Ford that I was able to button up my lip with iron rivets would he tell me his favorite motor car (excluding his own, of course).

"The best car," he said, "is the Franklin."

"Not too many persons think so," I put in. "The public doesn't appear to like the shape of the hood, for one thing. And I hear that the company is in for some rough times."

"The public," said Mr. Ford, "sometimes has a cinder in its eye. The Franklin is the most honest car, except the Ford. It is light, easier on tires, and it has an air-cooled engine. *All* engines could, and should, be air-cooled. Just as *all* batteries should be dry. But it would cost everyone a fortune to re-tool for these sensible things."

He said, also, that gasoline was not the best source of power for motor engines. We were walking on this hot day among some grain fields, and Mr. Ford gestured like a squire blessing the crops. "Alcohol would be a much better and endlessly available power. Instead of spoiling the brains of man with making liquor, the distilleries could be making alcohol cheaply for fuel. Besides, it would conserve the oil for other purposes."

I remember these and other matters much more vividly than the news-making events of the Ford-*Tribune* libel suit. How he could not remember who Benedict Arnold was, and the day he would win a verdict and six cents in damages, cannot compare in my interest with the time when Mr. Ford would give me the go-by and the good-by at—of all places—a drugstore soda fountain, and because of a pineapple ice-cream sundae!

That day we had taken our usual walk after a day in court, and it was a hot afternoon, indeed. The high-salaried courtiers marched a step or so behind the magnate, who, from some quirk of mind, insisted that I walk beside him. Mr. Ford sometimes would be hazy on facts when sprung upon him by someone bent upon losing a job. But he had a way of hearing, seeing, or coming upon some subject each day, and then would recite or lecture upon that text.

So it was this hot afternoon, and the Ford text was the food values contained in a pineapple ice-cream sundae. He spoke of the ice-cream itself, in terms of energy and other virtues. The pineapple and its juices, the sugar, the nuts, all were praised and analyzed.

At the close of the sermon, Mr. Ford asked me, "Would you like to stop in at the soda fountain?"

"If you are buying," I replied.

His courtiers winced at this sign of familiarity on my part; but Mr. Ford smiled a little and made up a joke of his own, at which everyone laughed ten times more than at a Buster Keaton pratfall. "I think that I can afford to treat everyone."

We all sat around our host at the small drugstore where we used to drink limeades for our hangovers. The waitress gave Mr. Ford

one of those tip-provoking smirks, and Mr. Ford offered a summary
of his lecture on the pineapple sundae and its dietetic wonders.

"Place your orders, gentlemen," he said.

The first order, as I recall it, was by William Cameron, editor of
Ford's Dearborn *Independent,* a lover of Bourbon and the man
who later would get Mr. Ford in bad with Semitic preachments.
Mr. Cameron ordered a pineapple ice-cream sundae. So on down
the line, everyone joyously asked for one of these Ford-approved
masterpieces; that is until it came to my turn.

"Miss," I said to the waitress, "would you bring me some chocolate ice-cream, with no whipped cream, no nuts, and a double
portion of chocolate syrup."

The waitress stopped noting our orders and looked toward our
host for his approval. The gentlemen present, stunned into silence
by this outrage, seemed to be watching Mr. Ford for a signal to
"throw the bum out."

Mr. Ford said, "I believe a pineapple sundae would be a more
healthful refreshment."

"No, chocolate will be fine," I said.

"You're sure, Mr. Fowler?"

"Yes, Mr. Ford, very sure."

The squire of Dearborn eyed me a moment; then, as if with
regret, he turned to the young lady and said, "Bring the young man
his order."

And now I'm back in this kitchen where I'm suddenly seventy
years old. I see the holly-green breadbox in which I happen to
know a birthday cake is hidden, frosted nicely, but so far lacking
its miniature forest of candles. I see the pie Agnes baked last night
for our longtime friend Jack Dempsey. I am to take it later on in
the morning to his home in Santa Monica. It is an apricot pie, his
favorite kind, as I happen to know because we used to eat apricot
pie at a Denver lunch counter when we both sold newspapers in
that city as boys. I feel very dishonest as I look at this pie.

Just who does Dempsey think he is to expect me to go hungry?

Agnes could very well bake another pie and let me have this one. Or, I could claim that I dropped it on the way to Santa Monica. No, for Agnes would be bound to see me sneaking out of the house with my hands empty and my belly full. This Dempsey fellow, a one-time champion, eh? I'll have him know that I once stole a pie—rather, some whipped-cream pastries—from no less a celebrity than Queen Marie of Romania.

I should like very much to steal a piece of this pie, but it would not be the safe thing to do. Not only is Dempsey still a powerful fellow, but, as I said many pages ago, Agnes is a crack shot. I lift the waxed-paper shield of the pie, and have not been as sorely tempted for . . . let me think back. . . . Oh yes, that time when an editor's sweetheart . . . This is a most wonderful pie . . . the old-fashioned kind that one seldom sees these days, with a lattice-work of crisp dough laid on the top of the fruit; dried apricots, soaked, sweetened, laced with lemon juice, stewed gently, then baked in the deep shell for forty minutes at an oven temperature of 450 degrees. Jack said yesterday that no one ever makes this masterpiece of pies in this day and age; not even the companies which supply pastry for the deep-freeze market.

"Almost everything is in a deep-freeze," Jack said. "And that goes for the emotions, too, and for a lot of other things."

When I go to Dempsey's today I mean to ask him about his father's point of view as to old age and how he got up to eighty-eight years with so much spirit. Old Hiram Dempsey was something of a philosopher. I remember that he once said to us, "Boys, never kick a cripple or go to bed with a fool."

He was well over six feet tall, skinny, old Hiram was; played the fiddle, sired eleven children, and was the nephew of Devil Anse Hatfield, a fact which I find in no stories printed of Jack. No, I think it best not to steal a pie, or any part of it, from a man with bloodlines touched by Devil Anse as well as by a bit of Cherokee Indian. Dempsey will get his pie, and I shall feel temporarily like a man of honor. I have also promised to help Jack repaint his library room. I mean to paint the edges of the shelves myself, leaving the walls and ceilings for him to cover. The still energetic ex-champion paints as he once fought in the ring: fast, furiously, effectively, with a sort of hysterical onset that seems in strange contrast to the gentle, shy nature of the man when away from the crowd, a side revealed only to a few friends. Few persons would believe that this son of fury actually is super-sensitive, blushes easily; has an excellent mind, but tries his best to hide the fact behind the image of his legend.

The Dempsey legend is like the larger saga of the age which sired his fame, the Roaring Twenties. Both the man and the era had gusto and raw color; but they also had other and less bombastic overtones. Not everyone danced the Charleston day and night; plunged on the stock exchange; drank bootleg gin for breakfast; gave bracelets to Peggy Joyce; patronized the floating crap games, or watched gambler Nick the Greek fade Arnold Rothstein for a hundred grand; or had William J. Fallon, the Great Mouthpiece, front for him in criminal courts. Nor did Dempsey fight Firpo every day.

We of the newspapers, who lived and worked in that time, unwittingly contributed to the lopsided reputations which were to take on a curious indelibility in printer's ink. In our juvenile enthusiasm to astound both ourselves and our readers, we neglected the genius of the worthwhile men among us; as when we passed by the genius of a young Robert Moses to elect an assortment of wind-bag patriots to the office of mayor. We exalted underworld punks, Legs Diamond, for example: that clay-pigeon sneak-thief who got his nickname because he could outrun the cops after robbing a pushcart. Today he is solemnly presented by the motion pictures as having won the name "Legs" because of his great ability to *dance!*

When you get up in years—or, as old Hiram Dempsey used to put it, *down* in them—your point of view changes in respect to the shape and meaning of things seen by your past. Most of the hobgoblins, as well as many of yesterday's loved angels, no longer are influential or readily identified. They seem suddenly small, distorted, unreal, as if seen through the bottom of a drained glass. I suddenly remember the password, a phrase which came to me so long ago, and as though by some instinctive means: "Keep the spirit unbroken until half-past Eternity."

I remember a discussion I had with my friend John Barrymore about Eternity. It was his sixtieth birthday. He was talking about his boyhood, a favorite topic of men no longer tempted nor tempting in the gardens of desire.

"I was a student, if you will allow me a slight exaggeration," said Jack. "Lionel and I were enrolled at Seton Hall. This is a somewhat celebrated Roman Catholic institution where learned priests stand for no monkeyshines whatsoever. I had just broken the rules, possibly all eleven of the Ten Commandments, I forget which or what, and was called on the carpet—I think it really was linoleum —in the office of the Reverend Father Linthicum—or a name something like it. Anyway he looked like an abandoned bird sanctuary, had the mind of six Greek philosophers, the voice of Thor, and the ability to make a sinner feel like an ice-cream cone in hell."

According to Jack's story, Father Linthicum let the eleven-year-old boy stand a full minute at attention, then said:

"Before you take another step downward to an eternal loss of soul, I wish to tell you what eternity is. First, imagine a globe one million times as big as the one where we live. Then imagine that this vast globe is made of a substance a million times as hard as the diamond. Now imagine a slight butterfly that flies against this globe one brief moment every million years, and each time merely brushes its wings against the surface of this huge hard globe. Well, then, my son, the time it takes for this butterfly to wear away the great hard globe we have described would comprise but the millionth part of the first *moment* of eternity! What have you to say to *that*, you careless young rascal?"

In recalling this lecture, Jack said that he had been terrified. "I wet my pants," he told me, "but one thing about this parable interested me above anything else. I stayed silent for a few moments, Father Linthicum's blazing eyes fixed on me. 'Answer me,' he roared. 'Answer me, if you can!' "

"Father," Jack said, "it is a *mighty tough* butterfly!"

You look at the present, too, with other eyes. I would not have understood this forty or more years ago when I first came to New York. I listened to the older men in the inns and bars, their voices in the wind. Of course there is one comforting thought: had you listened to sound advice you would have avoided some of your most valuable mistakes. It takes a bit of do-it-yourself philosophy to keep from growing sad or lonely. For example, when you see what has happened to the Camelot you once knew, the island of Manhattan. Or die on the installment plan whenever an old friend's name appears in the obituary pages of the *Times*.

Not only has the city changed in fact, but, more important to you, in fancy. Your reason tells you that young men and women are this moment finding it, as you once did, a region of magic, a city of dreams and singing stones. But with all its vaunt of size and importance and furies of voice, it makes you suddenly a stranger. Old symbols have been taken from the shrines. The mellowed brownstones are gone. The old nooks, the venerable inns, the lovely gloom of Park Row, Perry's alcoholic drugstore, Dr. DeGarmo's chestnut oven, and the flophouse where kidnaper Pat Crowe snored through his binges, and the monstrous post-office building at the southern tip of the tongue of City Hall's park—a thousand and seventy places you knew, and where you walked day upon day, and in the nights, too.

Blow, winds of yesterday! Blow across the stripped sands where the grassy dunes once dared to rise. Sing a wild song of remembrance at the place of the lost dunes, where youth once stood looking out upon the sea.

Till Kingdom Come.